W9-BDL-822

RUFF GUIDE

to the UNITED STATES

Second Edition

RUFF GUIDE

to the UNITED STATES

Second Edition

BringFido:

INTRODUCTION

At BringFido, we believe that dogs deserve a vacation, too! Since launching in 2006, our mission has been to sniff out every pet-friendly place on the planet and make finding them as easy as possible. Today, our website and mobile app feature nearly half a million dog-friendly hotels, vacation rentals, restaurants, activities, services, and events around the world. And over the past 15 years, we've helped millions of pet parents plan and book trips with their furry friends.

Along the way, we've logged countless miles crisscrossing the country on the hunt for the dog-friendliest destinations. And we've learned a lot about what makes an experience special for both two- and four-legged travelers. Now in its second edition, *Ruff Guide to the United States* is a compilation of many of our favorite places to stay and play with dogs in all 50 states.

In this book, you'll find a mix of luxury retreats, rustic getaways, and a treasure trove of other hidden gems where dogs are welcomed with a treat and a smile. As you flip through these pages, get ready to add dozens of drool-worthy destinations to Fido's bucket list. We hope you like reading about the featured attractions in this book as much as we enjoyed discovering them on our journeys across America. And, more importantly, we hope that you and your canine co-pilot get to experience them for yourselves during your own travels.

Although our team has worked hard to ensure that the information contained in this book is accurate at the time of printing, we encourage you to visit our website for the latest, most up-to-date pet policies and customer reviews about each of the places referenced in this book. We'd also love to hear from you. If you discover a new dog-friendly place or want to post a photo or review about the locations we've featured, please share them on our website or mobile app for other pet parents to enjoy.

Happy Travels,

Melissa Halliburton

Melissa Halliburton
Founder and CEO, BringFido

TABLE OF CONTENTS

Where to Stay:

After a long day of exploring Dauphin Island, you can rest your tired paws at the **Dauphin Island Harbor House**, a favorite among four-legged beach bums. Humans will enjoy a complimentary full southern breakfast each morning, and your water-loving pooch will enjoy the proximity to miles of dog-friendly beaches. Up to three dogs of any size are welcome for an additional fee of $25 per stay.

Dauphin Island Harbor House
730 Cadillac Avenue
Dauphin Island, AL 36528
(251) 861-2119
www.bringfido.com/go/1DIY
Rates from $110/night

Dauphin Island

Visit Dauphin Island for an exciting Gulf Coast getaway with Fido. Bring your binoculars and take your furry friend on over three miles of dog-friendly trails at the 137-acre **Audubon Bird Sanctuary**. Look for some of the 420 different bird species that have been spotted on the island, as well as butterflies, turtles, fish, and the occasional alligator. Audubon Bird Sanctuary is open daily from 7:00 am to 7:00 pm and is free to enter. Next, visit **Fort Gaines**, where Fido is welcome to explore a key site of the Civil War's Battle of Mobile Bay. The fort is open daily from 9:00 am to 5:00 pm, and admission is $9 for adults, $5 for children, and free for pups. For some beach time, head over to **Dauphin Island Beach**, where leashed dogs are welcome everywhere except the west end. Admission is $6 per car and $2 per walk-in. After working up an appetite, grab a bite to eat on the patio at **Islander's Restaurant**.

Audubon Bird Sanctuary
211 Bienville Boulevard
Dauphin Island, AL 36528
(251) 861-3607
www.bringfido.com/go/1DIM

Int'l Motorsports Hall of Fame

Does your dog have a need for speed? If so, start your engine and make a beeline for the **International Motorsports Hall of Fame** in Lincoln. Located just off Interstate 20 next to Talladega Superspeedway, NASCAR's biggest race track, this motoring experience is a must-visit for racing fans. The attraction features three exhibit halls and a pavilion area packed full of exhibitions of stock cars, road racing, motorcycles, and drag racing. From Jimmie Johnson to the Intimidator, Dale Earnhardt, you'll learn about the best racers who have ever crossed the finish line at the World's Fastest Superspeedway. The International Motorsports Hall of Fame is open daily from 9:00 am to 5:00 pm, and admission is $12 for adults and $5 for children. Your well-behaved, leashed pooch is welcome to accompany you for no additional charge.

International Motorsports Hall of Fame
3198 Speedway Boulevard
Lincoln, AL 35096
(256) 362-5002
www.bringfido.com/go/1DQS

Where to Stay:

When your weary pooch is ready for an overnight pit stop after his Talladega experience, make your way to the **Best Western Plus Bass Hotel & Suites** in Leeds. Located a half-hour drive from the International Motorsports Hall of Fame, this comfortable hotel offers complimentary daily breakfast for humans and ample green space for Fido. Two dogs up to 80 lbs are welcome for an additional fee of $30 per pet, per night.

Best Western Plus Bass
Hotel & Suites
1949 Village Drive
Leeds, AL 35094
(205) 640-5300
www.bringfido.com/go/1DQT
Rates from $90/night

Chugach Adventures

Discover The Last Frontier with your pooch on the 'Spencer Iceberg and Placer River Float' with **Chugach Adventures**. Board the **Alaska Railroad**'s Glacier Discovery Train in Portage for a brief 20-minute ride to the Spencer Glacier Whistle Stop (note: dogs must remain in a hard-sided carrier during transit). When you arrive, let your pup loose in one of Chugach Adventures' rigid inflatable boats. Take in the stunning mountain views while your guide navigates around icebergs on Spencer Lake and steers the boat along the scenic Placer River. Tours are offered from late May through early September, and rates start at $200 per person. Add $20 for Fido's train fare. After the tour, stretch your dog's legs on a hike along the **Winner Creek Trail** in nearby Girdwood, where you and Fido can climb into a unique hand tram to cross over roaring Glacier Creek.

Chugach Adventures
1553 Alyeska Highway
Girdwood, AK 99587
(907) 783-1860
www.bringfido.com/go/1DII

Where to Stay:

Before you take your hiking boots off and slide on your slippers at the **Ski Inn** in downtown Girdwood, have a stroll around the hotel's gardens and take in the views of the picturesque mountain town. This boutique hotel provides towels and sheets for dogs to clean up after a day on the trails or in the water. It's the perfect spot to warm up before your next outbound excursion with your adventurous hound. Two dogs of any size are welcome for an additional fee of $25 per pet, per night.

Ski Inn
189 Hightower Road
Girdwood, AK 99587
(907) 783-0002
www.bringfido.com/go/1DIJ
Rates from $100/night

Where to Stay:

Keep in the holiday spirit with a stay at the **Hotel North Pole**, where a crackling fire and Christmas decorations help spread the cheer to two- and four-legged guests. Fido is welcome in ground-floor rooms, providing easy access for early morning and late night walks. The hotel is just steps away from the Santa Claus House and the North Pole Plaza, where you'll find convenient shops and restaurants. Up to two dogs of any size are welcome for an additional fee of $35 per pet, per night.

Hotel North Pole
449 N Santa Claus Lane
North Pole, AK 99705
(907) 488-4800
www.bringfido.com/go/1DFQ
Rates from $125/night

North Pole

Thousands of letters are mailed to the man in the big red suit every Christmas, but do you ever wonder where they go? Wonder no more after you and Santa's Little Helper visit the Alaskan town of **North Pole**. Located 20 minutes from Fairbanks, this holiday-themed village allows you and your pup to view the World's Largest Santa outside the Santa Claus House. Next door to St. Nick's workshop, you'll find Antler Academy, where your fur child can get a good look at the resident reindeer from a safe distance. Take a walk through town along candy cane painted streets, stop for a photo op on Santa's sleigh, and, if Fido has been a good boy this year, he may even get to visit with Kris Kringle himself! There are no admission fees to tour this winter wonderland. When you are ready to leave, ask one of the elves to point you in the direction of the **North Pole Dog Park**, where your pup can have some off-leash fun.

North Pole
125 Snowman Lane
North Pole, AK 99705
(907) 488-2281
www.bringfido.com/go/1DFZ

A Day in the West

No trip to Sedona would be complete without an off-road adventure in one of the town's ubiquitous four-wheel drive Jeeps. Fortunately for Fido, **A Day in the West** offers you and your dog the chance to explore the area's canyons and natural rock formations on your own fur-flying escapade. The family-owned company offers a number of guided tours in and around the Coconino National Forest, including the Mogollon Rim Tour, which features breathtaking panoramic views courtesy of an exhilarating ascent to an elevation of 7,500 feet. If you want to see a particular site or attraction, customized tours are available for you and your pup. A Day in the West operates daily with private tours ranging from 90 minutes to three hours. Prices start at $275 per group (up to four people and a dog). Advance reservations are required.

A Day in the West
2900 W State Route 89A
Sedona, AZ 86336
(928) 282-4320
www.bringfido.com/go/1DFS

Where to Stay:

After a day of adventure on the Red Rocks, luxury awaits at the **El Portal Sedona**. Hotel dogs Dexter and Oliver are on duty to ensure that canine guests receive a special treat and other pet amenities at check-in. Each of this boutique property's guest suites is pet friendly, and several feature enclosed private patios. Dogs of any size are welcome for no additional fee. When it's dinner time, walk your pooch to nearby **Creekside American Bistro**, where he can order steak tartare from the doggy menu.

El Portal Sedona
95 Portal Lane
Sedona, AZ 86336
(800) 313-0017
www.bringfido.com/go/1DFT
Rates from $199/night

Where to Stay:

Wahweap Marina allows dogs of any size on houseboats for an additional fee of $10 per pet, per night. If you want to experience the lake, but aren't comfortable driving a 46-foot houseboat, you can rent a small powerboat for the day and stay at the **Lake Powell Resort** instead. Dogs of any size are welcome for an extra fee of $20 per pet, per night. Guests are also required to pay $25 per vehicle for entrance to the Glen Canyon National Recreation Area.

Lake Powell Resort
100 Lake Shore Drive
Page, AZ 86040
(928) 645-2433
www.bringfido.com/go/1DIU
Rates from $85/night

Lake Powell Houseboats

Located on the border of Arizona and Utah, Lake Powell is best known for two things - houseboating and the spectacular scenery of the **Glen Canyon National Recreation Area**. With a pet-friendly houseboat rental from **Wahweap Marina** in Page, you can easily enjoy both with man's best friend! After a brief introduction to houseboating at the full-service marina, set off on an adventure to Rainbow Bridge or explore the lake's 1,800 miles of shoreline. Lounge on the deck and soak up some sun as your home on the water floats through one of the scenic slot canyons. See the sunrise from the outer deck, drop a line over the side for an afternoon of fishing, and enjoy dinner under the stars with your canine companion. Rates vary depending on the season and vessel selected, and rentals are subject to a three-night minimum throughout the year.

Wahweap Marina
100 Lake Shore Drive
Page, AZ 86040
(928) 645-2433
www.bringfido.com/go/1DIT

Pima Air & Space Museum

Put on Snoopy's aviator hat and head to the **Pima Air & Space Museum** in Tucson. You and your furry co-pilot can meander through six hangers and view almost 400 aircraft on display, including a Wright Flyer, a Boeing 787, and a Douglas A-26 Invader from World War II. You can spend hours perusing the exhibits to learn about sea planes, amphibians, aircraft carriers, women in flight, and so much more. Included with your ticket is admission to the 390th Memorial Museum, which houses the last B-17 Flying Fortress flown by any branch of the US Military and details the experiences of the 390th Bomb Group who were captured during World War II. Pups are not allowed on trams or the AMARG tours. The museum is open daily from 9:00 am to 3:00 pm. Admission is $17 for adults and $10 for children. Dogs are welcome for no extra fee.

Pima Air & Space Museum
6000 E Valencia Road
Tucson, AZ 85756
(520) 574-0462
www.bringfido.com/go/1DIG

Where to Stay:

Touch down for the night at **Loews Ventana Canyon Resort**. Your pup will be treated to a 'Loews Loves Pets' amenity kit upon arrival. Don't miss the pet room service menu offering delicious, one-of-a-kind items from the hotel's executive chef. If you'd prefer to dine out alongside Fido, head to the hotel's dog-friendly Cascade Lounge or the patio of Bill's Grill. Two dogs of any size are welcome for an additional fee of $100 per stay.

Loews Ventana Canyon Resort
7000 N Resort Drive
Tucson, AZ 85750
(520) 299-2020
www.bringfido.com/go/1DIH
Rates from $115/night

Where to Stay:

At **Katie's Cozy Cabins**, dogs are welcomed with western hospitality. Located in the heart of the 'Town Too Tough to Die,' the cabins are within walking distance to all of Tombstone's pet-friendly attractions. During your stay, take Fido for a walk in Katie's Cozy Park and don't miss the beautiful Arizona sunset from your cabin porch. Three dogs of any size are welcome for an additional fee of $10 per pet, per night.

Katie's Cozy Cabins
16 W Allen Street
Tombstone, AZ 85638
(520) 559-0464
www.bringfido.com/go/1DIR
Rates from $99/night

Good Enough Mine

Take your furry outlaw to the dog-friendly town of Tombstone. Famous for the 1881 gunfight at the O.K. Corral, this wild west tourist hotspot is a great place to explore with your 'pawtner' in crime. Start with a 45-minute guided walk on the **Good Enough Mine Tour**, traveling underground to see what silver mining was like in the late 1880s. Admission is $15 for adults, $5 for children, and free for dogs. After sniffing out some silver, Fido can rest his paws during a 25-minute carriage ride on the historic 1880s **Butterfield Stage Coach** or a 40-minute ride on the **Good Enough Trolley**. The fare for both rides is $10 for adults and $5 for children. Pups ride for free. Take a break to let Fido enjoy an ice cream cone topped with a dog biscuit from **T. Miller's Tombstone Mercantile** before joining a **Tombstone After Dark** ghost tour. Tours are Friday and Saturday nights, and admission is $20.

Good Enough Mine Tour
501 E Toughnut Street
Tombstone, AZ 85638
(520) 255-5553
www.bringfido.com/go/1DIQ

Garvan Woodland Gardens

Dog lovers with a green thumb shouldn't pass up the chance to bring Fido to **Garvan Woodland Gardens** in Hot Springs. Pick up a self-guided tour map and roam the 210-acre meticulously manicured grounds. Leashed pups are welcome in all areas of the park except the ponds. The park is open daily from 9:00 am to 6:00 pm. Admission is $15 for adults and $5 for doggos. After your garden tour, take a short drive to Lake Hamilton for a cruise aboard the **Belle of Hot Springs Riverboat** with your furry friend. While you savor gorgeous views of the Ouachita Mountains, mansions and natural islands, the *Belle*'s captain will entertain you with an engaging narration. Sightseeing cruises are offered at least once daily throughout the year. Tickets are $39 for adults and $22 for children. Dogs ride on the upper deck for free.

Garvan Woodland Gardens
550 Arkridge Road
Hot Springs, AR 71913
(501) 262-9300
www.bringfido.com/go/1DFU

Where to Stay:

Beautiful views of Lake Hamilton await your arrival at the serene **Lookout Point Lakeside Inn** in Hot Springs. All of the inn's pet-friendly rooms feature a porch with access to the property's lush garden. When you aren't relaxing in your luxurious guest room, you can take Fido for a swim or canoe trip in the lake. Dogs of any size are welcome for an additional fee of $25 per pet, per night, and each pup receives a welcome treat upon arrival.

Lookout Point Lakeside Inn
104 Lookout Circle
Hot Springs, AR 71913
(501) 525-6155
www.bringfido.com/go/1DFV
Rates from $199/night

Crater of Diamonds State Park

Bring your fur-ocious digger to **Crater of Diamonds State Park** in Murfreesboro, where he can hunt for diamonds, minerals, and gemstones in their original volcanic source. You and your pup are invited to scour a 37-acre field, the site of an ancient volcanic crater. The largest diamond ever unearthed in the US was discovered here, and more than 33,000 have been found since the park opened in 1972. The park has a unique 'finders, keepers' policy, so any diamond or gem Fido sniffs out is his to keep. Before you start your search, visit the Diamond Discovery Center to see exhibits and watch a short video. When you get tired of digging, explore the walking trails together and enjoy a packed lunch in one of the picnic spots. The diamond search area is open daily from 8:00 am to 4:00 pm, with extended hours during summer months. Admission is $10 for adults and $6 for children. Dogs dig for free.

Crater of Diamonds State Park
209 State Park Road
Murfreesboro, AR 71958
(870) 285-3113
www.bringfido.com/go/1DID

Where to Stay:

After Fido has bagged the jewels for his new diamond-studded collar, retreat to the Codex Cabin at **Parker Creek Bend Cabins**. Your pup will feel right at home with the beagle-themed decor, covered deck, and fire pit. Dogs of any size are welcome for an extra fee of $15 per pet, per night. If you came up empty on your diamond hunt, you and your pooch can stay at a tree-shaded campsite at **Crater of Diamonds State Park Campground**. Dogs of any size sleep there for free.

Parker Creek Bend Cabins
89 Parker Creek Road
Murfreesboro, AR 71958
(844) 712-2246
www.bringfido.com/go/1DIE
Rates from $130/night

Where to Stay:

After catching some waves, check into the **Kimpton Shorebreak Huntington Beach Resort,** a beachfront property with an upscale surf motif. Your pooch will be greeted with treats, a plush pet bed, and bowls. After you unpack, relax with Fido by the courtyard fire pits as you enjoy a complimentary glass of wine or roast s'mores. Have dinner together at the on-site **Pacific Hideaway** restaurant, which offers a gourmet dog menu. Dogs of any size are welcome at the resort for no additional fee.

Kimpton Shorebreak
Huntington Beach Resort
500 Pacific Coast Highway
Huntington Beach, CA 92648
(714) 861-4470
www.bringfido.com/go/1DGD
Rates from $214/night

Huntington Dog Beach

Located on a mile-long stretch of sand between Seapoint Avenue and 21st Street on the famous Pacific Coast Highway, **Huntington Dog Beach** is a canine lover's paradise. Nicknamed 'Surf City USA' by the locals, this strand is home to several annual dog events, including the Surf City Surf Dog Competition. The event attracts four-legged competitors from around the world, seeking the title of canine surfing champion. Whether your pooch wants to ride a board or just romp leash-free on the sand, Huntington Beach is the place for some fun in the sun. After your day out, take a short walk with Fido to the **Dirty Dog Wash**. For the do-it-yourself price of $19 to $29 (depending on your pup's size), they will provide all of the equipment and supplies needed to get your dog freshened up for a night on the town. Be sure to stop by **Top Dog Barkery** and pick up a gourmet doggy delicacy for your good boy.

Huntington Dog Beach
100 Goldenwest Street
Huntington Beach, CA 92647
(714) 841-8644
www.bringfido.com/go/1DGC

Aqua Adventures

Spend a day on Mission Bay with your dog by renting a kayak or stand-up paddleboard from **Aqua Adventures** in San Diego. With a large variety of kayaks, canoes, and paddleboards to choose from, you'll find exactly what you need for an unforgettable day on the water. Beginners will appreciate the advice offered by the company's experienced staff. The outfitter will help you plan a route and make sure that the equipment is ready when you and your pooch get to the water. Gorgeous views of the Coronado Bay Bridge and San Diego skyline await you. If your pup is a novice at paddlesports, Aqua Adventures offers free clinics designed to introduce him to these activities to ensure success and enjoyment for both human and hound. Hone your skills with one of their regular dog paddles out to Fiesta Island Park for off-leash play time. Rental rates start at $20.

Aqua Adventures
1548 Quivira Way
San Diego, CA 92109
(619) 523-9577
www.bringfido.com/go/1DH1

Where to Stay:

Located in the vibrant Gaslamp Quarter, **Hotel Solamar** provides laid-back luxury for you and your four-legged companion. Canine guests receive delicious treats, a plush doggy bed, and feeding bowls in boutique-style rooms adorned with chic decor. There is a convenient grass parkway with a pet station right outside the front entrance for dog walking. Pet sitting arrangements can be made through the concierge. Dogs of any size are welcome for no additional fee.

Hotel Solamar
435 6th Avenue
San Diego, CA 92101
(619) 819-9500
www.bringfido.com/go/1DH2
Rates from $151/night

Where to Stay:

Glamp in a cabin, vintage trailer, or safari tent at **Flying Flags RV Resort & Campground**. Fido will enjoy meeting new friends in the off-leash dog park, at the Fireside Lounge, or while dining on the patio of the Campfire Café. Two dogs up to 60 lbs are welcome for an additional fee of $50 per stay. If your pup is on the larger side, head over to the **Royal Copenhagen Inn**, where two dogs of any size stay for an extra fee of $20 per pet, per night.

Flying Flags RV Resort
& Campground
180 Avenue Of The Flags
Buellton, CA 93427
(805) 688-3716
www.bringfido.com/go/1DI9
Rates from $189/night

OstrichLand USA

You and your pup can hang out with and feed ostriches and emus at **OstrichLand USA**. Over 100 of the large, flightless birds live on this central California ranch just outside the Danish-themed town of Solvang. Stop by the gift shop to purchase a bowl of food to feed the birds, or take home souvenirs and fresh eggs. If visiting in summer, you may even see some baby chicks. OstrichLand USA is open daily from 9:00 am to 5:00 pm. Admission is $5 for adults, $2 for children, and free for dogs. After your ostrich outing, stop by **Fresco Valley Café** for lunch and order Fido something delicious from the dog menu, like the Angus beef patty or wild salmon. Then drop by the dog-friendly tasting room at **Carivintas Winery**, where your pup can relax on a pet bed and munch on treats while you sample delicious wines featuring rescue dogs on the bottles.

OstrichLand USA
610 E Highway 246
Solvang, CA 93463
(805) 686-9696
www.bringfido.com/go/1DI8

Runyon Canyon Park

Take a hike along trails frequented by some of Hollywood's most famous celebrities and their dogs at **Runyon Canyon Park** in Los Angeles. Pretend like you're the 'pupparazzi' as you check out the scenery and the stars. For more fur-flying fun, make your way to **Lake Hollywood Park**, where the locals bring their dogs for playtime and socialization under the famous Hollywood Sign. If you want to get an even closer look at the iconic landmark, head to the **Bronson Canyon Trail** in Griffith Park. This 6.5-mile hike will take you and your pooch to the back of the Hollywood Sign in less than three hours. Just bring lots of water and be sure your pup can handle the heat. End your day with a visit to the **Hollywood Walk of Fame**, where you can snap Fido's picture next to the stars of *Lassie* and *Rin Tin Tin*. If you are lucky (or plan ahead), you may even witness an induction ceremony.

Runyon Canyon Park
2000 N Fuller Avenue
Los Angeles, CA 90046
(323) 666-5046
www.bringfido.com/go/1DM0

Where to Stay:

Want to make Fido feel like an A-list movie star on his visit to Los Angeles? **The Kimpton Everly Hotel** places you and your pampered pooch right in the heart of the glitz and glamour of Hollywood. Located just steps from the Hollywood Walk of Fame, the property welcomes furry friends with treats, beds, bowls, and plenty of attention during the hotel's nightly social hour. Dogs of any size are welcome for no additional fee.

The Kimpton Everly Hotel
1800 Argyle Avenue
Los Angeles, CA 90028
(213) 279-3532
www.bringfido.com/go/1DM1
Rates from $189/night

Where to Stay:

After seeing the highlights of Santa Barbara with DeeTours, you'll get an amazing view of the Pacific Ocean when you arrive at **Belmond El Encanto**. Unwind in one of the resort's private bungalows, which feature luxurious king-size beds, rainforest showers, and private patios. Fido will love exploring the botanical gardens that canvas the seven-acre property. Other pet amenities include welcome treats, doggy beds, and bowls. Up to two dogs of any size are welcome for an additional fee of $150 per stay.

Belmond El Encanto
800 Alvarado Place
Santa Barbara, CA 93103
(805) 845-5800
www.bringfido.com/go/1DIX
Rates from $447/night

DeeTours of Santa Barbara

Enjoy some fun in the California sun alongside your four-legged friend in an open-air Jeep limousine tour with **DeeTours of Santa Barbara**. Choose the Scenic Santa Barbara and Montecito City Tour for a fast-paced journey around some of the most famous landmarks and residences in the 'American Riviera.' Opt for the Wine Country Adventure Tour for a more relaxing pace, as you and your group are treated to a scenic drive to the Santa Ynez Valley for a day complete with three to four wine tasting stops, shopping time in Solvang, and a picnic lunch. City tour prices start at $25 for adults and $10 for children. Wine country tour prices (which include all tasting fees and lunch) are $140 per person for a five- to six-hour tour. Fully customized trips are also available. Well-behaved dogs of any size are welcome on all tours for no additional fee.

DeeTours of Santa Barbara
1 Garden Street
Santa Barbara, CA 93101
(805) 448-8425
www.bringfido.com/go/1DIW

Arroyo Burro Beach

For some fun in the sun, head to **Arroyo Burro Beach**. Known to Santa Barbara locals as Hendry's Beach, this strip of sand has a great dog-friendly area where Fido can run, play, and swim. Just be sure to keep your pooch on a leash until you reach the marked dog zone. Parking and beach access are free. If your pooch still has energy to burn after his swim, take a hike at the adjacent **Douglas Family Preserve**. This 70-acre park boasts gorgeous views of the surf below and offers three miles of trails for man's best friend to explore off leash. Access to the park is free. On your way back to the beach parking lot, stop by the convenient self-service dog wash to scrub down your dirty pooch. Then, finish your day with a delicious seafood dinner at the **Boathouse at Hendry's Beach**, where leashed pups are welcome in the designated outdoor seating area.

Arroyo Burro Beach
2981 Cliff Drive
Santa Barbara, CA 93109
(805) 687-3714
www.bringfido.com/go/1DN1

Where to Stay:

For a weekend getaway to Santa Barbara that won't break the bank, check out the charming **Beach House Inn**. Located only three blocks from the beach, restaurants, and shopping along Cabrillo Boulevard, the property offers comfortable accommodations at affordable prices. Many rooms feature fully furnished kitchens and gas fireplaces. At the end of the street, you'll find a park that is perfect for walking your furry friend. Up to two dogs of any size are welcome for an additional fee of $10 per pet, per night.

Beach House Inn
320 W Yanonali Street
Santa Barbara, CA 93101
(805) 966-1126
www.bringfido.com/go/1DN2
Rates from $158/night

The Original Dog Beach

Spend the afternoon basking in the sun while Fido splashes in the ocean at **The Original Dog Beach** in San Diego. Located at the end of Ocean Beach, this section of sand is possibly the most 'pupular' spot in town. There is no fee to enter, and canines can play off leash all day long. But, please be sure that Fido is up-to-date on all vaccinations before his visit. If your salty dog needs to be scrubbed and fluffed after rolling in the sand, head straight to **Dog Beach Dog Wash**. The affordable do-it-yourself scrub station is perfect for post-beach grooms! After cleaning up, make your way to **Sally's Fish House & Bar**, an ocean-to-table restaurant with several outdoor tables. Satisfy your pup's fur-ocious appetite with a dish from Sally's Dog Menu, such as the Sit, Stay, Roll (sushi made with seared tuna, steamed broccoli and brown rice wrapped in seaweed).

The Original Dog Beach
5156 W Point Loma Boulevard
San Diego, CA 92107
(619) 236-5555
www.bringfido.com/go/1DLW

Where to Stay:

Located across the street from The Original Dog Beach, **Ocean Villa Inn** is a great value stay in San Diego. Your pup will be greeted with a care package filled with treats, toys, and waste bags. Visiting canines will also love the communal, fenced dog run and grassy area for walks. Pet parents will appreciate the DIY dog wash station stocked with shampoo and towels. Up to four dogs of any size are welcome for an addi-tional fee of $30 to $75 per stay, depending on the number of pets.

Ocean Villa Inn
5142 W Point Loma Boulevard
San Diego, CA 92107
(619) 224-3481
www.bringfido.com/go/1DLX
Rates from $118/night

Where to Stay:

Continue your coastal California adventure with a stay at **The Tides Laguna Beach**, where two dogs of any size are welcome for a nightly fee of $25 each ($40 each for dogs over 25 lbs). After checking in, take a stroll over to the oceanfront **Heisler Park** and let Fido frolic around walking trails and landscaped gardens. Afterward, make your way to **Naked Dog Bistro** for some gourmet treats. Cap off the evening with dinner at **The Cliff**, offering panoramic ocean views and a doggy menu.

The Tides Laguna Beach
460 N Coast Highway
Laguna Beach, CA 92651
(949) 494-2494
www.bringfido.com/go/1DG1
Rates from $140/night

Fun Zone Boat Company

You and your pup can embark on a scenic harbor cruise with the **Fun Zone Boat Company** in Newport Beach. The company features a fleet of four vessels that welcome man's best friend on narrated 45-minute floats in and around the Newport Beach Harbor. Choose the Sea Lion Tour to venture into the Pacific Ocean or opt for smoother sailing with the Celebrity Home and Yacht Tour. If you can't decide, the company also offers a 90-minute trip that includes both options. Enjoy the captain's entertaining narration as you get a glimpse of Catalina Island. If you cruise in the winter, you may even spot a whale or two. Tours depart several times daily from the Harbor Cruise boat docks adjacent to the Balboa Island Ferry. Rates start at $15 for adults and $5 for children. Salty dogs are always welcome aboard for no additional fee.

Fun Zone Boat Company
700 Edgewater Place
Newport Beach, CA 92661
(949) 673-0240
www.bringfido.com/go/1DG0

Bay Cruisers

Traverse the crystal blue waters of Morro Bay with Fido as your first mate on a **Bay Cruisers** boat ride. Skipper your own canopy-topped electric boat that accommodates up to eight passengers and your furry friend. Zoom across the bay near Morro Rock, a massive dome-shaped volcanic plug that also serves as a bird sanctuary for Peregrine Falcons. Along the way, keep an eye out for sea lions swimming in the protected waters of the bay or lounging on their own floating dock. Private daytime and sunset cruises are offered, and rates start at $95 for one-hour rentals. Add $10 for four-legged captains. Bay Cruisers is open daily from 10:00 am to sunset (Tuesdays by appointment only). Fido can also view Morro Rock from another vantage point at **Morro Bay State Park**. Leashed dogs are permitted on designated walking trails that run along the shoreline.

Bay Cruisers
845 Embarcadero
Morro Bay, CA 93442
(805) 771-9339
www.bringfido.com/go/1DJH

Where to Stay:

Located within walking distance to Morro Rock, the **Bayfront Inn** offers cozy accommodations with amazing waterfront views. All guest rooms are pet friendly, and pups receive a welcome bag upon arrival that includes snacks, feeding bowls, and waste bags. While your furry bff is enjoying his treats, you can nosh on the inn's freshly baked cinnamon rolls. Up to two dogs of any size are welcome for an additional fee of $30 per stay. Add $20 for a third pet.

Bayfront Inn
1150 Embarcadero
Morro Bay, CA 93442
(805) 772-5607
www.bringfido.com/go/1DJI
Rates from $89/night

Where to Stay:

After a full day of hiking, Fido can rest his weary paws in a cozy cabin at **Convict Lake Resort**. These secluded mountain retreats just outside Mammoth Lakes come furnished with fully equipped kitchens, propane grills, and complimentary Wi-Fi. Wake up in the morning and take your pup for a walk around the three-mile trail encircling beautiful Convict Lake. After you've worked up an appetite, dine on the spacious, pet-friendly patio at the resort's on-site restaurant. Up to two dogs of any size are welcome for an additional fee of $12 per pet, per night.

Convict Lake Resort
2000 Convict Lake Road
Mammoth Lakes, CA 93546
(760) 934-3800
www.bringfido.com/go/1DGL
Rates from $199/night

Devils Postpile

Don't miss the chance to see a rare geologic wonder in Mammoth Lakes. **Devils Postpile National Monument** was formed a hundred thousand years ago when a volcanic eruption cooled into an impressive wall of columns. Today, the 60-foot-tall rock formation can be accessed via an easy half-mile hike. Dogs must be leashed at the monument but can remain under voice control on all other trails. Early birds may drive themselves to the Devils Postpile Ranger Station, but after 7:00 am, all visitors are required to take a shuttle bus from the **Mammoth Adventure Center**. The shuttle costs $8 for adults and $4 for children. Dogs ride for free but must be muzzled during the short trip. After returning to the Adventure Center, take the **Scenic Gondola** to the summit of the mountain for lunch at the **Eleven53 Café**. Tickets are $27 for adults and free for dogs.

Devils Postpile National Monument
Devils Postpile Access Road
Mammoth Lakes, CA 93546
(760) 934-2289
www.bringfido.com/go/1DGK

Monterey Bay Whale Watch

For a whale of a time with your pup, take a ride on *Sea Wolf II* with **Monterey Bay Whale Watch**. Tours on this 70-passenger vessel depart Monterey twice daily for three- to five-hour trips. All tours are guided by a marine biologist, and, depending on the season, your dog is almost sure to spot killer whales, humpbacks, blue whales, or gray whales in the Monterey Bay National Marine Sanctuary. Tour prices start at $60 for adults and $48 for children, with no additional charge for your pooch. After your adventure on the bay, park yourself at one of the outdoor tables at **Abalonetti Bar & Grill**. In addition to having the largest dog-friendly dining area on Fisherman's Wharf, they also feature a dog menu with tasty items like a grilled chicken breast or a hamburger patty. Both are served on a souvenir Frisbee that Fido can take home.

Monterey Bay Whale Watch
84 Fisherman's Wharf
Monterey, CA 93940
(831) 375-4658
www.bringfido.com/go/1DHI

Where to Stay:

You and your four-legged friend will be treated like VIPs at the lavish **Portola Hotel & Spa**. Sleep in elegant guest rooms, dine al fresco at one of the property's pet-friendly restaurants, or take a half-mile walk to **Cannery Row** on the Monterey Bay Coastal Recreation Trail. Dogs of any size are welcome for an extra fee of $50 for one night, and $25 for each additional night. A comfy dog bed, food and water bowls, and treats are provided at check-in.

Portola Hotel & Spa
2 Portola Plaza
Monterey, CA 93940
(800) 342-4295
www.bringfido.com/go/1DHJ
Rates from $249/night

Where to Stay:

Originally a fish shack and road-house, **Nick's Cove** features charming waterfront cottages perched on wooden stilts—the perfect setting to cap off your dog day on Tomales Bay. At check-in, you will be greeted with barbecued oysters and Fido will be offered freshly baked treats. Visit in April when your good boy will be spoiled with a canine massage and other surprises as part of the 'Pampered Pooch Package.' Up to two dogs of any size are welcome for an additional fee of $50 per pet, per stay.

Nick's Cove
23240 Highway 1
Marshall, CA 94940
(415) 663-1033
www.bringfido.com/go/1DV0
Rates from $365/night

Hog Island Oyster Co.

Bring your salty dog on an oyster crawl through Northern California. Start your day in Marshall with a visit to **Hog Island Oyster Co.**, which offers one-hour walking tours that take visitors on a deep dive into how oysters are commercially raised and harvested. Sample Hog Island's finest bivalves from a picnic table next to the waterfront oyster bar. Just a mile south, you'll find **The Marshall Store**, where you can sit on the patio with your pup to sample Pacific oysters from the Tomales Bay Oyster Company's family farm. Continue your journey south to the rocky shores of **Point Reyes National Seashore**, a beautiful backdrop for you to walk off those mid-day calories and let your pooch stretch his legs. Cap off your oyster adventure at idyllic **Nick's Cove Restaurant**. Kick back with Fido, sip on a tasty cocktail, and sample more award-winning shellfish from the waterfront patio overlooking Tomales Bay.

Hog Island Oyster Co.
20215 Shoreline Highway
Marshall, CA 94940
(415) 663-9218
www.bringfido.com/go/1DUZ

Skunk Train

Snaking through the majestic redwood forests, the famous **Skunk Train** offers human and canine passengers excellent views of gorgeous Mendocino County. Originally built as a logging railroad in 1885, the train takes its name from the description locals gave to the smell of gasoline-powered engines after the introduction of motorcars in 1925. Take the Pudding Creek Express Tour for a quick seven-mile trip to Glen Blair Junction where you can disembark to explore the redwood-lined trails. Catch the next train back approximately two hours later. Fares start at $42 for adults and $26 for children. Dogs are welcome for $11 more. When you return to Fort Bragg, head over to **Mendocino Coast Botanical Gardens** for a leisurely walk through the formal gardens, coastal bluffs, pine forests, and fern-covered canyons. The attraction is open year-round. Admission is $15 for adults and $8 for children. Dogs are free.

Skunk Train
100 W Laurel Street
Fort Bragg, CA 95437
(707) 964-6371
www.bringfido.com/go/1DG6

Where to Stay:

The town of Little River offers two Fido-approved lodging options. **The Inn at Schoolhouse Creek** welcomes dogs with a pet bed, bowl, beach towel, and treats. For amazing ocean views, choose the Water Tower cottage, which features an enclosed courtyard for your pup and a private hot tub and rooftop deck for you. Two dogs of any size stay for $25 per pet, per night. The **Little River Inn** offers treats, bowls, pet towels, and designated pet walking areas. You can even make arrangements for private dining with your pooch in the hotel parlor. Two dogs are welcome for an extra fee of $30 per pet, per night.

The Inn at Schoolhouse Creek
7051 N Highway One
Little River, CA 95456
(707) 937-5525
www.bringfido.com/go/1DG7
Rates from $159/night

17-Mile Drive

Nicknamed the dog-friendly capital of the world, Carmel caters to man's best friend like no other. Journey into town via picturesque **17-Mile Drive**. Along the way, be sure to stop at **Asilomar State Beach** where Fido can stretch his legs on boardwalks and trails meandering through coastal bluffs and sand dunes. Once you arrive in town, head to Carmel Plaza for an obligatory visit to the famous **Fountain of Woof**, a popular spot for dog- and people-watching. After Fido takes a sip in the fountain for good luck, explore the Carmel coastline on wheels with a vintage e-bike rental (with pup-friendly sidecar) from **Mad Dogs & Englishmen**. For some off-leash fun, head over to **Carmel Beach**, where spoiled dogs are free to roam on the gorgeous white sand beaches. Cap off your evening with a delicious meal and some California wine on the pet-friendly patio at **The Forge**.

17-Mile Drive
1700 17-Mile Drive
Pebble Beach, CA 93953
(831) 622-8307
www.bringfido.com/go/1DG3

Where to Stay:

After a day of exploring Carmel, rest those weary paws at **Cypress Inn**. Pet blankets, treats, and bowls are provided, and a pet wash station is located in the hotel courtyard. The property welcomes dogs of any size for an additional fee of $30 per night ($50 for two dogs). Or, make your way to **Svendsgaard's Inn**, where canine comforts include spacious grounds to roam, a pet bed and blanket, dog bowls, and treats available all day! Up to two dogs of any size are welcome for a fee of $25 per pet, per night.

Cypress Inn
Lincoln Street & 7th Avenue
Carmel, CA 93921
(831) 624-3871
www.bringfido.com/go/1DG4
Rates from $249/night

Where to Stay:

Go glamping with your pooch in an Airstream trailer at **Auto-Camp Yosemite**. Fully equipped trailers feature plush bedding and spa-inspired bathrooms for human comfort, and furry family members receive a blanket, treats, waste bags, and bowls. Two dogs up to 50 lbs are welcome for an additional fee of $75 per stay. If your pup is on the larger side, book a room at the **Narrow Gauge Inn** in Fish Camp, where two dogs of any size are permitted for an extra fee of $25 per pet, per stay.

AutoCamp Yosemite
6323 CA-140
Midpines, CA 95345
(888) 405-7553
www.bringfido.com/go/1DTV
Rates from $169/night

Yosemite National Park

Explore the great outdoors with your hound at **Yosemite National Park** in the Sierra Nevada Mountains. You'll feel like you're in another world while walking among granite monoliths, waterfalls, and Giant Sequoias. Take a hike with Fido along the Wawona Meadow Loop, a flat, 3.5-mile path through one of the park's largest meadows. In the spring and early summer months, it's filled with wildflowers. In the fall, vibrant foliage from the hardwoods will welcome you. For more scenic views, head to the Mirror Lake Trail, a paved two-mile path that passes beneath the base of the iconic Half Dome. If your pup isn't up for a big hike, check out the half-mile Bridalveil Fall Trail, which boasts a gorgeous overlook of a 620-foot waterfall. After you've worked up an appetite, stop for lunch on the patio at **Degnan's Deli** at Yosemite Village, the only pet-friendly restaurant in the national park.

Yosemite National Park
9035 Village Drive
Yosemite National Park, CA 95389
(209) 372-0200
www.bringfido.com/go/1DTU

Tahoe City Winter Sports Park

Pack your pup's earmuffs and ski boots and head to **Tahoe City Winter Sports Park**. This winter recreation complex allows you to cross-country ski and snowshoe with your canine companion in downtown Tahoe City, just steps from the shores of majestic Lake Tahoe. Furry extreme athletes can mush alongside as you navigate over two miles of wide open cross-country and snowshoe trails. All day fun passes are $40 for adults and $35 for children. Dogs ski for $3. If you are visiting the lake region in summer, bring Fido to **Kiva Beach** for a free swim, or charter a trip with **Tahoe Sport Fishing**. Cast your hook in search of mackinaw, trout, and kokanee salmon. Rates start at $140 per person and include bait, tackle, poles, and doggy life jackets, along with drinks and a continental breakfast. Dogs float for free.

Tahoe City Winter Sports Park
251 N Lake Boulevard
Tahoe City, CA 96145
(530) 583-1516
www.bringfido.com/go/1DUK

Where to Stay:

Dog lovers will find warm and inviting accommodations at the **Fireside Lodge** in South Lake Tahoe. Upon arrival, you'll be greeted as if you were staying at a friend's home. Travelers are welcomed with an afternoon wine and cheese reception and property tour. Families with children will particularly enjoy the nightly marshmallow roasts and retro game room. Complimentary bike, sled, and snowshoe rentals are also provided. Well-behaved dogs of any size are welcome for an additional fee of $35 per pet, per night.

Fireside Lodge
515 Emerald Bay Road
South Lake Tahoe, CA 96150
(530) 544-5515
www.bringfido.com/go/1DUL
Rates from $139/night

Where to Stay:

Nestled in the shadow of the Golden Gate Bridge and only minutes from the Sausalito Ferry Terminal, **Cavallo Point** rolls out the red carpet for its four-legged guests. The hotel's Eco Luxe Pups program treats Fido like royalty by lavishing him with organic biscuits, custom bowls from Sausalito Pottery, luxury pet bedding, and a Pet Swag Bag. He can also join you for dinner on the patio at the hotel restaurant, **Murray Circle**. Up to two dogs of any size are welcome for an additional fee of $150 per stay.

Cavallo Point
601 Murray Circle
Sausalito, CA 94965
(415) 339-4700
www.bringfido.com/go/1DJ7
Rates from $382/night

Blue & Gold Fleet

Spend a dog day on the bay with the **Blue & Gold Fleet**. Begin your journey in San Francisco's iconic Fisherman's Wharf. Make your way by foot and paw along The Embarcadero to Pier 39, where you will board a Blue & Gold vessel for your sightseeing excursion. Fido can sniff the salty sea air on a 90-minute 'Escape from the Rock' cruise that sails beneath the Golden Gate Bridge and around Alcatraz Island. Survey the storied home of America's most infamous maximum-security prison while learning about the institution's celebrated inmates and harrowing escape attempts on this fully narrated adventure. Tickets are $42 for adults and $31 for children. If Fido has sturdy sea legs, venture beyond the city on the Blue & Gold Fleet's ferry service to charming Sausalito. Boats depart several times daily from Pier 41, and dogs are welcome for free on all cruises.

Blue & Gold Fleet
Pier 41
San Francisco, CA 94133
(415) 705-8203
www.bringfido.com/go/1DJ6

Presidio of San Francisco

For a pawsome day in the Bay Area, bring Fido on a visit to the **Presidio of San Francisco**. The national park site, formerly a US Army post, today offers visitors free access to some of the city's best vistas, walking trails, and public open spaces. Take in some great views of the Golden Gate Bridge as you exercise your furry friend along **Baker Beach**, a one-mile stretch of coastline that is popular with active pups for its leash-optional policy. Slip on Fido's hiking boots and trek the **Presidio Ecology Trail**, a 1.7- mile loop that winds to the top of Inspiration Point, overlooking the bay and Alcatraz Island. Grab a bite to eat on the patio at **Presidio Café**, located across the street from the trailhead, or enjoy a picnic at **Crissy Field**. Much of the park can become quite crowded, especially on weekends. So, plan an early morning or mid-week visit if your pup prefers wide open spaces.

Presidio of San Francisco
103 Montgomery Street
San Francisco, CA 94129
(415) 561-5300
www.bringfido.com/go/1DUS

Where to Stay:

Once serving as quarters for military officers in the early 1900s, the **Inn at the Presidio** today provides modern, spacious rooms to tourists seeking a unique San Francisco lodging experience. After you and your pup's day of sightseeing, head to the hotel's outdoor patio and fire pit and enjoy the evening wine and cheese reception. Dogs of any size are invited for an additional fee of $40 per stay. The inn's sister property, **Lodge at the Presidio**, shares the same pet policy and welcomes guests with striking views of the Golden Gate Bridge.

Inn at the Presidio
42 Moraga Avenue
San Francisco, CA 94129
(415) 800-7356
www.bringfido.com/go/1DUT
Rates from $320/night

Where to Stay:

After a day on the Russian River, you and your pup can relax at **Healdsburg Inn on the Plaza** in downtown Healdsburg. Enjoy luxury accommodations, daily breakfast, and complimentary wine, cheese, and cookies each afternoon. Up to two dogs (40 lbs or less) are welcome for an additional fee of $65 per stay. If you have a larger dog, opt for the **Best Western Dry Creek Inn**, where four-legged guests receive a treat bag at check-in and two dogs of any size stay for an extra fee of $30 per night ($50 for premium rooms).

Healdsburg Inn on the Plaza
112 Matheson Street
Healdsburg, CA 95448
(707) 433-6991
www.bringfido.com/go/1DGA
Rates from $195/night

Russian River Adventures

Visit **Russian River Adventures** for a SOAR inflatable canoe trip down the Russian River in Healdsburg. The company's nine-mile, full-day float begins at the Memorial Beach Dam and covers a stretch of river that's unobstructed by buildings or roads, so Fido can remain off leash whenever and wherever you decide to pull ashore for a break from paddling. Cool down in one of the river's many swimming holes, play a game of fetch, show off on a rope swing, or enjoy a picnic lunch on the first sandbar that looks good to you. The company's trips are offered between April and October. Rentals are available seven days a week in the summer and every weekend in the fall. The fees are $75 per adult, $35 per child, and $15 per dog (with a guarantee that he'll be happy and tired at the end of the trip).

Russian River Adventures
20 Healdsburg Avenue
Healdsburg, CA 95448
(707) 433-5599
www.bringfido.com/go/1DG9

Catch a Canoe & Bicycles Too

If you'd like to paddle with your dog, but haven't tried it before, you might want to start by renting a handcrafted, redwood outrigger canoe from **Catch a Canoe & Bicycles Too** in Mendocino. Outriggers are the perfect vehicle for novice paddlers because they're extremely stable and easy to paddle on the water—even with an excited dog on board. And when Fido sees all of the herons, ducks, harbor seals, and river otters on the Big River estuary, he is definitely going to be excited! Families with multiple dogs should request the aptly named 'Canine Cruiser' outrigger. It can safely accommodate up to four dogs and has a raised fabric platform that allows them to walk, sit, and lie down comfortably. Catch a Canoe is open daily from 9:00 am to 5:00 pm. Rental fees start at $35 for adults and $15 for children. Doggos float for free.

Catch a Canoe & Bicycles Too
1 S Big River Road
Mendocino, CA 95460
(707) 937-0273
www.bringfido.com/go/1DHG

Where to Stay:

When you arrive at **The Stanford Inn by the Sea** following your Big River adventure, Fido will likely be greeted by the innkeeper's dogs, Ellie and Parker. While you warm up by the fire in the main lodge, the three of them can feast on organic sweet potato biscuits made by the inn's chef. But don't be jealous—you'll also be treated to one of his delicious creations at breakfast the next morning. One dog of any size is welcome for $45 per stay. Add $23 for each additional pet.

The Stanford Inn by the Sea
44850 Comptche Ukiah Road
Mendocino, CA 95460
(707) 937-5615
www.bringfido.com/go/1DHH
Rates from $277/night

Trees of Mystery

Massive Paul Bunyan and Babe the Blue Ox statues stand guard outside the **Trees of Mystery**, one of Northern California's most unique dog-friendly destinations. Located in the heart of Redwood National Park, this museum and nature attraction has been welcoming guests to explore the mighty redwoods up close since 1946. Measuring up to 20 feet in diameter, the massive trees are impressive to behold. Walk among 2,000-year-old behemoths with majestic monikers like The Brotherhood, Cathedral, and Elephant. When you're finished staring up at giants, soar above the towering forest canopy on a 10-minute ride on the SkyTrail Gondola. Fido is welcome to climb aboard to experience the bird's-eye view. General admission is $20 for adults, $11 for children, and free for dogs. Leashed pups are permitted in all areas except the Redwood Canopy Trail.

Trees of Mystery
15500 US-101
Klamath, CA 95548
(800) 638-3389
www.bringfido.com/go/1DJ3

Where to Stay:

Continue taking in the scenic views on a 25-mile drive north along the Redwood Highway to the **Anchor Beach Inn** in Crescent City. The hotel offers double-queen ocean-view rooms for guests traveling with fur kids. Dogs of any size are welcome for an additional fee of $15 per pet, per night. During your stay, enjoy the sunset and an ice cold brew on the dog-friendly deck at nearby **SeaQuake Brewing**. You may even spot a resident seal or sea lion on your walk around the harbor.

Anchor Beach Inn
880 Highway 101 S
Crescent City, CA 95531
(707) 464-2600
www.bringfido.com/go/1DJ4
Rates from $65/night

Where to Stay:

Located just outside of Winter Park, **Devil's Thumb Ranch** has been welcoming city folk (and their dogs) to the property since 1938. Today, the luxury resort boasts two gourmet restaurants, a full-service spa, and some of the best Nordic trails in North America. Each four-legged guest receives a dog bed, homemade treat, and leash to use while exploring the 6,000-acre property. Up to two dogs of any size are welcome in cabins for an additional fee of $50 per pet, per night.

Devil's Thumb Ranch
3530 County Road 83
Tabernash, CO 80478
(970) 726-5632
www.bringfido.com/go/1E3T
Rates from $279/night

High Country Dogs

Skijoring is a winter sport where a cross-country skier is pulled by a dog, several dogs, or even a horse! In the snow-covered Colorado Rockies, it's a great way to exercise and bond with your pooch while enjoying the jaw-dropping scenery all around you. Dogs of all breeds can participate, and most animals over 35 lbs are capable of pulling an average-sized skier. All they need is an innate desire to run down a trail and pull. If you'd like to give it a try, Louisa Morrissey of **High Country Dogs** offers private lessons and workshops at **Devil's Thumb Ranch**. Start with an indoor session on training tips and dog care before heading out on the snow for a hands-on lesson on basic commands and techniques. Lessons start at $75 per hour and include a dog harness, belt, and line (you need to provide your own ski equipment). Skijoring season generally runs from December through March.

High Country Dogs
3530 County Road 83
Tabernash, CO 80478
(970) 406-0158
www.bringfido.com/go/1DHR

Garden of the Gods

Garden of the Gods in Colorado Springs is known for its incredible red rock formations, beautiful hiking trails, and breathtaking views of Pikes Peak. Orient yourself with a 45-minute guided walk departing from the Visitor & Nature Center before exploring on your own. The park is open daily and admission is free. Guided tours are $5 per person with advance reservations. In the afternoon, make your way to the 1,000-year-old ruins at **Manitou Cliff Dwellings** for a look at the fascinating architecture of the ancient Anasazi people. The site is open daily. Admission is $12 for adults, $8 for children, and free for dogs. At the end of your day, grab a meal at **Pub Dog Colorado**, where you can dine indoors with your dog. Food is served counter-service style (in dog bowls!), and the restaurant boasts an impressive canine menu. Fido can burn off the calories at the restaurant's fenced dog park.

Garden of the Gods
1805 N 30th Street
Colorado Springs, CO 80904
(719) 634-6666
www.bringfido.com/go/1DGM

Where to Stay:

Located seven miles from Garden of the Gods in Colorado Springs, **The Broadmoor** defines modern elegance. Spectacular views of Cheyenne Mountain, Cheyenne Lake, or one of three on-site golf courses are available in most suites and cottages. Amenities include a full-service spa, tennis, three swimming pools, and numerous restaurants. Fido can sample canine cuisine from the gourmet pet menu. Bedding and bowls are provided. Up to two dogs of any size are welcome for an additional fee of $100 per pet, per night.

The Broadmoor
1 Lake Avenue
Colorado Springs, CO 80906
(719) 577-5775
www.bringfido.com/go/1DGN
Rates from $305/night

Telluride Gondola

Telluride is best known for its world-class alpine skiing, but with hundreds of pet-friendly trails originating in or near town, it is also heaven-on-earth for hounds that like to hike once the snow melts. Your adventure starts with a 13-minute trip on the **Telluride Gondola**. Free to ride, this popular attraction connects Telluride with Mountain Village via a scenic tram traversing the San Juan Mountains. Located halfway between the two towns, the Station San Sophia stop is your gateway to mountaintop hiking and biking. The gondola operates daily from 7:00 am to midnight, and pet-friendly cabins are marked with window stickers. After a day on the trails, give tired paws a break by heading into town for sightseeing aboard the **Galloping Goose**. The free shuttle bus will stop at any corner on town routes and runs every 20 minutes, seven days a week. Hours and schedule vary by season.

Telluride Gondola
300 W San Juan Avenue
Telluride, CO 81435
(970) 728-3041
www.bringfido.com/go/1DHM

Where to Stay:

With slope-side cabins and ski-in, ski-out access less than 100 yards away, you couldn't ask for a more convenient location for your Colorado vacation than the **Mountain Lodge at Telluride**. The pet-friendly Telluride Gondola is only a few blocks away too, so once you park your car at the lodge, you won't need it again until you leave. Just relax and enjoy the view. Dogs of any size are welcome for an additional fee of $50 per night (maximum $150 per stay).

Mountain Lodge at Telluride
457 Mountain Village Boulevard
Telluride, CO 81435
(970) 369-5000
www.bringfido.com/go/1DHN
Rates from $134/night

Where to Stay:

Settle in for the night in a cozy lodge room or spacious cabin at the **Sundance Trail Guest Ranch**. Rooms feature comfortable beds, private baths, outdoor entrances, refrigerators, and daily housekeeping. Cookies, lemonade, and coffee are available any time, and three hearty western meals are served daily. The dinner bell is rung before all meals, so you can enjoy your vacation without a watch. Dogs of any size are welcome at the ranch for no additional fee.

Sundance Trail Guest Ranch
17931 W County Road 74E
Red Feather Lakes, CO 80545
(970) 224-1222
www.bringfido.com/go/1DHQ
Rates from $150/night

Sundance Trail Guest Ranch

Bring Fido to Red Feather Lakes for an unforgettable experience at the **Sundance Trail Guest Ranch**. This northern Colorado dude ranch offers a variety of ranch activities, including rifle shooting, archery, roping lessons, rock climbing, hiking, fishing, and horseshoe tournaments. Explore the trails by horseback as Fido comes along for the ride. The ranch caters to a limited number of visitors each week, so all organized activities can be tailored for beginners or those with more advanced experience. Nightly offerings such as square dancing, cowboy poetry, and evening campfires are designed for the whole family to enjoy. Relax after a full day of fun with a soak in the hot tub, a massage, or a good book by the warm fire. Listen to cowboy stories on the expansive front porch in the company of your new friends. Well-socialized dogs can enjoy all of the ranch activities with their humans.

Sundance Trail Guest Ranch
17931 W County Road 74E
Red Feather Lakes, CO 80545
(970) 224-1222
www.bringfido.com/go/1DHP

Colorado River Runs

Let **Colorado River Runs** in Bond guide you and Fido on the perfect rafting trip down the beautiful Colorado River. The outfitter has created a special tour with dogs in mind, keeping everyone safe and ensuring fun for your four-legged friend. Your knowledgeable guide will lead you through light rapids, calm backwaters and deep canyons, stopping along the way for your pup to take a dip in cool swimming holes and dig his paws in sandy beaches. Life jackets for humans and canines are provided, and each raft can accommodate up to two dogs and eight people. The rate for a private group of up to four adults and their water-loving dogs is $490. Each additional person is $59. Arrive early for your rafting trip and enjoy lunch in the outfitter's designated picnic area. Fido can even say hello to the resident donkeys cared for by the Colorado River Runs team.

Colorado River Runs
43 County Highway 111
Bond, Colorado 80423
(970) 653-4292
www.bringfido.com/go/1DJ1

Where to Stay:

After a day on the rapids, take it easy at **The Inn at Riverwalk** in Edwards. Your pup will be welcomed with treats and his own comfy pet bed. Humans can relax in the outdoor hot tub or heated riverside pool. For some off-leash fun, take Fido to **Edwards Freedom Park**, located just steps down the recreation path that runs behind the hotel. Two dogs of any size are welcome for an additional fee of $25 per pet, per night.

The Inn at Riverwalk
27 Main Street
Edwards, CO 81632
(970) 926-0606
www.bringfido.com/go/1DJ2
Rates from $109/night

Leadville Railroad

Bring Fido on board the **Leadville Colorado & Southern Railroad** for a scenic ride through the Rocky Mountains. Choose a seat in an enclosed section of the train, or relax in an open-air car and enjoy the panoramic vistas of the Arkansas River Valley as you rise up 1,000 feet from the valley floor. There, you'll spot two of Colorado's highest peaks—Mt. Massive and Mt. Elbert. On the two-and-a-half hour tour through the breathtaking San Isabel National Forest, the conductor will educate passengers on the history of Leadville and share tales about legendary characters who once called the area home. Refreshments are available from the on-board concession stand, but you are free to bring your own food and drink to enjoy on the journey. Trains operate from the beginning of May through the first weekend of October. Tickets are $42 for adults and $22 for children. Dogs ride for free.

Leadville Colorado & Southern Railroad
326 E 7th Street
Leadville, CO 80461
(719) 486-3936
www.bringfido.com/go/1DIZ

Where to Stay:

Centrally located in Vail Valley, **The Ritz-Carlton, Bachelor Gulch** is a luxurious basecamp for your Rocky Mountain adventures. Fido will be impressed with services like in-room doggy massages and pup-friendly guided snowshoe tours. He'll also be happy to know that the pet menu has been taste-tested and approved by Bachelor, the hotel's canine ambassador. Two dogs of any size are welcome for a fee of $125 for the first three nights, and $50 for each additional night.

The Ritz-Carlton, Bachelor Gulch
0130 Daybreak Ridge
Avon, CO 81620
(970) 748-6200
www.bringfido.com/go/1DJ0
Rates from $189/night

Where to Stay:

Once you and Fido are finished hoppin' across the state, kick up your feet and paws at **Saybrook Point Resort & Marina**. This waterfront haven combines small-town charm with big-city elegance, offering luxury rooms and suites tastefully decorated in warm tones that convey a cozy, at-home ambiance. Four-legged guests receive tasty treats and sporty bandanas upon arrival. Two dogs of any size are welcome for an additional fee of $45 per night.

Saybrook Point Resort & Marina
2 Bridge Street
Old Saybrook, CT 06475
(860) 395-2000
www.bringfido.com/go/1DM6
Rates from $238/night

Hoppin' Around Connecticut

Beer enthusiasts and their brew dogs will enjoy a trio of stops on a day trip through Connecticut. Start your jaunt with a visit to **Hop Culture Farms & Brewing Co.** in Colchester to see the craft brewing process in action. If visiting in summer, sign up for a Hopyard Tour to learn how homegrown farm ingredients transform into uniquely flavored beers. At the end, grab some tasters of favorites like the American Hopic and Hop of Shame. Leashed dogs are always welcome. Continue your dog crawl to **Yankee Cider Company** in East Haddam. There, you can sample a New England Dry or Honeycrisp Blend in the cider barn alongside your pooch. Finally, head eight miles east to **Devil's Hopyard State Park** to exercise your furry friend along the half-mile Chapman Falls Loop. Entrance is free, and leashed dogs are permitted on multiple hiking trails.

Hop Culture Farms & Brewing Co.
144 Cato Corner Road
Colchester, CT 06415
(860) 305-9556
www.bringfido.com/go/1DM5

Mystic Seaport

Delve into American maritime history with a trip to **Mystic Seaport**. Fido is welcome to join in the fun as you explore the grounds of the nation's leading maritime museum. Stroll through the shipyard before visiting the re-creation of a 19th-century seafaring village with more than 30 historic trade shops and businesses. Historians, storytellers, and musicians in period dress bring an air of authenticity to the experience. Walk with your pup through Mystic Seaport's nine gardens to learn more about New England flora and fauna. Admission is $26 for adults, $17 for children, and free for dogs. If the setting inspires you to venture off shore, end a trip to the seaport aboard a rowboat with your pup. Rentals cost just $15 for a half-hour ride. For a more luxurious experience, take in the historic sites on a private two-hour cruise with **Mystic Yacht Charter**. Private cruise rates start at $350.

Mystic Seaport
75 Greenmanville Avenue
Mystic, CT 06355
(860) 572-0711
www.bringfido.com/go/1DHT

Where to Stay:

At the end of your seafaring expedition, bring your salty dog to **Hampton Inn & Suites Mystic** for a good night's rest. Located one mile north of the Mystic Seaport, the hotel welcomes guests with a daily hot breakfast and free parking. Pet-friendly rooms are located on the ground floor, and dogs of any size stay for no additional fee. Before you leave town, be sure to stop by the **Sea View Snack Bar** to enjoy fresh lobster rolls and clam chowder at an outdoor picnic table overlooking Mystic Harbor.

Hampton Inn & Suites Mystic
6 Hendel Drive
Mystic, CT 06355
(860) 536-2536
www.bringfido.com/go/1DHU
Rates from $76/night

Where to Stay:

The **Homestead Bed & Breakfast at Rehoboth Beach** is an adults-only bed & breakfast with two acres of grounds and a large fenced yard that is perfect for your pooch. During the off-season (when dogs are allowed on Rehoboth Beach), you'll find their doggy shower and towels convenient for cleaning up after a trip to the beach. Dogs up to 80 lbs are welcome for an additional fee of $30 per pet for the first night and $15 per pet for each additional night. Larger dogs may be allowed with prior approval.

Homestead Bed & Breakfast
at Rehoboth Beach
35060 Warrington Road
Rehoboth Beach, DE 19971
(302) 226-7625
www.bringfido.com/go/1DJA
Rates from $115/night

Anglers Fishing Center

Exercise Fido's sea legs with a charter boat rental from **Anglers Fishing Center** in Lewes. Located at the mouth of the Delaware Bay and the Atlantic Ocean, Anglers offers private fishing charters year-round. Captain Ted welcomes you and your furry first mate aboard either the *Angler Party & Head Boat* or the *Pirate King Two*—a 52-foot vessel equipped with radar, fish finder, and GPS plotter. Cruise the bay and ocean in waters ideal for catching sea bass, shark, tuna, marlin and swordfish. Full- and half-day charters are available, along with sightseeing and historic narrated tours. Rates start at $450 for private charters and increase based on tour type and passenger count. Prices include all rods, bait, and tackle. You are welcome to bring snacks and drinks aboard—just no glass containers. Afterward, head next door for some fish and chips on the pup-friendly patio at **Irish Eyes Pub & Restaurant**.

Anglers Fishing Center
213 Anglers Road
Lewes, DE 19958
(302) 644-4533
www.bringfido.com/go/1DJ9

Fenwick Island State Park

Fenwick Island is the ultimate destination for a quiet, serene vacation with the whole family, including Fido. Spend a day seaside at **Fenwick Island State Park**, where leashed pups are welcome to play year-round on a section of the beach at the northern dune crossing. The park is open daily from 8:00 am to sunset, and the entrance fee is $10 per vehicle ($5 for Delaware residents). Continue relaxing with your pup by renting a kayak or paddleboard from **Island Watersports** and float on the calm waters of Little Assawoman Bay. Dogs are also welcome on pontoon boat rentals. Rates start at $20 for kayak rentals. After a day in the sun, bring your well-behaved, leashed pooch along for a round of miniature golf at **Viking Golf**. Read up on viking history and be on the lookout for hidden trolls as you putt your way around the 19-hole course.

Fenwick Island State Park
36840 Coastal Highway
Fenwick Island, DE 19971
(302) 227-2800
www.bringfido.com/go/1DQU

Where to Stay:

Relax in comfort at **Seaside Inn** in Fenwick Island. Each room has its own balcony where Fido can bask in the sun or feel the sea breeze in his fur. While the hotel is just steps from the Atlantic Ocean, guests can also enjoy a dip in the outdoor pool. Up to two dogs of any size are welcome for an additional fee of $30 per pet, per night. After settling into your room, take your pup for an evening walk to nearby shops like **Seaside Country Store**, or grab dinner outdoors at **Just Hooked**.

Seaside Inn
1401 Coastal Highway
Fenwick Island, DE 19944
(302) 251-5000
www.bringfido.com/go/1DQV
Rates from $89/night

Where to Stay:

The Jefferson hotel is the perfect spot for your canine companion to rest his tired paws after a long day of touring Washington DC. Located just a few blocks from the White House, the hotel features elegant rooms, delectable dining, and an impressive private collection of antique furnishings, period artwork, and historical documents. Pet amenities include bedding, food dishes, and a tasty treat provided at check-in. Dogs are welcome for an additional fee of $50 per stay.

The Jefferson
1200 16th Street NW
Washington, DC 20036
(202) 448-2300
www.bringfido.com/go/1DR1
Rates from $324/night

Adventure DC Tricycle Tours

After a morning constitutional with Fido, sit back, relax and enjoy the view of the White House and Capitol on a pet-friendly pedicab ride with **Adventure DC Tricycle Tours**. Choose from one of the classic tour options, like the Monuments and Memorials Tour, or let your guide know where you'd like to go. These fully narrated tours are completely customizable, so you and your furry running mate can choose the places you'd like to visit. Plan on spending at least two hours circling the loop around the National Mall. Each pedicab seats up to three adults, and tours can be arranged for any time of day. Prices start at $297 per party, and there is no additional fee for your pooch. To see the nation's capital at its creepiest, take an evening tour with **DC Ghosts**. The hour-long walking tour includes eight stops at locations of political and paranormal importance. Tickets are $19 for adults, $12 for children, and free for dogs.

Adventure DC Tricycle Tours
1440 G Street NW
Washington, DC 20005
(202) 669-7274
www.bringfido.com/go/1DR0

Boating in DC

See Washington DC monuments as you've never seen them before on a guided SUP or kayak paddle tour with **Boating in DC**. You and your dog can take a plunge in the Potomac and Anacostia Rivers for a refreshing trip around Theodore Roosevelt Island and past iconic DC locations like Watergate, the Lincoln Memorial, and the Kennedy Center. Fido should be comfortable in the water, but no previous kayaking experience is required. If you are visiting in the spring, don't miss the Cherry Blossom tours around the Georgetown waterfront. Tours start at $55, and Fido floats for free. The company also rents stand-up paddleboards, canoes, and kayaks from several local marinas. Rentals start at $16 per hour. Doggy life jackets are provided for no extra charge. After your aquatic experience, treat your pup to a Bowser Beer or a Peanut-Banana Pupsicle on the patio at **Art and Soul**.

Boating in DC
Potomac Avenue SE & 1st Street SE
Washington, DC 20003
(202) 337-9642
www.bringfido.com/go/1DR3

Where to Stay:

Nestled among a row of quaint townhouses in Washington DC's historic Foggy Bottom neighborhood, you'll find **The River Inn**, a dog-friendly boutique hotel. Relax with your pup in one of the hotel's suites equipped with a full kitchen and comfortable sleeping, dining, and living areas. The property is convenient to several nearby parks for morning and evening walks. Dogs of any size are welcome for no additional fee.

The River Inn
924 25th Street NW
Washington, DC 20037
(202) 337-7600
www.bringfido.com/go/1DR4
Rates from $99/night

Sanibel Island

If your dog likes to walk where the wild things are, bring him to Sanibel's **J.N. Ding Darling National Wildlife Refuge**, part of the largest undeveloped mangrove ecosystem in the country. Follow the four-mile Wildlife Drive in your car, get out and hike one of the six nature trails, or rent a pontoon boat, kayak, or canoe from **Tarpon Bay Explorers** and see the refuge from the water. Admission is $10 per vehicle or $1 per hiker. Boat rentals start at $200 for a half-day, and kayak rentals start at $30 for two hours. Afterward, do the famous 'Sanibel Stoop' at **Gulfside City Park**, which is covered with shells and sand dollars at low tide. Simply bend down to pluck the perfect shell from the sand and repeat. After you and Fido have worked up an appetite, head to the outdoor patio of **The Island Cow** for 'udderly' delicious seafood and frozen concoctions.

Tarpon Bay Explorers
900 Tarpon Bay Road
Sanibel, FL 33957
(239) 472-8900
www.bringfido.com/go/1DV4

Where to Stay:

Just a short stroll from Gulfside City Park, you'll find the **Signal Inn**, a collection of 19 fully furnished condos that cater to man's best friend. Furry guests are welcomed with dog toys, and waste stations are located on the property. On-site amenities include a heated pool and spa, butterfly garden, charcoal grills, and a shell cleaning station. Two dogs of any size are permitted for an additional fee of $75 per three-night stay or $130 per week.

Signal Inn
1811 Olde Middle Gulf Drive
Sanibel, FL 33957
(239) 472-4690
www.bringfido.com/go/1DV5
Rates from $187/night

Where to Stay:

Located four blocks from downtown Apalachicola, the **Water Street Hotel and Marina** features 30 spacious guest suites, each with Hemingway-style furnishings, a full kitchen, and private balcony overlooking the Apalachicola River. Enjoy the complimentary continental breakfast and evening wine reception. Fishing and boating activities are right outside your door, courtesy of the full-service marina. You can also lounge by the pool and soak in the Florida sun. Two dogs up to 50 lbs are welcome for an additional fee of $35 per pet, per night.

Water Street Hotel and Marina
329 Water Street
Apalachicola, FL 32320
(850) 653-3700
www.bringfido.com/go/1DMG
Rates from $152/night

Captain Gill's River Cruises

You and your canine companion will love spending a day on the lower Apalachicola River with **Captain Gill's River Cruises**. Enjoy a private two-, three-, or four-hour tour aboard the *Lily*, a 28-foot Adventure Craft that features an air-conditioned cabin with a private bathroom. Captain Gill will entertain you with stories and history of the biologically diverse Apalachicola river system. A two-hour tour will provide you with an overview of the area and glimpses of the flora and fauna that inhabit the region. Longer tours will allow for more time to explore the scenic tributaries flowing into the river. Cruises can be tailored to your specific interests, and fishing charters are available. Departing from the Water Street Dock, tours are offered seven days a week. Rates start at $250 for a two-hour trip. Bring your own refreshments. Man's best friend is welcome to join in the fun for no additional fee.

Captain Gill's River Cruises
501 Bay City Road
Apalachicola, FL 32320
(850) 370-0075
www.bringfido.com/go/1DMF

St. Augustine Eco Tours

Take a dog-friendly cruise around St. Augustine on a serene boat tour with **St. Augustine Eco Tours**. Experience the popular Dolphin, Birding and Nature Tour, which takes you on a 90-minute journey around the rivers and creeks surrounding the historic city. Your boat captain will serve as your guide, educating you on marine ecology as you keep an eye out for turtles, bottlenose dolphins, and various bird species that call Florida home. If you're lucky, you may even spot a manatee or two. Tours start at $45 for adults and $35 for children. Dogs always ride for free. Private beachcombing and photography tours can also be arranged. Rates for private tours start at $260. After returning to port, walk over to **O.C. White's Restaurant** for delicious seafood and spirits on the dog-friendly garden patio.

St. Augustine Eco Tours
111 Avenida Menendez
St. Augustine, FL 32084
(904) 377-7245
www.bringfido.com/go/1DMH

Where to Stay:

Located in the heart of St. Augustine's historic district, **Bayfront Marin House** is a great place to rest and relax on your visit to America's oldest city. Each guest room has a private entrance, convenient for early morning and late night walks with your pup. Humans will enjoy the daily hot breakfast and evening happy hours. Parking is free, and dogs of any size are welcome for an additional fee of $35 per pet, per night.

Bayfront Marin House
142 Avenida Menendez
St. Augustine, FL 32084
(904) 824-4301
www.bringfido.com/go/1DMI
Rates from $248/night

Where to Stay:

Just across the border in Alabama, **Staybridge Suites Gulf Shores** offers a relaxing home away from home. The spacious accommodations feature living rooms and fully equipped kitchens. Rates include complimentary breakfast and frequent evening socials. Up to two dogs of any size are welcome for an additional fee of $75 for stays up to six nights. After checking in, head over to **The Flying Harpoon**, a po' boy pub on the bayou, for cajun eats and live music on the outdoor patio.

Staybridge Suites Gulf Shores
3947 Gulf Shores Parkway
Gulf Shores, AL 36542
(251) 975-1030
www.bringfido.com/go/1DSA
Rates from $123/night

Littleheads Kayak Rentals

Escape to picturesque Perdido Key on an eco-friendly adventure with **Littleheads Kayak Rentals**. Dogs are welcome to ride along as you explore uninhabited islands and pristine white-sand beaches on your own. If you'd rather have a guide, bring Fido on a two-hour eco-tour of the area. Fishing and snorkeling gear are also available. Rentals start at $40 for singles, and tours cost $55 per person. Dogs tag along for free. After enjoying the water, take a walk on the wild side at **Tarkiln Bayou Preserve State Park**, which is home to almost 100 species of rare flora and fauna. Leashed dogs are allowed on the park's hiking trails and nature walks. The half-mile Tarkiln Bayou Trail is an easy stroll over an elevated boardwalk, while the more challenging 6.5-mile Perdido Bay Trail offers access to bayshore beaches. Keep an eye out for deer, bobcats, and gopher tortoises along the way. Admission is $3 per vehicle.

Littleheads Kayak Rentals
14140 River Road
Pensacola, FL 32507
(251) 284-5107
www.bringfido.com/go/1DS9

De Leon Springs State Park

Experience Florida's wild beauty at **De Leon Springs State Park**. Admission is just $6 per vehicle, which gives you access to a full day of dog-friendly activities inside the park. Start your morning early with a tranquil hike along the 4.2-mile Wild Persimmon Trail. Following your trail jaunt, stop by the park's on-site restaurant, **The Old Spanish Sugar Mill**, for a hearty breakfast of pancakes and other treats served at their pup-approved walk-up window. After fueling up, head to the boat dock and sail away with Captain Frank and the **Fountain of Youth Eco/History Tours** on a 50-minute pontoon adventure through the Lake Woodruff National Wildlife Refuge. Keep an eye out for alligators, osprey, and other wildlife from the comfort of the boat. Tours are offered several times a day, and tickets are $14 per person and free for dogs.

De Leon Springs State Park
601 Ponce Deleon Boulevard
De Leon Springs, FL 32130
(386) 985-4212
www.bringfido.com/go/1DV9

Where to Stay:

Spend the night in nearby Orange City at **Alling House**, a charming bed & breakfast that welcomes furry guests in its five cottages. Each unit includes a kitchenette and is decorated in a unique theme, including the western Frontier Cottage and the elegant Victorian Cottage. A continental breakfast is included in the rate, but a full breakfast in the main house is also available. Up to two dogs of any size are welcome for an additional fee of $20 per stay.

Alling House
215 E French Avenue
Orange City, FL 32763
(386) 775-7648
www.bringfido.com/go/1DVA
Rates from $139/night

Where to Stay:

Located near Kings's Bay and the retail shops and restaurants in downtown Crystal River, the **Best Western Crystal River Resort** is a perfect overnight stop for Fido's Florida adventures. The hotel offers ample green space for morning walks, as well as complimentary daily breakfast for the humans. Two dogs up to 80 lbs are welcome for an additional fee of just $10 per pet, per night.

Best Western Crystal River Resort
614 NW US Highway 19
Crystal River, FL 34428
(352) 795-3171
www.bringfido.com/go/1DMP
Rates from $90/night

Florida Manatee Adventures

Bring Fido on a trip to see Florida's gentle giants with Captain Greg of **Florida Manatee Adventures**. Crystal River is one of the premier manatee-spotting destinations in the world, and the year-round warm waters also make it an ideal location to swim with the manatees in their natural habitat. With more than 25 years of experience as a captain, fisherman and scuba diver, Captain Greg has a wealth of knowledge about the Crystal River area. Climb aboard the boat with your pup and enjoy a three-hour tour, complete with narration, gear, snacks, and beverages. Dolphin-watching trips are also available. Rates start at $250 for a private charter (up to three passengers), and dogs are welcome to join for no additional charge. After the boat ride, Fido can stretch his legs at nearby **Crystal River Archaeological State Park**. The entrance fee is $3 per vehicle, and leashed dogs are welcome to sniff around.

Florida Manatee Adventures
2880 N Seabreeze Point
Crystal River, FL 34429
(352) 476-7556
www.bringfido.com/go/1DMO

Fountain of Youth

You and your canine explorer can walk in the footsteps of Juan Ponce de León with an expedition to the **Fountain of Youth Archaeological Park** in sunny St. Augustine. Begin your visit by meandering through exhibits on the Native Americans and Spaniards who once inhabited this land. After learning about the historic settlements, take your pup on a stroll along the Founders Riverwalk, a 600-foot-long observation platform overlooking the Matanzas Bay. When it's time to cool down, head inside to the park's Discovery Globe, where you and your pooch can watch a show in the comfort of an air-conditioned theater. Before leaving, stop by the Spring House and let Fido have his drink from the Fountain of Youth. The park is open daily from 9:00 am to 5:00 pm. Admission is $18 for adults and $10 for children. Dogs are welcome for no additional fee.

Fountain of Youth Archaeological Park
11 Magnolia Avenue
St. Augustine, FL 32084
(904) 829-3168
www.bringfido.com/go/1DQM

Where to Stay:

Enjoy a relaxing stay with your pooch at the **Saint Augustine Beach House**, where the innkeepers welcome Fido with open arms and yummy treats. After a comfy night's sleep, take a morning stroll on the pup-friendly **Vilano Beach** right outside your door. The property also boasts a fenced dog run and a dog wash station that makes for easy clean-up after a trip to the beach. Pet towels, beds, and blankets are available upon request. One dog of any size is welcome for an additional fee of $35 per stay. Add $25 for a second pet.

Saint Augustine Beach House
10 Vilano Road
St. Augustine, FL 32084
(904) 217-3765
www.bringfido.com/go/1DQN
Rates from $194/night

Palm Beach Lake Trail

Gaze at gorgeous, waterfront Palm Beach mansions and luxury yachts as you stroll down the **Palm Beach Lake Trail** with your pup. Fido will soon learn why it was nicknamed the Trail of Conspicuous Consumption! Stretching along the Intracoastal Waterway and lined with palm trees, this five-mile paved biking and walking pathway was constructed by Henry Flagler in 1894 as a promenade for elite guests staying at his Royal Poinciana Hotel. Start at the Flagler Museum for access to the public trail. If you prefer to bike with your pooch, rentals are available at the **Palm Beach Bicycle Trail Shop** (rates from $20). After enjoying the island, hit the water at **Jupiter Dog Beach**, located between beach markers 25 and 59 in nearby Jupiter. Furry friends under voice command are welcome to play off leash along more than two miles of sand and surf. Free parking is available along the public beach.

Palm Beach Lake Trail
1 Whitehall Way
Palm Beach, FL 33480
(800) 554-7256
www.bringfido.com/go/1DRN

Where to Stay:

Clean up those sandy paws and make the five-minute drive from the dog beach to the **Holiday Inn Express North Palm Beach Oceanview**. The hotel offers comfy accommodations in a prime location just across the street from the Atlantic Ocean. Up to three dogs of any size are welcome for an additional fee of $25 per pet, per night. After checking in, walk over to **Hurricane Café**, where Fido can join you for a gourmet meal on the patio.

Holiday Inn Express North Palm Beach Oceanview
13950 U.S. Highway 1
Juno Beach, FL 33408
(561) 622-4366
www.bringfido.com/go/1DRO
Rates from $94/night

Where to Stay:

Treat your pup to a slice of paradise at the **Islander Resort**. Spread across 24 acres of lush tropical landscape, this waterfront property invites leashed pups to join you on its private beach. Canine guests also have access to an on-site dog park for off-leash fun. Up to two dogs of any size are welcome for an additional fee of $75 per stay. When it's dinner time, walk over to the resort's restaurant, **Tides Beachside Bar & Grill**, where you can dine al fresco with your pooch.

Islander Resort
82100 Overseas Highway
Islamorada, FL 33036
(305) 664-2031
www.bringfido.com/go/1DML
Rates from $120/night

Theater of the Sea

At **Theater of the Sea**, your dog will quickly learn that he's not the only one who can do tricks. This open-air marine park has been delighting audiences since 1946 with its array of marine life shows and exhibits. Visiting pups can watch dolphin and sea lion performances and get up close and personal with sea turtles, fish, sharks, stingrays, alligators, and birds. They can even join you for a swim at the park's private lagoon-side beach. The only area that is off limits to dogs is the Parrot Theater. Park hours are 9:30 am to 5:00 pm daily. Admission is $40 for adults and $23 for children. Canine visitors are welcome for free, but they must remain leashed at all times. If Fido wants more time with Flipper, head south to the **Dolphin Research Center** in Grassy Key. This nonprofit facility welcomes furry friends to watch the resident dolphins and sea lions in action.

Theater of the Sea
84721 Overseas Highway
Islamorada, FL 33036
(305) 664-2431
www.bringfido.com/go/1DMK

Coopertown Airboats

Take a 30-mile drive west from Miami to bring your furry friend on a wild ride through one of the most unique ecosystems in the country with **Coopertown Airboats**. The company's flat-bottomed watercraft are ideally suited to navigate the marshes and wetlands of the Florida Everglades. Your pup will love feeling the wind in his fur as he skims across the sawgrass, keeping his eyes peeled for alligators, turtles, raccoons and various native bird species. Tours are $26 for adults, $15 for children, and free for dogs. Private tours start at $250 and are recommended for guests with pets. After romping through the Everglades, return to civilization at **Lincoln Road Mall** in Miami Beach, where you and your pup can people-watch as you dine al fresco at one of the many pet-friendly restaurants. While you're there, stop by the **Dog Bar** and pick up a treat for your good boy.

Coopertown Airboats
22700 SW 8th Street
Miami, FL 33194
(305) 226-6048
www.bringfido.com/go/1DO1

Where to Stay:

After a busy day of sightseeing, relax at Miami Beach's **Kimpton Surfcomber Hotel** and enjoy a cocktail in the courtyard with your furry friend. Pet amenities include beds, food and water bowls, and waste bags. Fido will enjoy socializing with other pet guests during the evening wine reception and can join you for dinner on the terrace at the resort's restaurant, **High Tide**. Dogs of any size are welcome for no additional fee.

Kimpton Surfcomber Hotel
1717 Collins Avenue
Miami Beach, FL 33139
(305) 532-7715
www.bringfido.com/go/1DO2
Rates from $91/night

Where to Stay:

Set in the heart of the Key West historic district, **Ambrosia Key West** is a cozy, tropical-themed bed and breakfast. Start your day with a morning meal served poolside, before strolling over to Duval Street, Mallory Square, and other island attractions. Upon your return, cool Fido off at the property's dedicated watering station, and let him lounge around the Ambrosia's lush gardens. Two dogs of any size are welcome for an additional fee of $25 per pet, per night.

Ambrosia Key West
622 Fleming Street
Key West, FL 33040
(305) 296-9838
www.bringfido.com/go/1DMS
Rates from $119/night

Lazy Dog Adventures

Bring your pooch on a two-hour guided tour with **Lazy Dog Adventures** in Key West. Paddle through mangrove creeks and shallow waters on a kayak or paddleboard, while spotting marine life such as jellyfish, conch, sea cucumbers, stingrays, and maybe even a shark or manatee. If you've never paddled with your pup before and would prefer to learn at your own pace, Lazy Dog also offers kayak and paddleboard rentals. Their staff will give you tips on how to introduce Fido to the sport and help you select the right board. Half-day rentals are $25, and guided tours start at $50. Dogs ride for no additional fee. If your doggo prefers to view marine life from dry land, take him to the **Key West Aquarium**, where he can participate in one of the guided walks and view the aquatic exhibits without getting wet. Admission is $17 for adults and $14 for children. Well-behaved dogs are welcome for free.

Lazy Dog Adventures
5114 Overseas Highway
Key West, FL 33040
(305) 295-9898
www.bringfido.com/go/1DMR

Oliver Bentleys

Savannah is home to many pet-friendly tour companies, but only one features a guide with four legs. Retailer **Oliver Bentleys** invites you to 'embark on a tour of tales' with its Historic Dog Walk Tour, led by the brand's official mascot, Abbie Girl. Tours are by reservation only and depart from Oglethorpe Square. Tickets are $29 for adults and $12 for children. Pups are free and receive signature treats! If your pooch is dog-tired after his walking tour, **Savannah Pedicab** will whisk you around town for a bit of sightseeing. Tour options start at $25, and dogs any size are welcome for no additional fee. Smaller pets can also learn a bit of Savannah history on a trolley ride with **Old Savannah Tours**. Dogs up to 25 lbs are welcome to ride on your lap as you enjoy on-and-off privileges from 9:00 am until 5:00 pm. Tickets are $35, and dogs ride for free.

Oliver Bentleys
Oglethorpe Square
127 Abercorn Street
Savannah, GA 31401
(912) 201-1688
www.bringfido.com/go/1DI0

Where to Stay:

Top off your Savannah getaway with a stay in one of the city's historic mansions. The **Foley House Inn** will welcome you with afternoon tea or an evening wine and cheese reception. Pups can join you for breakfast and evening amenities in the courtyard. Dogs of any size are permitted for an additional fee of $50 per pet, per stay. For a more modern vibe, head to **Kimpton Brice Hotel** where Fido will be greeted with treats, a plush pet bed and bowls. Relax with a glass of wine in their enclosed courtyard. Dogs of any size are welcome for no extra charge.

Foley House Inn
14 W Hull Street
Savannah, GA 31401
(912) 232-6622
www.bringfido.com/go/1DI1
Rates from $129/night

Where to Stay:

After you see Rock City, head down the mountain to stay at **Residence Inn by Marriott Chattanooga Downtown**, where two dogs of any size are welcome for an additional fee of $100 per stay. Humans will enjoy the free daily hot breakfast and the weekday evening socials in the lobby. Fido will dig the small garden on site and the walking paths along the Tennessee River, just one block away. If you are hungry, stop for waterfront dining at the dog-friendly **3rd Deck Burger Bar**, located atop the *Southern Belle* riverboat.

**Residence Inn by Marriott
Chattanooga Downtown**
215 Chestnut Street
Chattanooga, TN 37402
(423) 266-0600
www.bringfido.com/go/1DHW
Rates from $125/night

Rock City

Scenic views await you and your pup at **Rock City**, located high atop Lookout Mountain on the Tennessee-Georgia border. Stroll along the Enchanted Trail that winds through the manicured 14-acre property. Pose for some photos at the 100-foot waterfall or the 1,000-ton balanced rock. Conquer Fido's fear of heights by crossing the Swing-A-Long Bridge, or stay on solid ground by choosing the sturdy Stone Bridge. Perched 1,700 feet above sea level, Lover's Leap offers panoramic views of seven states, as well as breathtaking vistas of the Chattanooga Valley below. Amid the rock formations, you'll find expansive botanical gardens, displaying over 400 varieties of native flowers, shrubs, and trees year-round. To reward Fido for being a good boy, order a treat from the pet menu at Café 7. Rock City hours vary by season. Admission is $22 for adults and $13 for children. Dogs are admitted for no extra charge.

Rock City
1400 Patten Road
Lookout Mountain, GA 30750
(706) 820-2531
www.bringfido.com/go/1DHV

Barnsley Gardens

One of the few surviving antebellum gardens in the southern United States, **Barnsley Gardens** offers its visitors and their pups over 3,000 acres to explore just an hour's drive from Atlanta. Located in Adairsville, the 160-year old estate grounds were once home to a grand Italianate mansion, the ruins of which form the centerpiece of this attraction. A team of master gardeners maintains the property, where Fido can stop and smell the heirloom roses in spring, see a spectacular display of daylilies in summer, and pose for a picture-perfect Christmas card during the holidays (when the halls of the villa are decked with boughs of holly). After touring the gardens, you can hike 12 miles of trails or share a meal at the Beer Garden. Self-guided tours are complimentary for resort guests, but day visitors are also welcome Monday through Thursday. Tickets are $15 for adults, $10 for children, and free for dogs.

Barnsley Gardens
597 Barnsley Gardens Road
Adairsville, GA 30103
(770) 773-7480
www.bringfido.com/go/1DHY

Where to Stay:

Extend your visit by staying overnight at **Barnsley Resort**. Choose from an assortment of pet-friendly cottages featuring private entrances, front porches, hardwood floors, soaking tubs, and separate living rooms. The resort will ensure that your pup has an enjoyable stay by delivering treats, bottled water, a pet bed, and bowls to your room. Fido is also welcome to sit with you around the fire pit areas, on the front porch of Woodlands Grill, or in the Beer Garden on weekends. Dogs of any size are welcome for an additional fee of $150 to $250, depending on room type.

Barnsley Resort
597 Barnsley Gardens Road
Adairsville, GA 30103
(770) 773-7480
www.bringfido.com/go/1DHZ
Rates from $219/night

Bonaventure Cemetery

Savannah is well known for its elaborate burial grounds, and **Bonaventure Cemetery** is the city's most famous. Spanning over 100 acres and filled with live oaks towering over ornate tombs, the graveyard is a unique and interesting place to explore on foot with your canine companion. Visit on your own for free, but be sure to leave by 5:00 pm sharp. According to local legend, a pack of ghost dogs roam the grounds at night and will chase away any visitors still there after dark. If your pup's not afraid, check out **Ghost City Tours**, which offers nightly walking tours of Savannah. A 90-minute tour costs $20 for adults and $10 for kids. For another frightfully fun experience, enjoy a trip with **Hearse Ghost Tours**. Your mode of transportation is an authentic hearse once used to transport the dearly departed. Cruise around cemeteries and through the Historic and Victorian districts. Prices are $20 for adults and $12 for children. Dogs are free on both tours.

Bonaventure Cemetery
330 Bonaventure Road
Thunderbolt, GA 31404
(912) 412-4687
www.bringfido.com/go/1DJC

Where to Stay:

If you haven't had your fill of frights after a cemetery tour, plan to stay at **Olde Harbour Inn** in downtown Savannah, which boasts its own resident ghost. The all-suite property has large rooms with separate sitting areas overlooking the Savannah River. Pups are greeted at check-in with a treat bag, toy, and waste bags. The housekeeping staff is also known to leave human snacks during turn-down service. Dogs of any size are welcome for an additional fee of $50 per pet, per stay.

Olde Harbour Inn
508 E Factors Walk
Savannah, GA 31401
(912) 234-4100
www.bringfido.com/go/1DJD
Rates from $126/night

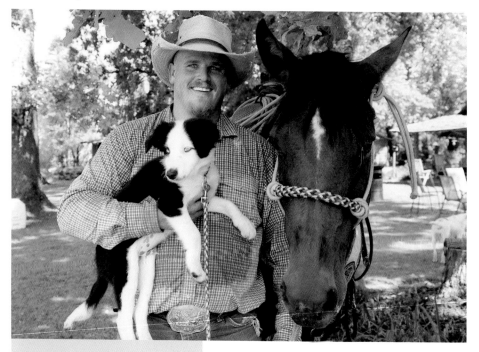

Where to Stay:

The Butler-Cape house at **Seventy-Four Ranch** allows pets in each of its four guest rooms, but, for a more rustic ranch experience, skip the main house in favor of the property's Saddle House. Originally designed as a cowboy bunkhouse, this room offers four full-size double bunk beds (which can sleep up to eight). The room shares a bathroom with the Porch Cabin, and both rooms may be reserved together for a family-friendly accommodation. Dogs of any size are welcome for no additional fee.

Seventy-Four Ranch
9205 Highway 53 W
Jasper, GA 30143
(770) 547-8580
www.bringfido.com/go/1DJG
Rates from $85/night

Seventy-Four Ranch

Give your pup an authentic dude ranch experience at **Seventy-Four Ranch** in Jasper. A working cattle farm and cozy bed and breakfast nestled in the foothills of the Blue Ridge Mountains, Seventy-Four Ranch provides an escape from daily life just an hour from Atlanta and Chattanooga. Their popular guided trail rides offer a taste of the cowboy life as you ride across thousands of acres of fields and creeks. This isn't your typical nose-to-tail trail ride. Your guide will set a course based on your experience and then let you ride to your heart's content. If Fido is comfortable around cattle, he can come along to enjoy a trail ride, too. The staff can create many adventures for you. During your stay on the ranch, you can also learn to rope like a cowboy or fish for your dinner in Parker Pond. They've got the poles, bait, and plenty of fish. Just bring your best fishing dog! They'll even set up breakfast on the lawn so Fido won't miss out.

Seventy-Four Ranch
9205 Highway 53 W
Jasper, GA 30143
(770) 547-8580
www.bringfido.com/go/1DJG

Cool River Tubing

Is your pup ready for a river adventure? On the outskirts of the Bavarian-themed town of Helen in the northeastern corner of Georgia, you'll find **Cool River Tubing**. The outfitter can equip you and your pooch with everything you need for a fun float down the crisp and refreshing waters of the Chattahoochee River. Smaller pups are welcome to sit on your lap, and larger dogs can ride their own tube. Rentals start at $10, and dogs ride for free. Once you've dried off, put on Fido's Lederhosen and make the short trip to nearby **Unicoi State Park**. There, you can hike along a half-mile paved trail to the spectacular **Anna Ruby Falls** and then take the **Unicoi to Helen Trail**, a three mile pathway that leads you to downtown Helen. When you arrive, swing by **Hofbrauhaus Restaurant**, where your hound will enjoy a free bratwurst while you dine riverside and sample some traditional German beers.

Cool River Tubing
590 Edelweiss Strasse
Helen, GA 30545
(706) 878-2665
www.bringfido.com/go/1DT2

Where to Stay:

If your poochie can't get enough of the Chattahoochee, he can sleep over at **Bear Creek Lodge & Cabins**. Featuring an assortment of lodging types, including a treehouse next to the river, Bear Creek offers something for everyone. Depending where you choose to stay, you can be within walking distance to the action in downtown Helen, enjoy views across the river, or find a pet-friendly trail just beyond your door. Dogs of any size are welcome for no additional fee.

Bear Creek Lodge & Cabins
219 Escowee Drive
Helen, GA 30545
(706) 773-1040
www.bringfido.com/go/1DT3
Rates from $242/night

Where to Stay:

Fido will be able to walk to the beach from his room at the **Holiday Inn Resort Jekyll Island**. In addition to stretching his paws in the sand, there are plenty of grassy spaces to sniff nearby. Explore more than 20 miles of pathways around the island, including the **North Loop Trail** and the **Ocean View Trail**. In the evening, get cozy around the fire pit with your canine as the sun sets over the water. Dogs of any size are welcome for an additional fee of $25 per pet, per night.

Holiday Inn Resort Jekyll Island
701 N Beachview Drive
Jekyll Island, GA 31527
(912) 635-2211
www.bringfido.com/go/1DT9
Rates from $123/night

Jekyll Island

Make your way to dog-friendly Jekyll Island for a charming retreat along the Georgia coast. Start your adventure at Jekyll Wharf on a cruise with **Jekyll Island Dolphin Tours**. Furry friends are welcome to join you in search of bottlenose dolphins frolicking in the East River and Jekyll Sound. Tickets are $25 for adults, $15 for children, and free for dogs. Private charters are also available starting at $300. After your cruise, enjoy delicious coastal cuisine on the dog-friendly deck at **The Wharf at Jekyll Island Club Resort**. In the afternoon, hop on a trolley tour with **Mosaic Jekyll Island Museum**, during which you'll learn more about Jekyll Island Club, once the winter escape for industry icons like Rockefeller, Vanderbilt, and Pulitzer. Finish the day with a swim at picturesque **Driftwood Beach**, where leashed pups can romp around a unique seaside landscape of gnarled, weather-beaten trees.

Jekyll Island Dolphin Tours
366 N Riverview Drive
Jekyll Island, GA 31527
(912) 635-3152
www.bringfido.com/go/1DT8

Creative Soul Scavenger Hunts

Load up the Mystery Machine and take your canine detective on an interactive adventure around the island of Kauai with **Creative Soul Scavenger Hunts**. Follow clues and complete imaginative tasks as you soak up the natural beauty of Hawaii's Garden Isle. Your experience begins and ends on the north shore of the island in the town of Hanalei. If you mention 'Ruff Guides' when reserving your hunt, a special canine clue will be added to your experience. Prices start at $33 per person, and dogs hunt for free. After Sherlock Bones has sniffed out all the clues, he's sure to be hungry. Bring him to one of Hanalei's famous food trucks for some fresh ahi or a burger patty, and then make your way to **JoJo's Shave Ice** for a cold treat. For some off-leash fun, head to Kauai **North Shore Dog Park**. Located in the Wai Koa Plantation in Kilauea, the park is open to the public and free to enter.

Creative Soul Scavenger Hunts
5-5161 Kuhio Highway F
Hanalei, HI 96714
(505) 692-0644
www.bringfido.com/go/1DTH

Where to Stay:

You and your island hound will enjoy the soothing sound of ocean waves from your room at the **Ko'a Kea Hotel & Resort**. Put on your pup's hula skirt and take a stroll around the lush landscaping and manicured grounds of the resort property. Canine guests are greeted with treats, bedding, and bowls at check-in. One dog up to 25 lbs is welcome for an additional fee of $300 per stay. Add $100 for a second pet.

Ko'a Kea Hotel & Resort
2251 Poipu Road
Koloa, HI 96756
(844) 236-3817
www.bringfido.com/go/1E6V
Rates from $399/night

Where to Stay:

After Fido learns to 'Hang 20' on the water, kick back and relax at **The Surfjack Hotel & Swim Club**, a trendy boutique property in the heart of Honolulu. The hotel offers dog-friendly rooms with private lanais and welcomes pups up to 80 lbs for an additional fee of $35 per pet, per night. After freshening up in the room, reward Fido with some treats from The **Public Pet** before heading to dinner at the **Barefoot Beach Café**. There, you'll enjoy authentic Hawaiian fare, as Fido lounges on the oceanfront patio.

The Surfjack Hotel & Swim Club
412 Lewers Street
Honolulu, HI 96815
(808) 923-8882
www.bringfido.com/go/1DPE
Rates from $96/night

Gone Surfing Hawaii

If you're planning a getaway to Honolulu and want to bring Fido along for the trip, reward him by catching some waves together on Waikiki Beach. Don't worry if you've never surfed before. The crew at **Gone Surfing Hawaii** offers beginner lessons for you and your dog and will equip you with all the necessary gear. During your private lesson, they'll provide an on-land demonstration of surfing basics before your paws get wet. After jumping in the ocean, you'll receive instruction on reading the waves, properly using the board, and the etiquette of wave riding. If surfing is not for you, the company also offers stand-up paddleboard lessons. You and your four-legged friend can enjoy either of these private 90-minute lessons for $165 per person, which includes all equipment. Gone Surfing Hawaii even has a videographer on staff to capture your adventure for posterity.

Gone Surfing Hawaii
330 Saratoga Road
Honolulu, HI 96815
(808) 429-6404
www.bringfido.com/go/1DPD

Long Drift Outfitters

The Idaho section of the Kootenai River flows through a serene canyon that's all but inaccessible except by boat. Book a scenic float trip in a classic wooden drift boat with **Long Drift Outfitters** in Sandpoint and enjoy the solitude of the river with your furry friend by your side. If you prefer a more active adventure, choose a guided fly fishing tour instead. Your helpful guide will offer tips to help you reel in a nice trout or whitefish. Rates start at $450 for up to two adults, and fishing trips include rods, reels, and flies. Dogs float for free. Let Fido stretch his legs afterward along 1,000 feet of lakefront shoreline at the nearby **Dog Beach Park**. Your furry friend can run off leash, and park admission is free. End your day with a stop at **Laughing Dog Brewing** in Ponderay, where you can sample the Alpha Dog IPA paired with an appetizer from the 'Not Beer' menu. Pups are allowed inside and out.

Long Drift Outfitters
Kootenai River
Sandpoint, ID 83864
(303) 917-2822
www.bringfido.com/go/1DRA

Where to Stay:

After an active day on the water, let your pup rest his tired paws at the **La Quinta Inn by Wyndham Sandpoint**. Four-legged guests are greeted with a treat and waste bags at check-in, and ample green space is just down the street at Farmin Park. The hotel offers free breakfast and is within walking distance to many other downtown shops and restaurants. Up to two dogs of any size are welcome for no additional fee.

La Quinta Inn
by Wyndham Sandpoint
415 Cedar Street
Sandpoint, ID 83864
(208) 263-9581
www.bringfido.com/go/1DRB
Rates from $115/night

Dog Bark Park Inn

Located near the border of Washington and Oregon, you'll find Idaho's most famous dog-friendly landmark in the sleepy town of Cottonwood. Nicknamed 'Sweet Willy' by the locals, the world's largest beagle stretches to a height of 30 feet. But this is no ordinary dog—it's actually a bed and breakfast! The **Dog Bark Park Inn** was created by a husband and wife team of chainsaw artists in 1997. The unusual structure has garnered worldwide attention as a slice of roadside Americana ever since, and travelers come from around the globe to spend a night 'in the dog house.' Even if you're not able to stay overnight, you can still browse the gift shop and watch Dennis and Frances carve wooden statues of more than 60 dog breeds in their studio. Passers-by can even take a potty break in the giant fire hydrant! Visitors are welcome daily from 11:00 am to 4:00 pm.

Dog Bark Park Inn
2421 Business Loop 95
Cottonwood, ID 83522
(208) 962-3647
www.bringfido.com/go/1DN5

Where to Stay:

No trip to the **Dog Bark Park Inn** is complete without an overnight stay. Inside the belly of the beast, you'll find a queen bedroom and full-size bathroom. Additional loft space (accessible by ladder) contains twin futons and a variety of books and games. A self-serve breakfast of homemade treats is included with your stay. Plan to get there early on your day of arrival, as check-in is from 3:30 pm to 5:30 pm. Well-behaved dogs are welcome for an additional fee of $15 each.

Dog Bark Park Inn
2421 Business Loop 95
Cottonwood, ID 83522
(208) 962-3647
www.bringfido.com/go/1DN5
Rates from $126/night

Where to Stay:

Check into the **Hotel Indigo Naperville Riverwalk** before venturing out for an evening on the town. Start with a stroll down **Naperville Riverwalk**, where Fido can frolic on the covered bridges and brick paths dotted with sculptures, artwork, fountains, and memorials. Make your way to **Two Bostons** dog boutique for a quick treat before finishing the evening with a meal from the dog menu at **Quigley's Irish Pub**. After you've had your fill, retire to the hotel for a well-deserved snooze. Two dogs of any size are welcome for an additional fee of $75 per pet, per night.

Hotel Indigo Naperville Riverwalk
120 Water Street
Naperville, IL 60540
(630) 778-9676
www.bringfido.com/go/1DJL
Rates from $141/night

Wag 'N Paddle

Shake off your pooch's wintertime blues with a trip to **Wag 'N Paddle** in Naperville. This indoor, climate-controlled park has three in-ground heated pools that are perfect for those days when your pup wants to swim but the lake is frozen over. Dog owners are encouraged to join their furry companions for half-hour, individual swimming sessions, and cleanup is made easy thanks to a self-service dog wash and special drying room supplied with towels and a dryer. The facility also boasts an indoor dog park with lots of play equipment, as well as an outdoor fenced dog run that is available when the weather warms up. All new fur-guests are evaluated by staff to make sure they are ready to join the fun. Before visiting, be sure to upload your pup's vaccination records to Wag 'N Paddle's website. A visit to the dog park starts at $15 for one hour, and private swims start at $45.

Wag 'N Paddle
1847 W Jefferson Avenue
Naperville, IL 60540
(331) 229-8660
www.bringfido.com/go/1DJK

Shawnee National Forest

With more than 270,000 acres across 10 counties in Southern Illinois, the **Shawnee National Forest** is a hiking enthusiast's dream. Dozens of trails in the area invite you and your canine companion to explore hundreds of miles of scenic landscape and amazing rock formations. Amateurs should feel comfortable starting out at the **Rim Rock National Recreation Trail** near Elizabethtown. Fido will enjoy the short one-mile hike around the forested bluffs, with interpretive signs guiding the way. More experienced hikers will be eager to backpack a nearby portion of the River to River Trail, which extends approximately 150 miles from Battery Rock on the Ohio River to Devil's Backbone Park on the Mississippi River. Finally, you won't want to miss the **Garden of the Gods Recreation Area**, with its unique rock formations and miles of interconnected trails. Leashed dogs are welcome on all trails throughout the Shawnee National Forest.

Shawnee National Forest
Karbers Ridge Road
Junction, IL 62954
(618) 253-7114
www.bringfido.com/go/1DVD

Where to Stay:

Located in the Shawnee Hills of Southern Illinois, **Rim Rock's Dogwood Cabins** are great for hiking enthusiasts who want to 'ruff it' for a few days with their dogs. This collection of five well-appointed cabins sits on 77 acres of forestland adjacent to the Rim Rock National Recreation Trail and only seven miles from the Garden of the Gods. Countless other trails are located in the surrounding area. Up to two dogs of any size are welcome to stay in the cabins for no additional fee.

Rim Rock's Dogwood Cabins
798 Karbers Ridge Road
Elizabethtown, IL 62931
(618) 264-6036
www.bringfido.com/go/1DVE
Rates from $86/night

Seadog Cruises

See the Windy City with your pooch on a **Seadog Cruises** speedboat tour. Departing from Chicago's famous Navy Pier, the company offers four pet-friendly cruise options. If you're short on time, opt for the half-hour Lakefront Speedboat Tour, which hits the highlights on a fast-paced cruise on Lake Michigan. With more time to spare, choose the 75-minute River & Lake Architecture Tour, which extends your trip through the Chicago River Locks. Cruises operate from April through October. Humans traveling with their pooch receive 15% off regular ticket prices, which start at $28 for adults and $21 for children. Dogs ride for free! If you'll be in town from July through September, check out **Mercury's** famous Canine Cruise. Taking place on Sunday mornings in late summer, the Canine Cruise highlights many of Chicago's pet-friendly restaurants, attractions, and parks. Rates are $37 for adults, $16 for kids, and $8 for Fido.

Seadog Cruises
600 E Grand Avenue
Chicago, IL 60611
(312) 321-7600
www.bringfido.com/go/1DOS

Where to Stay:

Located just one mile from the Navy Pier, the **Kimpton Hotel Palomar** will make your Chicago visit one to remember. Floor-to-ceiling windows in your luxurious guest room provide fantastic views of the Chicago skyline. Treat yourself to an in-room spa service or visit to the health club, while the concierge makes grooming arrangements for your canine companion. Dog treats, bowls, and bedding are provided for Fido during your stay. Dogs of any size are welcome for no additional fee.

Kimpton Hotel Palomar
505 N State Street
Chicago, IL 60654
(312) 755-9703
www.bringfido.com/go/1DOT
Rates from $196/night

Where to Stay:

If your pup is ready for a snooze after his park visit, settle in at the **Best Western Plus Champaign Urbana Inn**. Property amenities include a complimentary hot breakfast, indoor heated pool, and a designated dog walking area. Two dogs up to 75 lbs are welcome for an additional fee of $25 per pet, per night. When you are ready for dinner, head over to the pet-friendly patio tables at **Houlihan's Restaurant**, located only three blocks away.

Best Western Plus Champaign
Urbana Inn
516 W Marketview Drive
Champaign, IL 61822
(217) 355-5566
www.bringfido.com/go/1DVI
Rates from $62/night

Allerton Park & Retreat Center

Monticello's **Allerton Park & Retreat Center** is a 1,500-acre oasis of forests, hiking trails, gardens, statuary, sculptures, grassy fields, rivers, and ponds. You and your four-legged companion will find plenty to love about this park as you hike its 14 miles of trails, visit the 30-acre demonstration prairie, join a public tour, and gaze at more than 100 outdoor sculptures and ornamental pieces. Twelve park gardens, including the Chinese Maze Garden and Fu Dog Garden, offer amazing views that change with the seasons. In the warmer months, you can bring a picnic lunch or dine on the patio with your pup at the on-site **Greenhouse Café**. Allerton Park is open daily from 8:00 am to sunset with the exception of Thanksgiving, Christmas, and New Year's Day. Leashed dogs are welcome to join their humans throughout the park, and there are no admission fees.

Allerton Park & Retreat Center
515 Old Timber Road
Monticello, IL 61856
(217) 333-3287
www.bringfido.com/go/1DVH

Indiana Dunes

Sand dunes bordering the southern shore of Lake Michigan in Chesterton provide endless recreational opportunities for you and your pooch. Begin your trip at **Indiana Dunes State Park** where Fido can accept the Three-Dune Challenge, a hike up the three tallest dunes in the park. The 1.5-mile trail climbs 552 vertical feet and ends with breathtaking views. The state park is open daily from 7:00 am to 11:00 pm, and admission is $12 per vehicle ($7 for Indiana residents). After conquering the dune challenge, venture over to **Indiana Dunes National Park** for an afternoon swim. Dogs are permitted on all beaches in the park except the West Beach swimming area. Before departing, stop by the visitor center to have your pooch certified as an official National Park B.A.R.K. Ranger. There is no fee to visit the dog-friendly areas of the park, which is open daily from 6:00 am to 11:00 pm.

Indiana Dunes State Park
1600 N 25 E
Chesterton, IN 46304
(219) 926-1952
www.bringfido.com/go/1DVL

Where to Stay:

For a unique stay in Chesterton, spend the night with Fido in a repurposed New York Central Boxcar at **Riley's Railhouse**. Two- and four-legged train fans can marvel at decades' worth of railroad antiques, art, and memorabilia. Sit on the property's large covered deck along the Northfolk Southern line and watch as an average of 97 trains pass by daily. Two dogs of any size are welcome in boxcar rooms for an additional fee of $20 per pet, per stay.

Riley's Railhouse
123 N 4th Street
Chesterton, IN 46304
(219) 395-9999
www.bringfido.com/go/1DVM
Rates from $154/night

Where to Stay:

Inspired by the industrial heritage that Indiana is built upon, the **Ironworks Hotel** in Indianapolis is a work of art in its own right. The boutique property offers light-filled rooms with large industrial-style windows and stylish common spaces that invite guests to stay and socialize. Your pooch will find a dog water station and tasty treat awaiting him in the main lobby, and complimentary pet beds and bowls are also available. Dogs of any size are welcome for an additional fee of $20 per night.

Ironworks Hotel
2721 E 86th Street
Indianapolis, IN 46240
(463) 221-2200
www.bringfido.com/go/1E6H
Rates from $179/night

100 Acres at Newfields

Art lovers will want to bring their cultured critters to Indianapolis for a pair of outdoor exhibitions. The **Virginia B. Fairbanks Art & Nature Park: 100 Acres at Newfields** is one of the largest contemporary sculpture parks in the world and features a number of unique displays designed for human (and canine) interaction. At **Indianapolis Art Center ArtsPark**, more than 27 interactive sculptures dot the landscape of its 9.5-acre property. Both parks are open daily from sunrise to sunset and are free to enter. For an active day of sightseeing, ditch the car and walk Fido along a 4.5-mile stretch of trails connecting the two campuses. The **Central Canal Towpath** and the **Monon Trail** both offer scenic views and smooth walking surfaces. Break up the hike with a stop for lunch on the pet-friendly patio at **Flatwater**, located in the Broad Ripple district where the two trails intersect.

100 Acres at Newfields
4000 N Michigan Road
Indianapolis, IN 46208
(317) 923-1331
www.bringfido.com/go/1E6G

RV Motorhome Hall of Fame

Canine campers and RV enthusiasts will enjoy taking a detour to the **RV Motorhome Hall of Fame & Museum** in Elkhart. The museum features a rotating assortment of vintage recreational vehicles from Airstream, Winnebago and other American makers. Stroll with Fido through the RV Founders Hall to explore vehicles and memorabilia dating back to the 1920's, including Mae West's 1931 Chevrolet Housecar, a 1931 Tennessee Traveler Motorhome, and a 1969 Fleetwood Pace Arrow. In the Exhibitor Hall, view displays illustrating the history and products of the manufactured housing industry. Before concluding your tour, be sure to check out the selection of shiny new motorhomes on showcase. The museum is open daily (except Sundays in winter). Admission is $12 for adults and $9 for children. Well-behaved dogs are welcome for free.

RV Motorhome Hall of Fame & Museum
21565 Executive Parkway
Elkhart, IN 46514
(574) 293-2344
www.bringfido.com/go/1DMV

Where to Stay:

Conclude your stay in the RV Capital of the World with an overnight stop at the **Elkhart Campground**. Fido will love romping around the on-site dog park, and humans will enjoy the heated swimming pool, miniature golf course, and other recreational amenities. Full hook-up and pull-through sites are available. If you don't have an RV, you can stay in one of their pet-friendly cabins. Dogs of any size are welcome for no additional fee at RV sites and $10 per pet, per night in cabins.

Elkhart Campground
25608 County Road 4
Elkhart, IN 46514
(574) 264-2914
www.bringfido.com/go/1DMW
Rates from $30/night

Where to Stay:

You and your furry companion will find comfortable accommodations at the **GrandStay Hotel & Suites** in Ames. Spacious suites offer separate living areas and full kitchens, and property amenities include a complimentary daily breakfast, indoor swimming pool, and an outdoor sports court. Up to two dogs of any size are welcome for an additional fee of $15 per pet, per night. When it's time for dinner, make your way to the dog-friendly patio at **The Mucky Duck Pub**.

GrandStay Hotel & Suites Ames
1606 S Kellogg Avenue
Ames, IA 50010
(515) 232-8363
www.bringfido.com/go/1DVP
Rates from $79/night

Iowa Arboretum

On your next visit to the Hawkeye State, bring Fido to the **Iowa Arboretum**, an attraction featuring 160 acres of gardens, forests, and prairies populated with century-old oak trees and native grasses. You and your dog are welcome to explore the picturesque grounds and gardens that are home to more than 6,000 catalogued specimens of trees, plants, and shrubs. Exercise your leashed pup on the 0.8-mile outer loop and woodland hiking trails. Waste stations are positioned on the property for proper cleanup. Visit in the autumn and join the annual Woof Walk for a chance to meet and socialize with fellow dog lovers as you hike trails and marvel at the colorful fall foliage. The arboretum grounds and gardens are open daily from sunrise to sunset. Admission can be purchased online. The entrance fee is $7 for adults, $2 for children, and free for dogs.

Iowa Arboretum
1875 Peach Avenue
Madrid, IA 50156
(515) 795-3216
www.bringfido.com/go/1DVO

Living History Farms

Take your pup on a stroll through the past at **Living History Farms** in Urbandale. Visit exhibits designed to engage and educate you on life in the Midwest during the 1700s, 1800s, and 1900s. Each site is authentically farmed according to the time period and features interpreters dressed in period garb. The 1700 Iowa Farm boasts gardens, bark lodges, and demonstrations in tanning, cooking, and making pottery. At the 1850 Pioneer Farm, you might see men cultivating the fields while the women work on domestic projects inside the period cabin. See how farming changed with the arrival of machinery at the 1900 Horse-Powered Farm, or take in the sights and sounds of a bustling frontier community at the 1875 Town of Walnut Hill. Dogs must be leashed at all times and remain outside of the buildings. Hours vary by season. Admission is $16 for adults, $10 for children, and free for dogs.

Living History Farms
11121 Hickman Road
Urbandale, IA 50322
(515) 278-5286
www.bringfido.com/go/1DVR

Where to Stay:

In keeping with the pioneer theme of **Living History Farms**, the Stoney Creek Hotel and Conference Center in Johnston features Western-style suites with stone fireplaces. Families will love the bunk bed suites and free hot breakfast. Two dogs up to 50 lbs are welcome for an additional fee of $25 per pet, per night. Those traveling with larger pups should head to **Best Western Plus Des Moines West Inn & Suites**, where two dogs of any size are welcome for an additional fee of $25 per pet, per night.

Stoney Creek Hotel
and Conference Center
5291 Stoney Creek Court
Johnston, IA 50131
(515) 334-9000
www.bringfido.com/go/1DVS
Rates from $84/night

Shawnee Mission Park

Where to Stay:

When your pooch is dog-tired after a day of off-leash fun at Shawnee Mission Park, he'll find a comfy place to sleep at the **Hyatt Place Kansas City Lenexa City Center**. Fido can make himself at home in the oversized guest room, while you enjoy the complimentary breakfast or on-site restaurant. Up to two dogs (combined weight of 75 lbs) are welcome for an additional fee of $75 per stay.

Hyatt Place Kansas City
Lenexa City Center
8741 Ryckert Street
Lenexa, KS 66219
(913) 742-7777
www.bringfido.com/go/1DVX
Rates from $110/night

Fido can run free at **Shawnee Mission Park**, home to one of the largest off-leash areas in the country. This canine wonderland stretches across 44 acres of grasslands, wooded areas, and open fields that provide the perfect backdrop for a game of fetch. The highlight is the 120-acre lake, which features a dog beach and swimming hole. Your thirsty pup can hydrate at the water fountain located at the trailhead, before heading down for a leash-free swim. Afterward, explore miles of paved and unpaved trails that wind around the lake and through the woods. Keen-eyed pooches may spot deer, wild turkeys, and even a rare bobcat on their hike. Beyond the off-leash section, the park offers numerous picnic areas, shelters, and trails that welcome leashed pets. Dog park maps and trail guides are available at the Visitor Center. Hours vary by season. Admission is free.

Shawnee Mission Park
7900 Renner Road
Shawnee, KS 66219
(913) 438-7275
www.bringfido.com/go/1DVW

Dorothy's House & Land of Oz

Follow the Yellow Brick Road (with your little dog, too) to **Dorothy's House & Land of Oz** in Liberal. Decked out in her gingham dress and ruby red slippers, Dorothy herself will give you a tour through a replica of the Gale farmhouse featured in the *Wizard of Oz* film. Explore authentic memorabilia from the movie, including the actual model of the house used in the tornado scene from the 1939 classic, before traveling somewhere over the rainbow to the Land of Oz. Walk through the 5,000-square-foot animated exhibition with your pup and meet the Munchkins, the Scarecrow, the Tin Man, the Cowardly Lion, and the Wizard himself. Just watch out for the Wicked Witch. Fido is welcome to play the role of Toto as you wander along the magical road. Hours of operation vary by season. Tours are $7 for adults, $5 for children, and free for dogs.

Dorothy's House & Land of Oz
567 Yellow Brick Road
Liberal, KS 67901
(620) 624-7624
www.bringfido.com/go/1DVU

Where to Stay:

There's no place like home, but even Toto would feel comfortable in the spacious guest rooms at the **Holiday Inn Express & Suites Liberal**. Fido will find ample green space for his morning walk, and humans will enjoy the on-site amenities, which include a heated indoor pool and fitness center. A hot breakfast featuring the hotel's signature cinnamon rolls is offered every morning. Up to two dogs of any size are welcome for an additional fee of $25 per pet, per night.

Holiday Inn Express & Suites
Liberal
412 Ziegler Avenue
Liberal, KS 67901
(620) 624-2485
www.bringfido.com/go/1DVV
Rates from $85/night

Buffalo Trace Distillery

Many distilleries along Kentucky's famous Bourbon Trail welcome leashed dogs to explore their grounds. But, if you want a behind-the-scenes look at the bourbon-making craft, make your way to **Buffalo Trace Distillery** in Frankfort. There, Fido can join you on a 75-minute guided tour of the sprawling campus. The Trace Tour gives visitors a peek inside the company's aging warehouses and bottling rooms. You'll also learn about the different stages of the bourbon-making process. All tours end in the expansive tasting room, where you can sample some of Buffalo Trace's award-winning products, such as Eagle Rare and Blanton's Single Barrel. Operating hours are 10:00 am to 4:30 pm daily. Dogs are welcome on the tour, as well as in the tasting room and gift shop. The tours are complimentary and offered several times daily, but reservations are required.

Buffalo Trace Distillery
113 Great Buffalo Trace
Frankfort, KY 40601
(502) 696-5926
www.bringfido.com/go/1DMX

Where to Stay:

You'll need more than one day to explore Kentucky's bourbon heritage, so make the **21c Museum Hotel** in either Louisville or Lexington your home base. Both hotels feature contemporary art galleries highlighting specially-commissioned works from some of the world's most exciting artists, and both are very happy to accommodate your furry friend. Dogs of any size are welcome at either location for an additional fee of $75 per stay.

21c Museum Hotel Louisville
700 W Main Street
Louisville, KY 40202
(502) 217-6300
www.bringfido.com/go/1DMY
Rates from $160/night

Where to Stay:

Step out of the Jurassic period and into frontier times at **Yogi Bear's Jellystone Park**. Located a half-mile from Dinosaur World, the park's pet-friendly log cabins come equipped with full kitchens and feature covered porches and fire rings for grilling. Two dogs of any size are welcome for an additional fee of $10 per pet, per night. If you venture north, prolong your Kentucky stay at **Big Bone Lick State Historic Site Campground**. Campsites feature utility hookups and grills, as well as a community pool, showers, and restrooms. Dogs are welcome for free.

Yogi Bear's Jellystone Park
1002 Mammoth Cave Road
Cave City, KY 42127
(270) 773-3840
www.bringfido.com/go/1DJY
Rates from $89/night

Dinosaur World

Turn Fido into an amateur paleontologist by visiting a pair of prehistoric Kentucky attractions. At Cave City's **Dinosaur World**, more than 100 life-size replicas made from steel, concrete, and fiberglass line the paths of the attraction's Dinosaur Walk. This family-friendly activity also invites guests to hunt for fossils in the Fossil Dig, unearth life-size dinosaur bones in the Boneyard, and view the woolly creatures of Mammoth Gardens. Admission is $13 for adults, $10 for children, and free for leashed pups. If Fido would rather sniff out the real thing, drive a couple of hours north to **Big Bone Lick State Historic Site** in Union. There, he can hunt for fossils of ice age mammals that once called this area home and explore more than four miles of trails and salt springs. Keep an eye out for the resident bison who still roam the property year-round. The site is open daily and admission is free.

Dinosaur World
711 Mammoth Cave Road
Cave City, KY 42127
(270) 773-4345
www.bringfido.com/go/1DJV

Kentucky Horse Park

Aficionados of all things equestrian are certain to enjoy a visit to the **Kentucky Horse Park** in Lexington. Although the facility's museum is not pet friendly, dogs of any size are welcome at nearly all outdoor areas of the park. You can bring Fido along for a tour of the barns, rings, courses, and memorials sprinkled across the vast 1,032-acre campus. Don't miss the Memorial Walk of Champions and the famous Man o' War statue. You can also trot over to the stables to observe the guest horses residing at the park during the summer. Doggos may join you for a meal at one of the on-site restaurant's outdoor patios. Small pups that can be carried or wheeled in a stroller can even do a bit of browsing in the gift shop. Park hours are 9:00 am to 5:00 pm, and admission is $12 for adults and $6 for children. Dogs are free.

Kentucky Horse Park
4089 Iron Works Parkway
Lexington, KY 40511
(800) 678-8812
www.bringfido.com/go/1DK1

Where to Stay:

Located just 10 minutes from Kentucky Horse Park, the **Embassy Suites by Hilton Lexington UK Coldstream** is a stylish property in the heart of Bluegrass Country. Spacious suites offer many of the comforts of home, and your pup will love that the hotel is next door to the off-leash **Coldstream Dog Park**. Made-to-order breakfast is served each morning, and a complimentary reception takes place each evening in the hotel atrium. Up to two dogs of any size are welcome for an additional fee of $100 per stay.

Embassy Suites by Hilton
Lexington UK Coldstream
1801 Newtown Pike
Lexington, KY 40511
(859) 455-5000
www.bringfido.com/go/1DK2
Rates from $143/night

Where to Stay:

After trekking through the scenic Louisiana wilderness, you and Fido will welcome the charming appeal of the **Mouton Plantation** in Lafayette. Pet-friendly accommodations are available in the property's cottages, where up to two dogs of any size are welcome for an additional fee of $20 per pet. Don't miss the daily complimentary chef-prepared Cajun breakfast or the social hour from 4:30 pm to 6:30 pm each evening, where you can enjoy free hors d'oeuvres and cocktails.

Mouton Plantation
338 N Sterling Street
Lafayette, LA 70501
(337) 233-7816
www.bringfido.com/go/1DVZ
Rates $85/night

Atchafalaya Experience

Enjoy America's largest river swamp with your pup on the **Atchafalaya Experience** in Breaux Bridge. Louisiana's Atchafalaya River is a perfect place to spot beavers, deer, alligators, crocodiles, and over 30 bird species. Tour the swamp with experienced naturalists, whose love of the area and expertise make each trip memorable. Tours begin daily at the Atchafalaya Welcome Center, but you should call ahead for reservations. Prices are $50 for adults and $25 for children. Well-behaved, leashed pets are welcome for no additional fee. For another nearby adventure with Fido, travel to **Avery Island** for a visit to the Tabasco Country Store and the 170-acre Jungle Gardens. Dogs are welcome on the grounds of both attractions but should remain leashed at all times. Visitors pay a $1 toll per vehicle to enter Avery Island. Admission to Jungle Gardens is $8 for adults and $5 for children. Dogs are welcome for free.

Atchafalaya Experience
1908 Atchafalaya River Highway
Breaux Bridge, LA 70517
(337) 277-4726
www.bringfido.com/go/1DVY

Bloody Mary's Tours

If you're a fan of spooks and specters, enjoy a nighttime tour of New Orleans with **Bloody Mary's Tours**. On the French Quarter Supernatural Tour + Ghost Hunt, you'll conjure spirits and search for spooks with a real Voodoo priestess. History and haunts come to life as your guide entertains you with stories about 19th century vampires Marie Laveau and Madame LaLaurie. Tours depart from 941 Bourbon Street at 8:00 pm on Fridays, Saturdays, and Sundays. Tickets for the 2.5-hour tour cost $58 per person, and reservations are required. Well-behaved dogs are welcome for no additional fee. For a less-spooky look at New Orleans, pay $2 per pedestrian to climb aboard the pet-friendly **Algiers Ferry** and enjoy incredible views of the city as you and your pooch travel to Algiers Point. While you're there, stop in for a pint and a snack at **The Crown & Anchor**, which welcomes pups inside and out.

Bloody Mary's Tours
941 Bourbon Street
New Orleans, LA 70116
(504) 523-7684
www.bringfido.com/go/1DW1

Where to Stay:

When you check in at **The Old No. 77 Hotel & Chandlery**, a boutique property located just a few blocks from New Orleans' French Quarter, Fido will be treated like the VIP (very important pet) that he is. He'll be greeted with treats, a pet bed, bowls, and ID tags during his stay. When it's time to go for a walk, beautiful Lafayette Square is just around the corner. Up to three dogs of any size are welcome for an additional fee of $25 per stay.

The Old No. 77 Hotel & Chandlery
535 Tchoupitoulas Street
New Orleans, LA 70130
(504) 527-5271
www.bringfido.com/go/1DW2
Rates from $85/night

Where to Stay:

Constructed in 1900, the **Canterbury Cottage Bed & Breakfast** is a cozy alternative to traditional lodgings in Bar Harbor. The home is within walking distance to downtown shops and the harbor, as well as a short drive from the hiking trails in Acadia National Park. While you're there, you'll enjoy a hearty hot breakfast every morning. Dogs of any size are welcome in the property's Cottage and Garden rooms for an additional fee of $20 per night.

Canterbury Cottage Bed & Breakfast
12 Roberts Avenue
Bar Harbor, ME 04069
(207) 288-2112
www.bringfido.com/go/1DOW
Rates from $89/night

Acadia National Park

Spend a glorious day with your pup surrounded by the beauty of **Acadia National Park** on a tour with **Carriages of Acadia**. You and Fido will enjoy traveling down Acadia's historic roads in a horse-drawn carriage on one of four guided excursions. Tours start at $20. If you would rather explore on your own, take the free, pet-friendly **Island Explorer** shuttle into Acadia and wander the trails, hike the granite peaks, and savor the natural beauty of the flora and fauna. Visit the **Jordan Pond House** for famous popovers, lobster stew, or a refreshing glass of hand-squeezed lemonade on the lawn. See Acadia's wonders from the water with a scenic nature cruise aboard the **Sea Princess**. Narrated by an Acadia Park Ranger, the pet-friendly cruise will take you to the Great Harbor of Mount Desert and Somes Sound Fjord. Rates start at $27 for adults and $17 for children. Dogs ride for free.

Acadia National Park
25 Visitor Center Road
Bar Harbor, ME 04609
(207) 288-3338
www.bringfido.com/go/1DOV

Seashore Trolley Museum

Chug over to the world's largest and oldest electric railway museum with your canine conductor and hop on board a restored street car at the **Seashore Trolley Museum**. Stroll with Fido through the visitor center, three public exhibit buildings and the observation gallery, where you can see restoration work taking place. Take your pup for a ride on one of several restored street cars that travel a 1.5-mile private railway. You can hop off and hike a nearby trail system and then complete the loop with a return ride to the visitor center. The museum is open from 10:00 am to 5:00 pm daily between May and October. Admission is $12 for adults and $10 for children. Dogs are welcome for free. After your visit, make your way to the Cape Porpoise Pier for a fresh seafood or Maine lobster dinner with your pup at the **Cape Pier Chowder House**.

Seashore Trolley Museum
195 Log Cabin Road
Kennebunkport, ME 04046
(207) 967-2800
www.bringfido.com/go/1DSK

Where to Stay:

Extend your dog-friendly Maine getaway with a night at **The Colony Hotel** in Kennebunkport. You'll relish the spectacular ocean views from this historic coastal resort. Take a dip in the Atlantic Ocean or the hotel's heated saltwater pool. Fido is free to play on the hotel's private beach and explore the famous Maine tidal pools. Up to two dogs of any size are welcome for an additional fee of $30 per pet, per night.

The Colony Hotel
140 Ocean Avenue
Kennebunkport, ME 04046
(207) 967-3331
www.bringfido.com/go/1DSL
Rates from $164/night

Casco Bay Lines

Explore the islands of Casco Bay with Fido aboard one of the daily cruises offered by **Casco Bay Lines** in Portland. Start your morning with a beautiful 'Sunrise on the Bay' cruise, a two-hour tour that starts at the peak of dawn, giving you opportunities for great early morning photographs. If island hopping is more your style, check out the 'Mailboat Run' instead. As the name implies, the Mailboat navigates the many small islands of Casco Bay, delivering mail and freight, as well as hauling passengers and their furry friends. Roundtrip cruises take approximately three hours and depart twice daily. Ticket prices are $17 for adults, $9 for children, and $4 for dogs. Dogs must remain leashed at all times. After you've worked up an appetite helping to deliver mail, stop by the **Portland Lobster Company** to enjoy a classic Maine lobster roll. The restaurant welcomes your pooch with ample outdoor seating.

Casco Bay Lines
56 Commercial Street
Portland, ME 04101
(207) 774-7871
www.bringfido.com/go/1DSH

Where to Stay:

Located a short drive from Portland, **Inn by the Sea** is a true doggy delight on Crescent Beach. The hotel offers an 'Inncredible Pets' package, which includes a two-night stay in a one-bedroom suite, personalized L.L. Bean dog bed and toy, Inn by the Sea dog bowl, nightly dining from the gourmet pet menu, and evening turndown service (complete with a locally made seasonal dog treat). The property's human perks are great too, and dogs of any size stay for no additional fee.

Inn by the Sea
40 Bowery Beach Road
Cape Elizabeth, ME 04107
(207) 799-3134
www.bringfido.com/go/1DSI
Rates from $259/night

Where to Stay:

Conclude your Boothbay visit with a stay at **Spruce Point Inn Resort & Spa**, a seaside retreat offering sensational views of Boothbay Harbor. Choose from several pet-friendly room types, each decorated with authentic New England furnishings. Fido will get plenty of exercise on the many wooded walking trails located around the property, which sits on 57 acres of shoreline. You can also sail aboard Maine's only wooden lobster boat from the resort's dock. Dogs of any size are welcome for an additional fee of $35 per pet, per night.

Spruce Point Inn Resort & Spa
88 Grandview Avenue
Boothbay Harbor, ME 04538
(207) 633-4152
www.bringfido.com/go/1DSE
Rates from $195/night

Cap'n Fish's Cruises

Begin your trip to Boothbay by embarking on an Audubon Puffin and Scenic Cruise with **Cap'n Fish's Cruises**. A 2.5-hour tour will take you around Eastern Egg Rock—North America's southernmost nesting island for the Atlantic Puffin. Onboard, marine biologists and naturalists will answer questions as you spot seals, herons, the occasional whale and, of course, puffins. The cruises are offered from mid-May through late August. Other tours are available through October. Rates are $45 for adults, $35 for children, and $20 for dogs. Call ahead for reservations and departure times. After your cruise, walk a block down the street to **Two Salty Dogs Pet Outfitters**, where good pups will receive a special treat. Then head north for a ride on an authentic steam and diesel locomotive at **Boothbay Railway Village**. The Village is open May through October. Admission is $15 for adults, $8 for children, and free for dogs.

Cap'n Fish's Cruises
42 Commercial Street
Boothbay Harbor, ME 04538
(207) 613-7339
www.bringfido.com/go/1DSD

Appalachian Trail

Take a fantastic day hike with your pup along a 10-mile stretch of the Appalachian Trail from Crampton's Gap in Maryland to Harpers Ferry in West Virginia. Start your adventure by staying overnight at **The Treehouse Camp**, located just a quarter of a mile from the trailhead in **Gathland State Park**. Spend some time learning about the Civil War Battle of the South Mountain and admire the War Correspondent's Arch before heading south toward Harpers Ferry. The mild elevation change along this portion of the Appalachian Trail makes the trek appropriate for both skilled and novice hikers. Stop for a picnic lunch before crossing the banks of the Potomac River into West Virginia. Don't worry about the hike back once you've reached Harpers Ferry. **River & Trail Outfitters** will shuttle you to your accommodations for a small charge. Dogs must remain leashed on the trail and during the shuttle ride.

Gathland State Park
900 Arnoldstown Road
Jefferson, MD 21755
(301) 791-4767
www.bringfido.com/go/1DK5

Where to Stay:

Located just a stone's throw from the Appalachian Trail, **The Treehouse Camp** in Rohrersville features 18 elevated tree cottages and treehouses that welcome Fido. Cottages are insulated for year-round use and come furnished with tables, mattresses, and wood stoves. Tree houses are rustic, screened-in structures without stoves or mattresses. Campground amenities include fire pits, charcoal grills, picnic areas, and private bathrooms. Remember to bring your own bedding and a lantern. Dogs are welcome for no additional fee.

The Treehouse Camp
20716 Townsend Road
Rohrersville, MD 21779
(301) 432-5585
www.bringfido.com/go/1DK4
Rates from $43/night

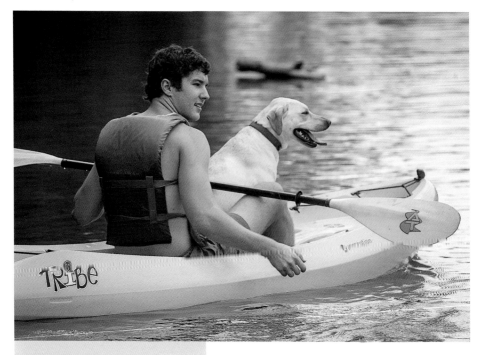

Where to Stay:

Sheltered on the shores of Sinepuxent Bay, **Castaways Campground** offers pet-friendly cottage and RV rentals. The property features dog-friendly perks including a bark park, bark beach, and dog wash station. Fido is also welcome to join you for a drink at the on-site Jackspot Waterfront Tiki Bar, which features live entertainment during the summer. Up to three dogs of any size are welcome for an additional fee of $8 per pet, per night.

Castaways Campground
12550 Eagles Nest Road
Berlin, MD 21811
(410) 213-0097
www.bringfido.com/go/1DU8
Rates from $53/night

Ayers Creek Adventures

Experience Maryland's coastal waterways with **Ayers Creek Adventures** in Berlin. Located just a stone's throw from Ocean City, the family-owned business can introduce you to the quiet side of this bustling beach town with a kayak, canoe, or stand-up paddleboard rental. As you paddle Ayers Creek with your canine companion, he's likely to see bald eagles, herons, egrets, and osprey nesting in the salt marsh. If you'd prefer to paddle Sinepuxent Bay, boats can also be delivered to **Castaways Campground** by request. Either way, you'll get a brief lesson, water trail map, and guide to the local wildlife before you set off. The outfitter is open daily from 8:00 am to 5:00 pm between May and October. Rental rates start at $15. Half-day, full-day, and weekend rates are also available. Dogs paddle for free, but advance notice of Fido's participation is requested.

Ayers Creek Adventures
8628 Grey Fox Lane
Berlin, MD 21811
(443) 513-0889
www.bringfido.com/go/1DU7

Watermark Cruises

You and your canine compatriot can cruise the Chesapeake Bay in style with **Watermark Cruises** in Annapolis. Whether you have just an hour or want to enjoy an entire day on the water, the company has you covered. Enjoy a quick 40-minute trip around the bay as you learn about Annapolis history, or set off on a 90-minute excursion highlighting the scenic Severn River. If you want to see more of coastal Maryland, spend an entire day on the bay with a tour to St. Michaels on the Eastern Shore. There, you'll disembark for three hours of shopping, sightseeing, and dining along the town's charming streets before completing the return journey to Annapolis. If your dog needs to shake off his sea legs, head to **Quiet Waters Park** after your cruise for off-leash playtime in the dog park or along the hiking trails. Cruise prices start at $19 for adults and $6 for children. Well-behaved dogs ride for free.

Watermark Cruises
1 Dock Street
Annapolis, MD 21401
(410) 268-7601
www.bringfido.com/go/1DQP

Where to Stay:

After a day on the water, you and your furry friend can take it easy at the **Graduate Annapolis**, located in the heart of the Annapolis Arts District. In addition to offering first-rate rooms and amenities, the hotel welcomes visiting pups with an assortment of treats and toys from BarkBox. Fido can also meet furry friends in the outdoor dog park located on the second floor. Two dogs up to 60 lbs are welcome for an additional fee of $25 per pet, per night.

Graduate Annapolis
126 West Street
Annapolis, MD 21401
(410) 263-7777
www.bringfido.com/go/1DQQ
Rates from $101/night

Savage River Lodge

Spend some quality time with your hound on an outdoor adventure at **Savage River Lodge** in Frostburg. Located within the 700-acre **Savage River State Forest**, the lodge provides a year-round peaceful oasis from the distractions of daily life. In the spring, try your hand at fly fishing for trout in the cold mountain streams. Summer is the perfect time to take man's best friend for a hike along the 13 miles of maintained trails looping through the property and surrounding state forest. Relax amid the changing scenery during the brilliant fall foliage season. Enjoy a winter escape on the cross-country ski trails, or take a snowshoe expedition with Fido by your side. Regardless of season, pups are welcome anywhere on the property except inside the lodge and on the porches. A dog wash station is available from May through October.

Savage River Lodge
1600 Mount Aetna Road
Frostburg, MD 21532
(301) 689-3200
www.bringfido.com/go/1DN6

Where to Stay:

From the acres of outdoor fun to the daily homemade dog biscuits given to all visiting pooches, **Savage River Lodge** is a doggy paradise. When it's dinner time, Fido can savor canine casserole and mutt meatballs from the 'Bone Appetit' menu. After a full day, cozy up in one of the private, two-story cabins appointed with everything you and your pooch need to enjoy a comfortable night. Dogs of any size are welcome for an additional fee of $30 per pet, per night.

Savage River Lodge
1600 Mount Aetna Road
Frostburg, MD 21532
(301) 689-3200
www.bringfido.com/go/1DN6
Rates from $250/night

Where to Stay:

Located just one block from Provincetown Harbor, the **Provincetown Hotel at Gabriel's** is made up of four historic buildings that surround a lovely courtyard (which serves as the gathering spot for a made-to-order breakfast each morning). With beautiful gardens, decks, private sitting areas, and a fire pit, it's easy to forget you are just steps away from bustling Commercial Street. Dogs of any size are welcome for an additional fee of $25 per pet, per night.

Provincetown Hotel at Gabriel's
102 Bradford Street
Provincetown, MA 02657
(508) 487-3232
www.bringfido.com/go/1DO7
Rates from $115/night

Dog Gone Sailing Charters

Strap a doggy life vest on your pup and go sailing with **Dog Gone Sailing Charters** in Provincetown. After climbing aboard *The Moondance II* with Captain Ro and her trusty sea dog Spinnaker, you'll sail to Long Point—the site of the original Provincetown settlement. Choose a 90-minute sunrise or sunset tour, or relax on a half-day or full-day sailing adventure. Rates start at $40 for shrimp sails to Toro. Sunrise and sunset cruises are $45 per person. Half-day charters begin at $350 and can accommodate up to six passengers. Life vests are available for pups of all sizes. If your salty dog is up for more water fun, take a whale watching cruise with **Dolphin Fleet of Provincetown**. An interpretive guide accompanies each three- to four-hour cruise to narrate the natural history of Cape Cod and to help identify marine life spotted on the trip. Prices are $57 for adults and $35 for children. Dogs float for free.

Dog Gone Sailing Charters
10 MacMillan Pier
Provincetown, MA 02657
(508) 566-0410
www.bringfido.com/go/1DO6

Nantucket Island

Travel with your dog by air or sea to beautiful Nantucket Island. Start your adventure with a flight from Hyannis on **Cape Air & Nantucket Airlines**. One dog up to 80 lbs can sit in the aisle beside you for a $30 fee. If your pup would rather float than fly, dogs ride for free on the **Steamship Authority**'s high-speed ferry. Either way, once you arrive in Nantucket, it's time to catch **'The Wave'** (the island's public bus service). Take the Madaket Route to **Sanford Farm** for a six-mile Ocean Walk, or visit the island's unofficial dog park at **Tupancy Links**. For more beach fun, head to **Nobadeer Beach**, where Fido can run off leash year-round. If you want to explore the island with your own set of wheels, visit **Young's Bicycle Shop** to rent a bicycle for yourself and a bike trailer for Fido. Before your day is over, grab a cold beer and local seafood at dog-friendly **Cisco Brewers**.

Cape Air & Nantucket Airlines
660 Barnstable Road
Hyannis, MA 02601
(800) 227-3247
www.bringfido.com/go/1DOF

Where to Stay:

For a quintessential Nantucket experience, spend the night in a 'Woof Cottage' at **The Cottages & Lofts at the Boat Basin**—a waterfront property located right on the dock at Straight Wharf. The staff will ensure that Fido is provided a comfy pet bed, food and water bowls, and a basket of nautical chew toys during your stay. Doggy turndown service is also provided nightly. Up to two dogs of any size are welcome for an additional fee of $49 per night.

The Cottage & Lofts at Nantucket Boat Basin
24 Old South Wharf
Nantucket, MA 02554
(508) 325-1499
www.bringfido.com/go/1DOG
Rates from $165/night

Where to Stay:

At the end of a long day of sightseeing, make your way to the **Hampton Inn & Suites Plymouth** for a well-deserved snooze. Up to two dogs of any size are welcome for an additional fee of $35 per pet, per night. When it's time for dinner, head to the **Lobster Hut**, where you can sample some fresh New England seafood. Pups are allowed to join you at the waterfront eatery's covered outdoor seating area.

Hampton Inn & Suites Plymouth
10 Plaza Way
Plymouth, MA 02360
(508) 747-5000
www.bringfido.com/go/1E4J
Rates from $123/night

Pilgrim Memorial State Park

Bring Fido to see Plymouth Rock at **Pilgrim Memorial State Park**, the landing site where America's first European settlers disembarked the *Mayflower* over 400 years ago. Explore the area with your pooch on a self-guided tour of the monuments and memorials, view the replica *Mayflower II*, and listen to one of the historical talks offered throughout the day. There is no admission fee to access the park. Just be sure to keep Fido leashed at all times. After your park visit, your salty dog can hit the high seas on a fishing charter with **Captain John Boats**. Cast your line in the deep sea along the Cape Cod peninsula in search of sharks, striped bass, blue fish, and tuna. Fishing trip prices start at $45 for adults, and dogs sail for free. If Fido prefers being a landlubber, take him on a hike along one of the five dog-friendly trails at nearby **Myles Standish State Forest**.

Pilgrim Memorial State Park
79 Water Street
Plymouth, MA 02360
(508) 747-5360
www.bringfido.com/go/1E4I

The Freedom Trail

Fido can walk in the footsteps of America's founding fathers by following the **Freedom Trail** through downtown Boston. All you need to enjoy this free attraction is your dog's leash and a good pair of walking shoes. The 2.5-mile red brick trail will lead you right to 16 of Boston's most historic sites, so you don't even need a map! Starting at the **Boston Common**, America's oldest public park, you'll pass by Faneuil Hall, Paul Revere's House, and the site of the Boston Massacre, before ending at the USS Constitution in Charlestown. Once there, you can hitch a ride back to Faneuil Hall on the **Boston Water Taxi** for a $15 fare. Or, better yet, ask to be dropped off at Boston's Long Wharf, where you can stop for 'chowdah' and freshly shucked oysters at **State Street Provisions**. The Boston Water Taxi allows dogs for no additional fee.

The Freedom Trail
139 Tremont Street
Boston, MA 02111
(617) 357-8300
www.bringfido.com/go/1DO9

Where to Stay:

After conquering the Freedom Trail, Fido can rest his weary paws at **XV Beacon Hotel**. Centrally located in Beacon Hill, the property offers a boutique hotel feel with full-service amenities, including dog treats at check-in. Dogs of any size are welcome for an additional fee of $50 per stay. After a restful night's sleep, bring your pooch to the nearby **Public Garden** to enjoy a morning constitutional through America's first public botanical garden.

XV Beacon Hotel
15 Beacon Street
Boston, MA 02108
(617) 670-1500
www.bringfido.com/go/1DOA
Rates from $333/night

deCordova Sculpture Park

Bring your furry art critic to explore over 60 large-scale modern and contemporary sculptures at the **deCordova Sculpture Park**, located along the shore of Flint's Pond in Lincoln. This 30-acre park is the largest of its kind in New England. Most of the exhibits are on loan to the museum and are constantly changing, making each visit to this attraction unique. Your pup is welcome to wander the trails with you as you marvel at the beautiful lawns, gardens, fields, and forests. Take a guided tour of the grounds, or set your own pace and pause for a picnic in the park. Dogs must remain leashed at all times. The park is open daily during the summer and Wednesdays through Sundays during the winter. Admission is $14 for adults. Children under 12 and dogs enjoy complimentary admission when accompanied by a paying adult.

deCordova Sculpture Park
51 Sandy Pond Road
Lincoln, MA 01773
(781) 259-8355
www.bringfido.com/go/1DK7

Where to Stay:

Following your art walk, rest up at the **Westin Waltham Boston**. Just 15 miles from downtown Boston, this hotel offers Fido plenty of grassy space to stretch his legs. In the evening, you are invited to sip a glass of champagne or have a cocktail in the Lobby Lounge or outdoor terrace. Other perks include complimentary treats at check-in and a Westin Heavenly Dog Bed for your pup. Two dogs up to 75 lbs are welcome for no additional fee.

Westin Waltham Boston
70 3rd Avenue
Waltham, MA 02451
(781) 290-5600
www.bringfido.com/go/1DK8
Rates from $116/night

Where to Stay:

Nicknamed 'Michigan's Little Bavaria' for its German heritage and architectural style, the town of Frankenmuth is home to many Bavarian-themed shops and attractions. Extend your visit with Fido by staying at the **Drury Inn & Suites Frankenmuth**. Located on Main Street, within easy walking distance to all the downtown attractions, the hotel offers comfortable rooms, free hot breakfast, and a nightly happy hour. Two dogs up to 80 lbs (combined weight) are welcome for an additional fee of $35 per night.

Drury Inn & Suites Frankenmuth
260 S Main Street
Frankenmuth, MI 48734
(989) 652-2800
www.bringfido.com/go/1DPR
Rates from $119/night

Bavarian Belle Riverboat

The **Bavarian Belle Riverboat** is a popular attraction for visitors to the German-themed town of Frankenmuth, and tail waggers are welcome to join in the fun. Board the vessel with your pup to enjoy views of town from the Cass River and learn more about the history of the region. The authentic, stern-driven paddlewheel riverboat has an open-air canopied upper deck and a fully enclosed lower deck. Plan ahead and visit during the annual Dog Bowl Festival at the end of May when the company offers a special 'Canine Cruise.' Tours depart several times daily between early May and mid-October. Tickets are $15 for adults, $5 for children, and free for dogs. After your ride, head next door to the **River Place Shops**, where furry friends are welcome inside many of the retail stores. Stop by **Hello Cats & Dogs** to pick up a yummy treat for your good boy.

Bavarian Belle Riverboat
925 S Main Street
Frankenmuth, MI 48734
(866) 808-2628
www.bringfido.com/go/1DPQ

Silver Lake Buggy Rentals

Take your pooch on a wild dune buggy ride with a rental from **Silver Lake Buggy Rentals** in Mears. Pick up a two-seat or four-seat cart for an off-road adventure between the shores of Lake Michigan and Silver Lake. Your dog is welcome to ride along as you speed across the sand. You'll need eye protection when navigating the dunes, so don't forget to pack Fido's goggles! Bring a change of clothes and a towel for your pup, too—you'll probably get wet. The recreation area is open from April through October, and buggy rentals are available from May through September. Rates start at $245 for a two-hour rental. When your ride is over, bring your pup on a walk or bike ride through the nearby **Hart-Montague Trail State Park**, a scenic 22-mile paved path that was formerly a railroad line. Pack a lunch and take a break at one of the picnic tables found along the trail.

Silver Lake Buggy Rentals
8288 W Hazel Road
Mears, MI 49436
(231) 873-8833
www.bringfido.com/go/1DRR

Where to Stay:

Hop off the trail in Montague for a stay at **The Weathervane Inn**, a waterfront property on beautiful White Lake. Guest rooms feature hot tubs, fireplaces, and private balconies overlooking the lake. Enjoy a complimentary breakfast before taking your pup for a walk on the adjacent Hart-Montague Trail. Kayak, stand-up paddleboard, and bike rentals are available on-site through **WaterDog Outfitters**. Up to two dogs of any size are welcome for an additional fee of $20 per pet, per night.

The Weathervane Inn
4527 Dowling Street
Montague, MI 49437
(231) 292-9092
www.bringfido.com/go/1DRS
Rates from $89/night

Where to Stay:

Extend your outdoor adventure in Michigan's Upper Peninsula with an overnight stay at **Northland Outfitters** in Germfask. Located adjacent to the **Seney National Wildlife Refuge** (where leashed pets are welcome on all trails), their heated and furnished cabins are available from May through October. Dogs of any size are welcome for an additional fee of $5 per night. You and your pooch can also sign up for Northland Outfitters' overnight canoe and fishing trips down the Fox and Manistique Rivers.

Northland Outfitters
8174 Highway M-77
Germfask, MI 49836
(906) 586-9801
www.bringfido.com/go/1DKL
Rates from $75/night

Toonerville Trolley

Climb aboard the **Toonerville Trolley** in Soo Junction to set off on an adventure with Fido through the thick forests of Michigan's Upper Peninsula. Operating since 1927, the train gives you the chance to see deer, bears, moose, wolves, and birds from the comfort of your seat. Let Fido sit on your lap, and he'll help you spot them! At the end of the line, you'll get your first peek of the Tahquamenon River and board the *Hiawatha* riverboat for a 21-mile cruise to its rapids. Well-behaved, leashed dogs can ride on the top deck of the boat. After reaching the rapids, disembark for a half-mile hike to Tahquamenon Falls with your pooch. Tours operate multiple times per week from mid-June through early October and depart at 10:30 am. The journey takes approximately six hours to complete and costs $49 for adults and $27 for children. Dogs ride for free.

Toonerville Trolley
7195 Co Road 381
Soo Junction, MI 49000
(888) 778-7246
www.bringfido.com/go/1DKK

Mackinac Island

Mackinac Island is filled with fun activities you can enjoy with your pup, and nearly all of the historic sites and buildings allow leashed pets. Your adventure begins with a 15-minute ride to the island aboard **Shepler's Ferry**. Roundtrip fares start at $27 for adults and $16 for children. Dogs ride for free. Motorized vehicles are not allowed on the island, so you'll have to get around on two (or four) legs. With a circumference of only eight miles, it is possible to walk around the entire island. However, if you'd prefer not to 'hoof it,' you can pay a horse to do it for you! **Mackinac Island Carriage Tours** offers fully narrated two-hour tours of the island with stops at Arch Rock, Fort Mackinac, and several other points of interest. Tickets are $30 for adults and $11 for children. Lap dogs are free, and larger dogs ride for the price of a child's ticket.

Mackinac Island
7274 Main Street
Mackinac Island, MI 49757
(906) 847-3783
www.bringfido.com/go/1DUO

Where to Stay:

Extend your visit to Mackinac Island with a stay at the pet-friendly **Mission Point Resort**. Plan ahead and book the hotel's 'Pooch at the Point' package, which includes accommodation in the resort's historic Straits Lodge, roundtrip transfers on Shepler's Ferry, an assortment of welcome amenities for the doggos, and daily breakfast for the humans. Up to two dogs of any size are welcome for an additional fee of $100 per stay.

Mission Point Resort
6633 Main Street
Mackinac Island, MI 49757
(906) 847-3312
www.bringfido.com/go/1DUP
Rates from $124/night

Argo Park Canoe & Kayak

Meander down the Huron River with Fido in beautiful Ann Arbor. Start your day at **Argo Park Canoe & Kayak**, where you'll get outfitted with a life jacket and canoe or kayak. Although you're in the heart of the city, you'll enjoy the peaceful vibe of the river as you spot turtles, cranes, and ducks. End your float 3.7 miles down the river at Gallup Park, where you can return your equipment and get a van ride back to your starting point. The cost is $27 (including transportation) for a two-person kayak. Fido can stop to stretch his legs at several points along the way, including **Broadway Park**, which also features an off-leash dog run (permit required). Plan ahead and pack a picnic for a lunch break at **Fuller Park**. After your river adventure, take a stroll along the garden paths of **Nichols Arboretum**, which is open daily from sunrise to sunset. Admission is complimentary.

Argo Park Canoe & Kayak
1055 Longshore Drive
Ann Arbor, MI 48105
(734) 794-6241
www.bringfido.com/go/1DK9

Where to Stay:

After your day of floating fun, call it a night at the **Graduate Ann Arbor**. Furry guests are greeted with treats, bowls, and blankets. You will enjoy the retro cocktail lounge, 24-hour fitness center, and complimentary bike rentals. The hotel welcomes dogs of any size for an additional fee of $25 per night. When it's dinner time, walk to **Grizzly Peaks Brewing Company**, where you can grab a cold one and Fido can order from their 'Pups on the Patio' menu.

Graduate Ann Arbor
615 E Huron Street
Ann Arbor, MI 48104
(734) 769-2200
www.bringfido.com/go/1DKA
Rates from $109/night

Where to Stay:

Your dog-tired pup won't have far to walk after your day of adventure in the Minnesota Northwoods. **Gunflint Lodge** offers a variety of pet-friendly accommodations to keep you warm at night. Standard cabins feature wood-burning fireplaces, plush bedding, and kitchenettes. For a budget-friendly experience, rent one of the rustic Voyageur cabins, which offer four individual bunks and shared bathroom facilities (bring your own sleeping bags and towels). Dogs of any size are welcome for an additional fee of $25 per pet, per night, except during 'Dog Lover's Weekends' when they stay for free!

Gunflint Lodge
143 S Gunflint Lake Road
Grand Marais, MN 55604
(218) 388-2296
www.bringfido.com/go/1DKN
Rates from $79/night

Gunflint Lodge

No matter the season, treat your canine companion to a Northwoods adventure at **Gunflint Lodge**, located 40 miles up the Gunflint Trail from the dog-friendly town of Grand Marais. In the warmer months, snag a trophy walleye on a guided fishing trip, rent a pontoon boat to explore Gunflint Lake at your leisure, or take advantage of the resort's free use of canoes and kayaks. Pups are also welcome to play in the sand and cool off with a swim in the lake. In winter, the lodge offers a dog-friendly ski trail for snowshoeing and cross-country skiing. Hiking trails are open year-round, and reservations can be made for a dog hike with a naturalist guide. Plan your visit during one of the popular 'Dog Lover's Weekends' when the lodge offers classes and seminars geared toward man's best friend. At the end of the day, enjoy sunset views and dinner with your furry friend on the patio of the resort's lakeside restaurant.

Gunflint Lodge
143 S Gunflint Lake Road
Grand Marais, MN 55604
(218) 388-2296
www.bringfido.com/go/1DKN

Lake Country Air

Even the most well-traveled pups will find a unique experience awaiting them at **Lake Country Air & Beaver Air Tours** in Duluth. You and your pooch are welcome to hop aboard a de Havilland Beaver floatplane for a scenic flight tour of the Twin Ports and Duluth areas. Customize a private trip or choose from one of the company's curated outings. Listen by headset as your pilot narrates the tour and soars over historic landmarks. Some tours will dock, giving passengers time to explore on land. Want to learn more about flying? Book the company's 'Learn the Basics of Float Flying' session to learn about landings and take-offs, radio communication, and the principles of flight work. Forty-five minutes to full-day tours are available with rates starting at $119 per adult. Fido flies for free! Advance registration is required for guests traveling with pets. Tours depart from Duluth's Sky Harbor Airport.

Lake Country Air & Beaver Air Tours
5000 Minnesota Avenue
Duluth, MN 55802
(612) 812-1223
www.bringfido.com/go/1DW5

Where to Stay:

Make **Fitger's Inn** your base for exploring dog-friendly Duluth. This historic lakefront hotel is home to a brewery, spa, mall, and many restaurants. Your furry fashionista can shop 'til she drops at most retailers, including **A Place for Fido**. After browsing the mall, head out for a walk along the shores of Lake Superior on Duluth's **Lakewalk**. On your way back to the inn, stop by **Portland Malt Shoppe** for a scoop of banana ice cream to share with your pup. Two dogs of any size are welcome at Fitger's Inn for no extra fee.

Fitger's Inn
600 E Superior Street
Duluth, MN 55802
(218) 722-8826
www.bringfido.com/go/1DW6
Rates from $180/night

Where to Stay:

Choctaw Hall, a historic pre-war mansion constructed in the 1830s, will be your pampered pup's choice for accommodations in Natchez. All of the property's Queen rooms are pet friendly, and rooms at the front of the building have direct outdoor access. Up to two dogs of any size are welcome for no additional fee. When the sun begins to set, stroll down to the Natchez Bluff to enjoy magnificent views across the Mississippi River.

Choctaw Hall
310 N Wall Street
Natchez, MS 39120
(601) 807-0196
www.bringfido.com/go/1DXZ
Rates from $135/night

Natchez Trace Parkway

Bring Fido on a road trip across Mississippi by way of the historic **Natchez Trace Parkway**. Start your journey in Tupelo with a visit to the **Elvis Presley Birthplace**, where your hound dog can explore the grounds and trails surrounding the childhood home of the King of Rock and Roll. Then, make your way to the Parkway Visitor Center at milepost 266, where humans can learn some Natchez Trace history and doggos can earn their B.A.R.K. ranger certification. From there, you will drive 270 miles south to Natchez. Along the way, stop at **Jeff Busby Park** to take a short 1.6-mile roundtrip hike to the overlook at **Little Mountain**. Further south, walk along the boardwalk through the canopy of trees growing in the marshy waters of the **Cypress Swamp Trail**. At the end of the parkway, you'll find the **Natchez National Historical Park**, where you can explore Civil War sites and more dog-friendly trails with your furry friend.

Natchez Trace Parkway
Natchez, MS 39120
(800) 305-7417
www.bringfido.com/go/1DXY

Biloxi Shrimping Trip

Bring your canine companion to the Mississippi Gulf Coast for an educational outing with **Biloxi Shrimping Trip**. Climb aboard the *Sailfish* for a 70-minute journey into the unexpectedly fascinating world of shrimping. The crew will tell you everything you ever wanted to know about shrimp, from the life cycle of the crustaceans to the best ways to catch, cook, and eat them. Watch the crew demonstrate the proper techniques for catching the tasty shellfish as they drop the net and drag the bottom of the Mississippi Sound. After learning some history of the industry, the day's catch will be hauled in, and the captain will help you identify the various sea creatures that found their way into the net. Rates start at $20 per adult and $12 for children. Dogs float for free. After your tour, stop by **Shaggy's Beach Bar & Grill** to enjoy some tasty barbeque shrimp at a beachfront table.

Biloxi Shrimping Trip
693 Beach Boulevard
Biloxi, MS 39530
(228) 392-8645
www.bringfido.com/go/1DWA

Where to Stay:

If you and your four-legged friend are feeling lucky, your best bet is to head to the **Hard Rock Hotel & Casino Biloxi**. Your pampered pooch will enjoy the view from your suite. Resort amenities include a full-service spa, fitness center, pool with swim-up bar, live entertainment, and multiple on-site dining options. Dogs up to 25 lbs are welcome for an additional fee of $75 per pet, per stay. The fee doubles for larger dogs.

Hard Rock Hotel & Casino Biloxi
777 Beach Boulevard
Biloxi, MS 39530
(228) 374-7625
www.bringfido.com/go/1DWB
Rates from $69/night

Where to Stay:

Only two miles from the heart of Branson, a relaxing stay awaits you at **Lilleys' Landing Resort & Marina** on Lake Taneycomo. Fish from the covered dock, lounge on the poolside sundeck, play a game of horseshoes, or gather with friends and family at the outdoor pavilion overlooking the lake. Fido is free to sniff the grounds as long as he remains leashed. Dogs of any size are welcome for an additional fee of $12 per pet, per night.

Lilleys' Landing Resort & Marina
367 River Lane
Branson, MO 65616
(417) 334-6380
www.bringfido.com/go/1DWE
Rates from $72/night

National Tiger Sanctuary

Introduce Fido to the big cats at the **National Tiger Sanctuary** in Saddlebrooke. This 501(c)(3) nonprofit facility is home to over 40 exotic animals, including a black leopard, mountain lion, African lion, and many tigers. What sets the sanctuary apart is the stress-free environment in which the animals live, along with the love and care given to the animals for their entire lives. The 75-minute 'Awareness Tour' includes a brief classroom presentation and the chance to see tigers from three feet away. The 'Feeding Tour' highlights the different personalities of each cat and lets tour-goers tag along for the feeding. Well-behaved, leashed pets are welcome on all tours. The National Tiger Sanctuary is only open to visitors during scheduled tours, which take place Wednesday through Sunday between 10:00 am and 4:00 pm. Prices start at $30 for adults and $18 for children. Dogs visit for free.

National Tiger Sanctuary
518 State Highway BB
Saddlebrooke, MO 65630
(417) 587-3633
www.bringfido.com/go/1DWD

Gateway Arch National Park

Enter the Gateway to the West with Fido on a visit to the **Gateway Arch National Park** in downtown St. Louis. Leashed pups can explore trails, relax on a grassy hillside overlooking the Mississippi River, and have their photo taken with the iconic monument. The park grounds are open from 5:00 am to 11:00 pm year-round, and there is no admission fee. Plan your trip to coincide with the annual 'Purina Pooches in the Ballpark' baseball game at nearby Busch Stadium and let Fido cheer on the St. Louis Cardinals from a seat in the stands. If you miss the event, baseball mutts can still watch a game with other sports fans at **The Doghaus**, a dog park sports bar that welcomes pups to play while you enjoy televised Cardinals games all summer long. Dogs can even pick up free treats from the quick serve window and meet new friends at the incredible fenced-in dog park.

Gateway Arch National Park
11 N 4th Street #1810
St. Louis, MO 63102
(314) 655-1600
www.bringfido.com/go/1DXV

Where to Stay:

Fido is in for a special treat during his stay at **Four Seasons Hotel St. Louis**. Pet amenities provided at check-in include a comfy dog bed, bowls, snack, and bottled water. The hotel is situated on the banks of the Mississippi River, within walking distance to Gateway Arch National Park and Busch Stadium. Book an Arch-View room or admire skyline views from a poolside cabana. Dogs up to 100 lbs are welcome for an additional fee of $40 per pet.

Four Seasons Hotel St. Louis
999 N 2nd Street
St. Louis, MO 63102
(314) 881-5800
www.bringfido.com/go/1DXW
Rates from $267/night

Fantastic Caverns

Discovered by a farmer's dog in 1862, **Fantastic Caverns** was first explored by a dozen local women who answered a Springfield newspaper ad seeking explorers. During Prohibition, the massive cave was used by bootleggers as a speakeasy and casino. In the 1950's, it was transformed into an underground auditorium by country greats like Buck Owens. Today, your dog can 'mark his territory' on America's only Jeep-drawn cave tour. During the one-hour tour, you'll hear more fascinating tales about this Springfield landmark and see stunning stalactites and stalagmites at every turn. With a natural temperature of 60 degrees year-round, Fantastic Caverns is a perfect spot to visit with your pooch in any season. The caverns are open daily from 8:00 am until dusk. Because no walking is required, the tour is appropriate for guests of all ages and abilities. Admission is $28 for adults, $17 for children, and free for dogs.

Fantastic Caverns
4872 N Farm Road 125
Springfield, MO 65803
(417) 833-2010
www.bringfido.com/go/1E4G

Where to Stay:

After a day of spelunking with your canine companion, spend a night in downtown Springfield at the **Hotel Vandivort**. This industrial-chic urban retreat offers Fido treats and toys upon arrival. Contemporary rooms and suites come outfitted with luxury bedding, hardwood floors, minibars, and spacious bathrooms with walk-in showers. Relax by the fireplace in the cozy lobby sitting area and gaze at the cityscape from the rooftop lounge. Two dogs of any size are welcome for an additional fee of $50 per stay.

Hotel Vandivort
305 E Walnut Street
Springfield, MO 65806
(417) 832-1515
www.bringfido.com/go/1E4H
Rates from $125/night

Where to Stay:

Located in the middle of Missouri's wine country, the **Best Western Plus Washington Hotel** caters to travelers with four-legged family members. After a comfortable night's rest, wake up and enjoy your morning coffee alongside Fido on the hotel's outdoor patio. After breakfast, venture out for some fun at Purina Farms or **Mount Pleasant Estates**, a dog-friendly winery in nearby Augusta. Two dogs up to 80 lbs are welcome for an additional fee of $25 per night.

Best Western Plus
Washington Hotel
2621 E 5th Street
Washington, MO 63090
(636) 390-8877
www.bringfido.com/go/1DWG
Rates from $102/night

Purina Farms

If your pup always has a ball or Frisbee in his mouth, bring him to **Purina Farms** in Gray Summit. Check in at the information desk to pick up a free visiting pet pack. Then, make your way to the Incredible Dog Arena to witness the high flying action of the Purina Incredible Dog Team. Fido may learn a new trick or two as he watches professional canine athletes perform feats of skill and agility at several demonstrations daily. When the show is over, stroll through the interactive exhibits, take your good boy on a wagon ride, and stop by the gift shop to pick up some Purina swag. The facility hosts many special events throughout the year, including egg hunts and trick-or-treating. You can even hold a 'Pooch Pawty' to celebrate your pup's birthday. Purina Farms is open to the public from 9:30 am to 3:30 pm Wednesday through Sunday. Admission and parking are free.

Purina Farms
200 Checkerboard Drive
Gray Summit, MO 63039
(314) 982-3232
www.bringfido.com/go/1DWF

Whitefish Tours & Shuttle

Whitefish Tours & Shuttle will pick you up at your Whitefish-area hotel and take you and your furry beast on a custom adventure around Montana's stunning backcountry. Hop in a Subaru for a half-day ride around the Whitefish Range, or add a guided hike for a full-day tour. Your experienced driver will give you a rundown of the area's rich history, fill you in on the nature you may encounter, and take you to pet-friendly places that would be tricky to find on a self-guided tour. Rates start at $150 per person, and dogs travel for free. After a day on the trails, bring your pooch to **Hugh Rogers WAG Park**. Etched into the foothills of the Rocky Mountains, the off leash park offers panoramic views of the soaring peaks, along with agility equipment and a pond for water dogs. Reward your good boy with a dog pop from **Sweet Peaks Ice Cream** before visiting the buzzing **Bonsai Brewing Company** for dinner.

Whitefish Tours & Shuttle
541 Spokane Avenue
Whitefish, MT 59937
(406) 212-0080
www.bringfido.com/go/1DXQ

Where to Stay:

Make **The Pine Lodge** in White-fish your basecamp for exploring the Montana wilderness. Located on the banks of the Whitefish River, the hotel offers loads of amenities for human and canine guests. Pet-friendly ground floor rooms provide convenient access to the paved trail that runs along-side the river, and all guests have complimentary use of the hotel dock and kayaks during their stay. Pick up a free s'mores kit from the front desk to enjoy at the outdoor fire pit. Dogs up to 80 lbs are welcome for an additional fee of $25 per night.

The Pine Lodge
920 Spokane Avenue
Whitefish, MT 59937
(406) 204-4519
www.bringfido.com/go/1DXR
Rates from $80/night

Where to Stay:

Located on a beautiful ranch just outside of Yellowstone National Park, **Under Canvas Yellowstone** offers the comforts of home for humans and canines alike. Sleep in luxury tents outfitted with cozy beds, plush linens, private bathrooms and wood-burning stoves. Book a Stargazer tent, which features a unique overhead window for viewing the night sky from your bed. Howl the night away singing by the campfire and roasting s'mores before turning in. Dogs of any size are welcome for an additional fee of $25 per pet, per night.

Under Canvas Yellowstone
890 Buttermilk Creek Road
West Yellowstone, MT 59758
(406) 219-0441
www.bringfido.com/go/1E4E
Rates from $95/night

Under Canvas Yellowstone

Dreaming of sleeping under the stars with Fido? Camping is a great way to escape the stress of modern life, immerse yourself in nature, and breathe some fresh air. But if you really want to take the stress away, plan a dog-friendly 'glamping' getaway to West Yellowstone. **Under Canvas Yellowstone** takes camping to another level by doing all of the prep work for you and elevating the experience for hounds who still require creature comforts in the great outdoors. The safari-inspired glampsite offers uninterrupted views of the picturesque Montana landscape and convenient access to **Yellowstone National Park**'s West Entrance, which is just a 10-minute drive away. For a $35 park entry fee, your pup can scratch Old Faithful off his bucket list. Just be aware that dogs aren't permitted on park hiking trails or boardwalks for their safety.

Under Canvas Yellowstone
890 Buttermilk Creek Road
West Yellowstone, MT 59758
(406) 219-0441
www.bringfido.com/go/1E4E

Fort Robinson State Park

Nestled in the northwest corner of the Cornhusker State, **Fort Robinson State Park** in Crawford invites two- and four-legged tourists to unearth a treasure trove of midwest history and beauty. For much of its existence, Fort Robinson served as an active military post. It was the site of Chief Crazy Horse's death in 1879, and during World War II, it operated as a POW camp and K-9 training facility. Today, the property is managed as a state park catering to large family groups, campers, and well-traveled canines. Plan on spending a full day exploring more than 60 miles of pristine pine ridge trails, fishing for bass in crystal blue lakes, and driving through 22,000 acres of scenic prairies. Leashed dogs are welcome on all trails, including the popular Red Cloud Butte Trail, which offers scenic views of Lovers Leap Butte. The daily entrance fee is $8 per vehicle.

Fort Robinson State Park
3200 Highway 20
Crawford, NE 69339
(308) 665-2900
www.bringfido.com/go/1DWI

Where to Stay:

You and Fido won't have to look far for a place to lay your head after exploring Fort Robinson. The Old West buildings that once served as housing for officers and enlisted soldiers now welcome tourists. The **Fort Robinson State Park Cabins** have been renovated to accommodate modern traveler needs without sacrificing the lodging's rustic charm. Each unit comes equipped with stoves, refrigerators, cooking utensils, blankets, and towels. Dogs of any size are welcome for an additional fee of $15 per stay.

Fort Robinson State Park Cabins
3200 Highway 20
Crawford, NE 69339
(308) 665-2900
www.bringfido.com/go/1DWJ
Rates from $170/night

Where to Stay:

Following your airboat adventure, drive into Omaha for a stay at the **Element Omaha Midtown Crossing**. This hotel boasts large, apartment-style rooms, complete with fully furnished kitchens. The area around the property offers ample green space, dog-friendly shops, and outdoor dining establishments. Take Fido for a stroll across the street to Turner Park to stretch his legs. The Element welcomes two dogs of any size for no additional fee.

Element Omaha Midtown Crossing
3253 Dodge Street
Omaha, NE 68131
(402) 614-8080
www.bringfido.com/go/1DPV
Rates from $99/night

Bryson's Airboat Tours

If Fido loves riding in your car with his head out the window, he is sure to enjoy an adventure with **Bryson's Airboat Tours** in Fremont, about 40 miles outside of Omaha. Bryson's 21-foot Panther airboat comfortably seats 11 passengers and, thanks to its theater-style seating, provides a great view of the water to everyone. During your journey on the Platte River, you and your pup might encounter several species of wildlife, including bald eagles, deer, turkeys, river otters, and beavers. This 700-horsepower boat can reach speeds of 60 mph, so it's a good idea to bring eyewear and a jacket. Ear protection is provided by Bryson's. Prices start at $150 for two passengers, and children can ride for an additional fee of $20 each. Dogs are welcome for no extra charge. Tours take place from May to September and can be scheduled from 10:00 am to dusk.

Bryson's Airboat Tours
839 County Road 19
Fremont, NE 68025
(402) 968-8534
www.bringfido.com/go/1DPU

Red Rock Canyon

For a day trip away from the glitz and glamour of the Las Vegas strip, rent a Jeep and take your pup on a visit to **Red Rock Canyon National Conservation Area**. Enjoy stunning panoramic views at several points along the 13-mile scenic drive. If the weather cooperates, venture off the road on a hike along one of 26 marked trails. Pack a lunch (and plenty of water for you and your pooch!) and find a quiet spot in the Willow Springs picnic area for a memorable meal. Keep your eyes peeled for dinosaur tracks in the Aztec sandstone of the Mojave Desert. The park is open year-round, and daily admission is $15 per vehicle. For visits between October and May, be sure to purchase a timed entry reservation in advance of your trip. It you have a second day to explore beyond Sin City, head to **Valley of Fire State Park** in Overton, where you and Fido can spot petrified trees dating back more than 2,000 years.

Red Rock Canyon National Conservation Area
1000 Scenic Loop Drive
Las Vegas, NV 89161
(702) 515-5350
www.bringfido.com/go/1DN8

Where to Stay:

After a day in the desert, put your pup's posh paws up at the **Delano Las Vegas**. The hotel's Doggie Butler Service can provide in-room treat delivery, fresh bowls of water, daily brushings, and trips to the on-site AstroTurf dog run. Fido will also want to order dinner from the Doggie Delights room service menu. Two dogs up to 100 lbs (combined weight) are welcome for an additional fee of $100 per pet, per night.

Delano Las Vegas
3970 Las Vegas Boulevard S
Las Vegas, NV 89119
(877) 632-5400
www.bringfido.com/go/1DN9
Rates from $89/night

Mount Charleston

If you're looking to escape the desert heat, head to **Mount Charleston** for some cool outdoor adventures with your pooch. Located less than an hour's drive from downtown Las Vegas, Mount Charleston offers the chance to explore over 50 miles of hiking trails in a climate with temperatures averaging 20 degrees lower than Sin City. That means from November through April, there is snow on the mountain! The Bristlecone Trail is particularly great for snowshoeing, but the most popular wintertime activities are sledding, snowman building, and good old-fashioned snowball fights. In fact, there's even a designated location for it at the **Foxtail Winter Snowplay Area** in Lee Canyon. For $20 per vehicle, you'll have access to plenty of parking, heated restrooms, concessions, and lots of open space to play in the snow with Fido. The gates are open daily from 10:00 am to 4:00 pm.

Mount Charleston
2525 Kyle Canyon Road
Las Vegas, NV 89124
(702) 872-5486
www.bringfido.com/go/1DTF

Where to Stay:

Following his mountain activities, your pooch will be happy to come home to a cozy cabin at the **Mount Charleston Lodge & Cabins**. Relax in a jetted tub, warm up by the fire, or unwind on a private balcony overlooking the mountain. Take Fido for a walk on the 1.4-mile Cathedral Rock Trail, which is located across the street from the cabins. One dog of any size is welcome for an additional fee of $35 per night. Add $20 for a second pet.

Mount Charleston Lodge & Cabins
5355 Kyle Canyon Road
Las Vegas, NV 89124
(702) 872-5408
www.bringfido.com/go/1DTG
Rates from $150/night

Where to Stay:

Treat Fido to a much-needed break at **The Glen House** in Gorham. The spacious Shaker-style accommodations offer panoramic views of Mount Washington, and your pup will be greeted with a welcome note, yummy treats, pet bed, and food bowls upon arrival. Up to two dogs of any size are permitted for an additional fee of $20 per night. During your stay, walk across the street to **Great Glen Trails**, where leashed dogs are welcome to join you as you hike, bike, cross-country ski, or snowshoe.

The Glen House
979 NH Route 16
Gorham, NH 03581
(603) 466-3420
www.bringfido.com/go/1DXJ
Rates from $350/night

Mt. Washington Auto Road

If you and your pooch are experienced hikers looking for a challenge, hike up New England's tallest peak, Mount Washington, and then take the pet-friendly shuttle back down. If your pup isn't up for the difficult ascent, you can still enjoy stunning views by driving the **Mt. Washington Auto Road** to the top of the mountain. Your $35 toll includes a bumper sticker and audio guide detailing the famous road's history and geography. Enjoy breathtaking views of New Hampshire's White Mountains as you drive the famous **Kancamagus Highway** through the **White Mountain National Forest**. The Kanc, as it's known by the locals, is most popular during the fall foliage season, but this scenic byway is frequented year-round for its beautiful natural setting. Grab Fido's leash and spend some time outside the car, hiking on one of the many trails found along the highway.

Mt. Washington Auto Road
1 Mount Washington Auto Road
Gorham, NH 03581
(603) 466-3988
www.bringfido.com/go/1DXI

Conway Scenic Railroad

For breathtaking views of the White Mountain region, 'pawsengers' should climb aboard the **Conway Scenic Railroad**. Departing from North Conway, the **Mountaineer** will take you and your canine conductor on the Iconic Notch Scenic Train Ride. This five-hour trip offers dramatic mountain views and crosses Frankenstein Trestle and Willey Brook Bridge. Boarding begins at 11:30 am, and lunch may be purchased from the on-board concession cart. If you don't have time for a full-day adventure, the company also offers shorter tours, like the Bartlett Excursion Train Ride, which rolls through the Saco River Valley in under two hours. Rates range from $19 to $62 for adults and $13 to $43 for children. Leashed dogs ride for free in coach cars on all trips. The railroad operates year-round except for maintenance closures in March. Train schedules vary, and reservations are recommended.

Conway Scenic Railroad
38 Norcross Circle
North Conway, NH 03860
(603) 356-5251
www.bringfido.com/go/1DKO

Where to Stay:

Rest your caboose in a guestroom or private cottage at **Whitney's Inn at Jackson**. Just a short drive from North Conway, the hotel is situated on 12 acres with a stocked trout pond (bring your fishing gear) and surrounded by miles of hiking trails for you and Fido to explore. Ask for Room #20, a ground floor unit with rustic wood beam ceilings and a private entrance ideal for early morning or late night walks with your pup. Dogs of any size are welcome for an additional fee of $25 per pet, per night.

Whitney's Inn at Jackson
357 Black Mountain Road
Jackson, NH 03846
(603) 383-8916
www.bringfido.com/go/1DKP
Rates from $89/night

Where to Stay:

Built in 1850, the **Highland House** is an ultra pet-friendly B&B in Cape May. The innkeepers are dog lovers, and all of the rooms are decorated with canine-themed knickknacks. The result is charmingly homey, so you may feel like you're sleeping over at grandma's house. Spend an afternoon lounging on the front porch, walk four blocks to the beach, or let Fido play with the other pet guests in the fenced yard. Dogs of any size are welcome for no additional fee.

Highland House
131 N Broadway
Cape May, NJ 08204
(609) 898-1198
www.bringfido.com/go/1DKR
Rates from $169/night

Cape May Whale Watcher

Furry friends are invited to come aboard the 110-foot Cape May Whale Watcher for an unforgettable Jersey Shore experience. Departing from the Miss Chris Marina in Cape May, the company offers three tours daily from May through October. The morning and evening tours both circle the island in two hours, providing a unique view of Cape May's picturesque Victorian homes and lighthouse. The afternoon cruise is all about whales! On this three-hour 'Cetacean Spectacular' tour, Captain Jeff Stewart takes you deep into the Delaware Bay Estuary and guarantees you'll see whales, dolphins, or porpoises (or your next trip is free). Rates start at $35 for adults. Dogs and children under seven are free. After your cruise, Fido can walk off his sea legs with a stroll through the 150-acre vineyard at **Cape May Winery**. Admission is free, and you can sample six wines for $10 in the dog-friendly tasting room.

Cape May Whale Watcher
1218 Wilson Drive
Cape May, NJ 08204
(609) 884-5445
www.bringfido.com/go/1DKQ

8th Avenue Dog Beach

If your hound was born to run, plan an off-leash romp at the **8th Avenue Dog Beach** in Asbury Park. After a game of fetch or Frisbee, jump in the water with your pooch for a refreshing swim. Dogs are always allowed on the beach between mid-September and mid-May. If you are visiting in summer, schedule an early morning or late evening visit, as dogs are not permitted between 8:30 am and 6:00 pm. After Fido's beach time, get him cleaned up with a grooming appointment at **The Dawg Joint**, before an evening out together at the **Wonder Bar**. The rock 'n' roll beach bar has hosted some of the biggest legends of the music world over the years, but none more prominent than New Jersey local Bruce Springsteen, who has been spotted at its famous Yappy Hour. The bar's outdoor space—Tillie's Landing—is fenced and equipped with a dog agility area. Entry is free mid-week and $5 on the weekends.

8th Avenue Dog Beach
8th Avenue & Ocean Avenue
Asbury Park, NJ 07712
(732) 616-0749
www.bringfido.com/go/1DKT

Where to Stay:

If you're looking for a rock-n-roll stay in comfort, **The Asbury** is the place for your furry VIP. Located just a short walk from the dog beach and Wonder Bar, the hotel features a rooftop lounge and a swimming pool area, which is the perfect spot for hanging out with your pooch during the summer months. When the temperature drops outside, head inside and enjoy live music in the lobby together. Up to two dogs of any size are welcome for an additional fee of $75 per stay.

The Asbury
210 5th Avenue
Asbury Park, NJ 07712
(732) 774-7100
www.bringfido.com/go/1DKU
Rates from $135/night

Where to Stay:

Hotel Parq Central is the perfect base for two- and four-legged tourists looking to explore New Mexico's largest city. Your pooch will be welcomed by the hotel's pet ambassador, Mollie, who personally delivers treats, toys, beds, and water bowls to furry guests. In addition, Fido will love socializing with other pampered pups in the hotel's fenced dog run. For a longer walk, take a stroll to nearby **Highland Park**. One dog up to 75 lbs is welcome for an additional fee of $75 per stay. Add $25 for a second pet.

Hotel Parq Central
806 Central Avenue SE
Albuquerque, NM 87102
(505) 242-0040
www.bringfido.com/go/1DY9
Rates from $148/night

ABQ Trolley Company

'The best first thing to do in Albuquerque' is the motto for the **ABQ Trolley Company**. Climb aboard the trolley with your pup for a comprehensive overview of Duke City's rich history and a unique perspective on all that Albuquerque has to offer. Operating twice daily from April through October, owners Jesse Herron and Mike Silva personally guide visitors on each tour. If it's your first time in Albuquerque, choose the 'Best of ABQ' city tour. You and Fido will enjoy an 85-minute ride beginning in historic Old Town that highlights Route 66, Museum Row, and the Barelas Neighborhood, among other attractions. Tour prices start at $30 per person, and dogs are free. After being cooped up on the trolley, Fido can stretch his legs on a hike along the 1.5-mile trail through Piedras Marcadas Canyon at **Petroglyph National Monument**, where you can see up to 400 ancient rock carvings.

ABQ Trolley Company
303 Romero Street NW
Albuquerque, NM 87104
(505) 200-2642
www.bringfido.com/go/1DY8

Santa Fe Mountain Adventures

You and your canine companion can explore the mountains and canyons around Santa Fe on a guided tour with **Santa Fe Mountain Adventures**. With several half-day and full-day hiking tours to choose from, hikers of all skill levels are sure to find an excursion of interest. Take a four-mile hike though a magical grove of Aspen trees in the Sangre de Cristo Mountains. Or start at the rim of White Rock Canyon and descend 800 feet to the Rio Grande River. For the easiest hiking option, choose the Sunset Diablo Canyon Tour, which takes you on an off-road adventure in a GE230 Wagon or Pinzgauer all-terrain vehicle and ends with a short hike. Fun 4x4 tours that start with a history lesson in Santa Fe and end in Sangres mountains are also available. Leashed dogs are welcome on all tours, and prices start at $46 per person. The tour company mascot, Murjo, might even join you and your pup on the adventure.

Santa Fe Mountain Adventures
Don Diego Court
Santa Fe, NM 87505
(505) 988-4000
www.bringfido.com/go/1DTS

Where to Stay:

Santa Fe's **Inn of the Turquoise Bear** welcomes four-legged guests with creature comforts including delicious treats, in-room sleeping pads, food and water dishes, and waste bags for potty breaks. Fido is invited to play off leash in the lush one-acre garden located on the property grounds. Afterward, he can snooze on the spacious main patio while you mingle with other guests and enjoy a glass of wine during the inn's happy hour. Dogs of any size are welcome for an additional fee of $25 per night.

Inn of the Turquoise Bear
342 E Buena Vista Street
Santa Fe, NM 87505
(505) 983-0798
www.bringfido.com/go/1DTT
Rates from $174/night

Where to Stay:

If the thought of little green martians doesn't scare Fido away, book a room at **The Roswell Inn**, the self-proclaimed crash pad recommended by 9 out of 10 aliens. The hotel is centrally located to Roswell's dog-friendly UFO attractions and **Woof Bowl Dog Park**. Be sure to snap your pup's photo beside the alien sign out front. Up to two dogs of any size are welcome for an additional fee of $10 per pet, per night.

The Roswell Inn
2101 N Main Street
Roswell, NM 88201
(575) 623-6050
www.bringfido.com/go/1DTO
Rates from $41/night

International UFO Museum

For an out-of-this-world experience with your pup, look no further than the **International UFO Museum** in Roswell. The museum is committed to chronicling the stories and preserving materials related to the infamous 1947 'Roswell Incident,' as well as other UFO events from around the globe. Put a tin foil hat on Fido and bring him to the museum to explore decades of supernatural history, research, and science. Before you leave, stop by the gift shop to purchase an 'Alien Hunter' dog shirt for your canine earthling. The museum is open daily from 9:00 am to 5:00 pm. Admission is $5 for adults, $2 for children, and free for dogs. Afterward, visit **Roswell UFO Spacewalk** to take your pooch on a blacklight adventure through a spaceship and alien planet and view retro sci-fi art and unique space toys. End the day with a stop at **Alien Zone** for more souvenirs and wacky photo ops.

International UFO Museum
114 N Main Street
Roswell, NM 88203
(575) 625-9495
www.bringfido.com/go/1DTN

Robert H. Treman State Park

Enjoy the wild beauty of the Finger Lakes region of New York at the **Robert H. Treman State Park**. With over nine miles of pet-friendly hiking trails, your pup will have plenty of room to explore this state treasure just outside of Ithaca. The popular Enfield Glen Gorge Trail will bring you past 12 waterfalls, including the 115-foot Lucifer Falls, while providing stunning views of the wooded gorge. Continue your outdoor adventure by visiting nearby **Buttermilk Falls State Park**, which offers several more rim and gorge hiking trails. To extend the adventure, you can camp overnight in either park. Dogs are welcome in tent sites and cabins, which are rustic and offer no bedding, cookware, or heat. Both parks are open year-round, but some trails might be inaccessible during winter. Admission to each park is $8 per vehicle. Dogs must remain leashed at all times.

Robert H. Treman State Park
105 Enfield Falls Road
Ithaca, NY 14850
(607) 273-3440
www.bringfido.com/go/1DYD

Where to Stay:

If you don't want to 'ruff it' in the state park all night, bring your pooch to **La Tourelle Hotel & Spa** in Ithaca, which welcomes dogs of any size to stay in traditional king guest rooms for no additional fee. From May to October, you also have the option of glamping on the grounds of the resort. **Firelight Camps** invites dogs of any size to stay in a furnished safari tent with their humans for an extra nightly fee of $25.

La Tourelle Hotel & Spa
1150 Danby Road
Ithaca, NY 14850
(607) 273-2734
www.bringfido.com/go/1DYE
Rates from $170/night

Gold Coast Mansions

Enjoy a day of history and adventure as you tour the grounds of Long Island's Gold Coast Mansions. In the morning, start your sightseeing with a visit to **Sands Point Preserve**. There, you can explore six trails that wind through 216 acres of property that is home to four historic mansions, including the Hempstead House and Castle Gould. Dogs must remain leashed at all times on the trails, but you can let Fido loose in the preserve's fenced dog run. Bring a picnic lunch to enjoy on the manicured grounds before heading over to your second stop—Theodore Roosevelt's beloved **Sagamore Hill**. Although only humans are permitted to enter the historic Roosevelt home, you and your leashed pup can spend hours exploring the 83 acres of forests, meadows, and salt marshes on the property's trails and boardwalks. At the end of your day, enjoy a well-deserved brew with your furry friend at nearby **Oyster Bay Brewing Company**.

Sands Point Preserve
127 Middle Neck Road
Sands Point, NY 11050
(516) 571-7901
www.bringfido.com/go/1DYJ

Where to Stay:

Guarded by magnificent formal gardens and infused with rich Long Island history, the French-style chateau known as **Oheka Castle** is an amazing estate hotel that conjures images from the classic novel *The Great Gatsby*. Dogs are not permitted on the historic mansion tours, but Fido can sleep like a king in the guestrooms and suites of this storied mansion (and filming location for numerous movies and TV series). Dogs of any size are welcome for an additional fee of $200 per pet, per stay.

Oheka Castle
135 W Gate Drive
Huntington, NY 11743
(631) 659-1400
www.bringfido.com/go/1DYI
Rates from $270/night

Where to Stay:

Emerald Glen Getaway offers a variety of lodging options during your canine-centric retreat. For those who prefer to 'ruff it,' there are three creekside tents furnished with a futon and two camping chairs. Well-equipped cottages and cabins with electricity are available for those who love nature but prefer to sleep indoors. For the ultimate in privacy and comfort while at the farm, enjoy an air-conditioned RV, complete with separate living and sleeping areas, a bathroom, and a kitchen.

Emerald Glen Getaway
217 Pegg Road
Morris, NY 13808
(510) 552-3500
www.bringfido.com/go/1DWM
Rates from $140/night

Emerald Glen Getaway

Give your pup an unforgettable vacation at **Emerald Glen Getaway** in Morris. The property's 120 acres of meadows, trails, and forests in upstate New York provides the perfect backdrop to relax and recharge alongside man's best friend. Fido is free to roam off leash during his visit, and he'll enjoy getting his feet wet at one of several dog beaches along Butternut Creek. On-site amenities include water stations, a dog wash, and a practically limitless supply of toys. In the evening, you and your pup will love hanging out at The Hound Hub, a central gathering spot where you can socialize with other guests, fire up the wood-burning grill to cook a tasty dinner, and catch a lovely sunset over the meadow. Cap off the night around the campfire, toasting s'mores with your new dog-loving friends to end an amazing day. The Getaway accepts visitors from late May through September.

Emerald Glen Getaway
217 Pegg Road
Morris, NY 13808
(510) 552-3500
www.bringfido.com/go/1DWL

Seneca Lake Wine Trail

When traveling through the Finger Lakes region of New York with your four-legged friend, be sure to sample some of the first-class vino being produced along the **Seneca Lake Wine Trail**. Many of the member wineries invite your pup to join you as you taste what makes them unique. Visit **Ravines Wine Cellars** for a dry Riesling, **Penguin Bay Winery** for a spicy Gewurztraminer, and **Atwater Estate Vineyards** for a bubbly Pinot Noir. Throughout the year, you can take in special events on the trail, like the Grapehound Wine Tour held annually in July. Celebrating greyhounds and other sighthounds, the event is a popular pet-friendly festival filled with tastings, art events, vendors, and music at different venues. Some of the wineries on the trail welcome dogs off leash, but others require Fido to be restrained when visiting (so it's best to ask). Most are open for tours throughout the year, but hours vary by season.

Seneca Lake Wine Trail
2 N Franklin Street, Suite 320
Watkins Glen, NY 14891
(877) 536-2717
www.bringfido.com/go/1DL0

Where to Stay:

After a fun day roaming New York wine country, your pooch will be dog-tired and ready for a comfy stay at The **Gould Hotel** in Seneca Falls. Situated in the heart of the village, the hotel is a great jumping-off point to explore both the Seneca Lake Wine Trail and the nearby **Cayuga Lake Wine Trail**, which boasts more than a dozen dog-friendly wineries. Up to two dogs of any size are welcome for an additional fee of $50 per stay. In the morning, you can take Fido on an art walk at the nearby **Ludovico Sculpture Trail**.

The Gould Hotel
108 Falls Street
Seneca Falls, NY 13148
(315) 712-4000
www.bringfido.com/go/1DL1
Rates from $101/night

Where to Stay:

After a long day of hiking, rest your weary paws in the cozy guest rooms at the **High Peaks Resort**. Catering to man's best friend, the hotel's exclusive 'Peak Pup' program offers your good boy an assortment of amenities, including complimentary treats, a plush dog bed, bowls and mat to use during your stay, and a souvenir bandana to take home. There is a fully stocked refrigerator in each cabin, and a prepared-to-order breakfast is served each morning. Two dogs up to 75 lbs are welcome for an additional fee of $25 per pet, per night.

High Peaks Resort
2384 Saranac Avenue
Lake Placid, NY 12946
(518) 523-4411
www.bringfido.com/go/1DL8
Rates from $99/night

Whiteface Mountain

Adventurous climbers and their active canine companions will enjoy the challenge of trekking to the summit of **Whiteface Mountain** in Wilmington. At an elevation of 4,876 feet, the mountain is New York's fifth-highest peak. Begin your ascent by taking the **Wilmington Trail**, a 5.2-mile, one-way hike with an elevation gain of nearly 3,700 feet. If you or Fido aren't quite up to the challenge of making the full climb, you can still enjoy the beauty of the mountain on a scenic drive up **Whiteface Veterans' Memorial Highway**, followed by a short climb to the top. Park your car at the summit parking area, and make your way on foot up the alpine nature trail located behind the stone castle. Be sure to wear appropriate shoes because the final ascent can be steep and slippery. Entrance fees start at $15 but vary based on the number of passengers in your vehicle.

Whiteface Mountain
5021 State Route 86
Wilmington, NY 12997
(518) 946-2223
www.bringfido.com/go/1DL7

Central Park

From a dog's point of view, no trip to New York is complete without a visit to **Central Park**. You and your pup can hike to waterfalls in the North Woods, meander through woodland trails in the Ramble, stroll the formal Conservatory Garden, or jog around the Reservoir. Furry fans of The Beatles can wander through the 2.5-acre Strawberry Fields, and all dogs will want to pose for a photo with the statue of Balto. Fido can hydrate at one of 29 dog fountains and is allowed to roam leash-free before 9:00 am and after 9:00 pm. When your pooch needs a break from walking, he can ride in style with **NYC Horse Carriage Rides**. The carriages have covers and warm blankets available, so your pug can stay snug and dry even in bad weather. Prices start at $57 per trip, and dogs ride for free. If he gets hungry, head over to **Shake Shack** and order your good boy a Pooch-ini or Bag O' Bones from the dog menu.

Central Park
59th Street & 5th Avenue
New York, NY 10022
(212) 310-6600
www.bringfido.com/go/1E5X

Where to Stay:

The Sherry-Netherland is a great choice for canine comfort when visiting the Big Apple. Located next to Central Park, this iconic boutique hotel is known for its elegance and service. Humans are greeted with a welcome gift of Louis Sherry chocolates, fresh flowers, and complimentary beverages. Furry guests are spoiled with natural dog treats and the use of a comfy dog bed and bowls during their stay. Up to two dogs of any size are welcome for no additional fee.

The Sherry-Netherland
781 5th Avenue
New York, NY 10022
(212) 355-2800
www.bringfido.com/go/1E5Y
Rates from $399/night

Brooklyn Bridge

Completed in 1883, the **Brooklyn Bridge** is one of New York's most iconic landmarks, and crossing it is a quintessential experience when visiting the city with your dog. For the best views, start in Brooklyn and cross the 1.3-mile span into Manhattan. Alternatively, if Fido prefers to take in the sights by water, he is welcome to accompany you on the **NYC Ferry** as long as he remains muzzled or in a carrier for the short journey. Once in Manhattan, bring your furry friend to **The Battery**, which serves as the gateway to Ellis Island and the Statue of Liberty. Fido can greet Lady Liberty from a distance as he sniffs the grassy Woodland and meanders along the park's paved pathways. Walk a block up Broadway to take his photo with the **Charging Bull** statue outside the New York Stock Exchange before making the return trip across the East River.

Brooklyn Bridge
Brooklyn Bridge, NY 10038
(212) 639-9675
www.bringfido.com/go/1E5P

Where to Stay:

Enjoy the skyline views from your dog-friendly guest room at **1 Hotel Brooklyn Bridge**. Adjacent to **Brooklyn Bridge Park**, this modern and hip property greets furry visitors with fluffy pet beds, as well as food and water bowls. One dog of any size is welcome for no additional fee. If you've worked up an appetite from a day of sightseeing, head a block up the street to the walk-up window at **Luke's Lobster**. Then, let your pup burn some energy with a bit of off-leash play at **Hillside Dog Park**.

1 Hotel Brooklyn Bridge
60 Furman Street
Brooklyn, NY 11201
(347) 696-2500
www.bringfido.com/go/1E5Q
Rates from $273/night

Where to Stay:

Located a block from the boutiques and galleries of East Hampton, the **Mill House Inn** is a lovely bed and breakfast with incredible service and creature comforts like down-stuffed dog beds, nightly turn-down treats, and a fenced yard. The inn is known for serving the best breakfast in the Hamptons, and the chef will even prepare a fresh breakfast for Fido upon request. Two dogs of any size are welcome for an additional fee of $60 per pet, per night.

Mill House Inn
31 N Main Street
East Hampton, NY 11937
(631) 324-9766
www.bringfido.com/go/1DWO
Rates from $210/night

The Hamptons

Fido can get a taste of the good life during a visit to the Hamptons. Begin his adventure aboard a lobster yacht with **Sag Harbor Charters**. The company offers fishing trips and sightseeing cruises to hidden coves and beaches around Long Island. Prices start at $300 for up to six people, and dogs sail for free. From Sag Harbor, make the 15-minute drive south to **East Hampton Main Beach**. There, pups can play on the sand leash-free at any time in the off-season or between 6:00 pm and 9:00 am during the summer. Feeling flexible? Join **Claudia Matles Yoga** for a stretch on the beach with your downward dog. Afterward, Fido can clean up with a bubble bath, hot towel wrap, and blueberry facial at **The Classy Canine**. Before heading home, be sure to visit Montauk, where your pup can zoom off leash along miles of white sand beaches or join you for a coastal walk framed by rolling dunes and views of **Montauk Point Lighthouse**.

Sag Harbor Charters
23 Marine Park Drive
Sag Harbor, NY 11963
(631) 459-1823
www.bringfido.com/go/1DWN

Chimney Rock State Park

Novice and experienced hikers alike will enjoy bringing their furry companions on an outdoor adventure at **Chimney Rock State Park**. Panoramic views of Hickory Nut Gorge and Lake Lure await those who ascend the 499 steps of the Outcroppings Trail to the top of the rock. For another vantage point, you can climb the Exclamation Point Trail to an elevation of 2,480 feet. During your visit, don't miss Hickory Nut Falls, one of the tallest waterfalls east of the Mississippi River. Admission to the park is $17 for adults, $8 for children, and free for dogs. After your climb, stop for lunch at the **Old Rock Café**, where you and your pooch can enjoy a delicious meal on the back deck overlooking the Rocky Broad River. Then, head to Lake Lure and explore the water in a pontoon boat rental from **Lake Lure Adventure Company**. Rentals start at $85 per hour and come equipped with pool noodles and a cooler.

Chimney Rock State Park
431 Main Street
Chimney Rock, NC 28720
(828) 625-9611
www.bringfido.com/go/1DLQ

Where to Stay:

After a fun day in Chimney Rock, make your way to Mills River for a restful night's sleep at **Barkwells**, a canine-centric retreat in the heart of the Blue Ridge Mountains. With more than eight acres of fenced-in meadows and a pond, your best friend will have plenty of room to run, swim, and play. Two dogs of any size are welcome for no extra fee. Add $25 for a third pet. During your stay, be sure to visit **Sierra Nevada Brewing Company**, which has a dog-friendly beer garden and a nature trail that leads to the French Broad River.

Barkwells
290 Lance Road
Mills River, NC 28759
(828) 891-8288
www.bringfido.com/go/1DLR
Rates from $129/night

Bald Head Island

For a dog-friendly escape from the mainland, plan a visit to beautiful **Bald Head Island**. Start your adventure at **Deep Point Marina** in Southport, where a scheduled ferry service will take you and your pooch on a 20-minute trip to the island. Roundtrip tickets are $23 for adults, $12 for children, and free for dogs. Upon arrival, take a short walk to **Cary Cart Company** to rent a golf cart, which will serve as your mode of transportation on this car-free island. Daily rentals start at $75. If you prefer to pedal instead, daily and weekly bike rentals (with bike trailers or baskets for Fido) are available from **Riverside Adventure Company**. After securing your wheels, cruise the cart path and explore 14 miles of sandy beaches, hit the surf for some fun on the water, and take a hike with your canine companion on one of the lovely trails running through this island community.

Bald Head Island–Deep Point Marina
1301 Ferry Road SE
Southport, NC 28461
(910) 457-5003
www.bringfido.com/go/1DLB

Where to Stay:

Extend your visit to Bald Head Island by renting a dog-friendly vacation home from **Bald Head Island Limited**. All rentals are fully furnished with expansive living rooms, gourmet kitchens, and luxurious master retreats. Many of them are also oceanfront with screened porches, outdoor showers, and direct beach access. The use of a golf cart is included for free with every vacation rental. Dogs of any size are welcome in select homes for an additional fee of $200 per stay.

Bald Head Island Limited
6 Marina Wynd
Bald Head Island, NC 28461
(910) 457-5002
www.bringfido.com/go/1DLC
Rates from $450/night

Biltmore Estate

Your dog will love strolling through the hundreds of manicured acres on the **Biltmore Estate** in Asheville. Nestled in the Blue Ridge Mountains, this 8,000-acre property offers you and your furry friend over 20 miles of hiking trails and 2.5 miles of paths through manicured gardens. Relax with a glass of wine at Biltmore Winery's Bistro or have a bite to eat at Cedric's Tavern (named for George Vanderbilt's Saint Bernard). Dogs must remain leashed at all times and are not allowed in any buildings. Admission fees start at $94 for adults. Children under 10 and dogs are admitted for no extra fee. For an alternative view of the estate's lush grounds, take a six-mile kayak tour with **French Broad Outfitters**. Enjoy paddling with your pooch past the 19th-century house, stables, Inn, Antler Hill Village, and winery. The kayak tour operates from April through October, and trips start at $45. Dogs float for free.

Biltmore Estate
1 Lodge Street
Asheville, NC 28803
(828) 225-1333
www.bringfido.com/go/1DLF

Where to Stay:

Located just outside the gates of the Biltmore Estate, the luxurious **Grand Bohemian Hotel Asheville** awaits your pooch's arrival. This Tudor-inspired property will greet Fido with treats and bowls at check-in. Once you are settled in, stroll through the hotel art gallery, relax with a cocktail in the lounge, or visit the neighboring shops at Biltmore Village, where you will find an assortment of dog-friendly restaurants and boutiques. The hotel welcomes one dog of any size for an additional fee of $150 per stay. Add $50 for a second pup.

Grand Bohemian Hotel Asheville
11 Boston Way
Asheville, NC 28803
(828) 505-2949
www.bringfido.com/go/1DLG
Rates from $179/night

Where to Stay:

Four Paws Kingdom caters to RV owners by providing full hook-up sites with free cable and wireless internet, along with a bathhouse and laundry facilities. Don't have an RV? Air-conditioned and heated cabin and trailer rentals are also available. Those accommodations include a Queen-size bed with futon or sofa sleeper, full kitchen or kitchenette, and an outdoor grill. Linens and bedding are not provided. Up to four dogs are welcome in RV sites for no extra fee (two dogs maximum in rental units).

Four Paws Kingdom
335 Lazy Creek Drive
Rutherfordton, NC 28139
(828) 287-7324
www.bringfido.com/go/1DLP
Rates from $64/night

Four Paws Kingdom

Enjoy the great American tradition of camping with your pooch at **Four Paws Kingdom** in Rutherfordton. This canine paradise is a full-service campground catering exclusively to adults and their furry friends. Fido will enjoy hours of fun in the kingdom's eight fully fenced dog parks. He can take a dip in the swimming pond, practice jumps and weave through poles on the agility equipment, or fetch a stick from the stream. Afterward, cleaning up is a breeze at the grooming station and doggy spa. Four Paws Kingdom is open seasonally from March through November, and special events are held throughout the year. Whether you come for the Barktoberfest, Memorial Day Rib Fest, Tailgating and Chili Cook-Off Weekend or Agility Beginners Boot Camp, you are sure to have an unforgettable vacation with like-minded humans and their dogs.

Four Paws Kingdom
335 Lazy Creek Drive
Rutherfordton, NC 28139
(828) 287-7324
www.bringfido.com/go/1DLP

US National Whitewater Center

The **US National Whitewater Center** in Charlotte offers numerous outdoor adventures, whether you're on two legs or four! Dogs aren't allowed on the rafts or zip lines for safety reasons, but water-loving pups can join you on a kayak, canoe, or stand-up paddleboard trip down the scenic Catawba River. Snag a 'Flatwater Kayaking and SUP Pass' for $30, or opt for a full-day, all-access pass for $59. Land lovers enjoy complimentary access to hike, bike, or run with Fido on over 20 miles of trails. Doggos are always welcome at special events, festivals, Family Camping Weekends, and concerts held throughout the year. So, be sure to check the center's online calendar before planning your visit. For refreshments, head to the facility's outdoor restaurant and biergarten, where you and your pup can take a snack break while watching rafters brave the whitewater course.

US National Whitewater Center
5000 Whitewater Center Parkway
Charlotte, NC 28214
(704) 391-3900
www.bringfido.com/go/1DLM

Where to Stay:

After tiring your pooch out at the USNWC, check into the **Drury Inn & Suites Northlake** in time for their nightly 'kickback' hour at 5:30 pm. While Fido chills out in the comfortable suite, you'll be treated to some free hot food and cold drinks. Two dogs up to 80 lbs (combined weight) are welcome for an additional fee of $35 per night. Once your furry pal is rested, head to **Lucky Dog Bark & Brew Charlotte**, a dog-friendly bar with an indoor and outdoor dog park.

Drury Inn & Suites Northlake
6920 Northlake Mall Drive
Charlotte, NC 28216
(704) 599-8882
www.bringfido.com/go/1DLN
Rates from $95/night

Where to Stay:

Less than a mile from Corolla Outback Adventures, you'll find the **Inn at Corolla Light**, a pet-friendly hotel offering waterfront accommodations on the Currituck Sound. The property is located within the renowned Corolla Light Resort. Walk, take a free trolley, borrow a bike to cruise to the ocean, or stroll along the resort's trails to visit the grounds of the **Whalehead Club**. Up to two dogs of any size are welcome for an additional fee of $30 per pet, per night.

Inn at Corolla Light
1066 Ocean Trail
Corolla, NC 27927
(252) 453-3340
www.bringfido.com/go/1DRK
Rates from $109/night

Corolla Outback Adventures

Bring Fido to the Outer Banks of North Carolina to see wild horses on a tour with **Corolla Outback Adventures**. With private access into the Wild Horse Conservation Easement, the company can take you into refuge areas and sanctuary sites that are home to Colonial Spanish Mustangs. On the two-hour adventure, you're likely to see dozens of horses walking along the beach and playing in the surf, while knowledgeable guides provide commentary on the history of the horses and the local area. Tour prices are $50 for adults and $25 for children. Well-behaved dogs are welcome for no additional charge, but be sure to call ahead to let them know Fido is coming. After your tour, head to the shaded deck of **Corolla Cantina** to enjoy a great view of the sunset and lighthouse, along with a house margarita and yummy fish tacos.

Corolla Outback Adventures
1150 Ocean Trail
Corolla, NC 27927
(252) 453-4484
www.bringfido.com/go/1DRJ

Wright Brothers Memorial

Aviation and history buffs will enjoy bringing their furry co-pilots to the **Wright Brothers National Memorial** in Kill Devil Hills. Stand on the spot where Orville and Wilbur changed the world with their first flight and view full-scale replicas of their 1902 glider, 1903 flying machine, and first wind tunnel. Take a walk up Big Kill Devil Hill, where the duo conducted their glider experiments. Admission is $10 for adults and free for kids and dogs. If you want to do some flying of your own, head to nearby **Outer Banks Airlines** for a sightseeing flight. Pilot Charlie Snow will take you and your pooch on an aerial tour of the memorial, Roanoke Island, and Bodie Island Lighthouse. Rates start at $275 per half-hour flight for up to five people. Once your feet are back on the ground, visit the **Cape Hatteras National Seashore** for some free fun in the sand and surf.

Wright Brothers National Memorial
1000 N Croatan Highway
Kill Devil Hills, NC 27948
(252) 473-2111
www.bringfido.com/go/1DRE

Where to Stay:

Following Fido's day of fun in the Outer Banks, retire for the evening to the **Sandbar Bed & Breakfast** in beautiful Nags Head. The inviting three-story cottage offers beachfront convenience paired with Southern hospitality. Complimentary breakfast and evening refreshments are served daily. For an afternoon treat, take a short walk to **Surfin' Spoon**, where Fido can enjoy a cup of frozen vanilla yogurt topped with a dog treat. Dogs of any size are welcome at the Sandbar for an additional fee of $30 per stay.

Sandbar Bed & Breakfast
2510 S Virginia Dare Trail
Nags Head, NC 27959
(252) 489-1868
www.bringfido.com/go/1DRF
Rates from $89/night

National Buffalo Museum

Hit the highway on a dog-friendly road trip across North Dakota to visit several of the largest creatures on planet Earth. Your cross-state trek along I-94 begins at the **National Buffalo Museum** in Jamestown, where your pup can visit mighty **Dakota Thunder**, the world's largest buffalo. While there, you can stroll through **Frontier Village**, a replica prairie town constructed using original buildings from frontier days. Drive west 50 miles to the tiny town of Steele to visit **Sandy—The World's Largest Sandhill Crane**. After Fido feeds the bird, head 70 miles west to New Salem to moo at **Salem Sue**, the world's largest Holstein Cow. Finally, take a quick detour off I-94 near Gladstone to cruise along the 30-mile stretch of asphalt called the **Enchanted Highway**. Dogs can stretch their legs at one of several giant roadside metal sculptures, including Deer Crossing, Grasshoppers in the Field, and Fisherman's Dream.

National Buffalo Museum
500 17th Street SE
Jamestown, ND 58401
(701) 252-8648
www.bringfido.com/go/1DYP

Where to Stay:

After a long day of roadtripping, the **La Quinta Inn & Suites Dickinson** is a great place to take a breather. Settle back in comfy rooms with separate sitting areas. Take advantage of quality amenities like a complimentary breakfast buffet, fitness center, and an indoor pool with hot tub. Up to two dogs of any size are welcome for no additional fee. In the morning, make your way to nearby **Dickinson Dog Park** for some off-leash exercise before continuing your road trip.

La Quinta Inn & Suites Dickinson
552 12th Street W
Dickinson, ND 58601
(701) 456-2500
www.bringfido.com/go/1DYQ
Rates from $76/night

Where to Stay:

The **Hawthorn Suites by Wyndham Minot** serves as a comfortable overnight stop as you traverse between Dunseith and Washburn. All of the suites in this apartment-style property feature pillow-top beds and full kitchens. Two dogs up to 80 lbs are welcome for an additional fee of $10 per pet, per night. While in Minot, be sure to visit **Scandinavian Heritage Park**, an outdoor museum dedicated to all five Nordic countries. Admission is free of charge, although donations are encouraged.

Hawthorn Suites by
Wyndham Minot
800 37th Avenue SW
Minot, ND 58701
(701) 858-7300
www.bringfido.com/go/1DYM
Rates from $67/night

International Peace Garden

Lying on the 49th parallel at the Canada–United States border near Dunseith, the **International Peace Garden** is a living tribute to world peace. This 2,339-acre park is accessible to visitors from both countries without the need for a passport. Over 150,000 flowers are planted in the formal garden every spring, but the star attractions are always the American and Canadian flags made out of flowers. The gardens are open year-round, but mid-July through August tends to be the best time to view the colorful floral displays. The entrance fee is $20 per vehicle. Your leashed pup is welcome to join you throughout the park for free. As you continue your journey across North Dakota, take a detour to Washburn to visit the **Seaman Overlook**, featuring a 1,400-pound, steel sculpture of the dog that accompanied Lewis and Clark on their expedition across America.

International Peace Garden
10939 Highway 281
Dunseith, ND 58329
(701) 263-4390
www.bringfido.com/go/1E2M

The Canine Country Club

When the weather outside is frightful, take your pooch to **The Canine Country Club** in North Olmsted. This Cleveland-area business is a hub for pet parents looking for some recreation and socialization opportunities for their pups. Your furry friend can release some of his pent-up energy with a swim session in the facility's indoor, heated pool. All dogs are welcome regardless of swimming ability, but first-time visitors must complete an orientation session before participating in an open swim. If the water doesn't suit your pup, you can also schedule private play time in the activity room, which is furnished with toys and agility equipment. The facility is open daily (except Mondays), and pricing starts at $15 for play sessions and $30 for swims. Pamper your pooch even more by booking a canine massage session with Modern Dog Massage, which performs services at the club.

The Canine Country Club
29929 Lorain Road
North Olmsted, OH 44070
(440) 455-9337
www.bringfido.com/go/1DYZ

Where to Stay:

Stay in downtown Cleveland at **Metropolitan at The 9**. The historic property oozes class and sophistication, and it's the country's only four-star hotel with an indoor dog park. Located on the 29th floor, this petite paradise for pups contains a potty area with fire hydrants and artificial turf. The long hallway offers just enough space for playing a game of fetch. Two dogs up to 75 lbs are welcome for an additional fee of $100 per stay.

Metropolitan at the 9
2017 E 9th Street
Cleveland, OH 44115
(216) 239-1200
www.bringfido.com/go/1DZ0
Rates from $199/night

Where to Stay:

With so much for Fido to explore, you'll want to spend a night (or more!) in the state park to experience all it has to offer. The **Hueston Woods Lodge & Conference Center** provides efficiency cabins that welcome furry guests. Each cabin includes some modern amenities of home such as a gas fireplace, fully equipped kitchen, TV, outdoor grill, and fire ring. Up to two dogs of any size are welcome for no additional fee.

Hueston Woods Lodge
& Conference Center
5201 Lodge Road
College Corner, OH 45003
(513) 664-3500
www.bringfido.com/go/1DYY
Rates from $82/night

Hueston Woods State Park

You and your canine companion can enjoy four seasons of fun at **Hueston Woods State Park** in College Corner. In the springtime, take a hike on one of the eight dog-friendly trails running through the nearly 3,500-acre park, and enjoy fossil hunting and geocaching along the way. When the weather heats up in summer, Action Lake offers boating, canoeing, and fishing for catfish and bass. Fido can splash around at the dog beach or let loose inside the park's three-acre, fenced-in dog park. The fall is a great time to explore the park as the leaves change. Grab some grub to-go from the on-site Smoke-house Restaurant to enjoy at one of the picnic areas located throughout the park, and cozy up around the bonfire on the cool nights. In the winter, visitors can enjoy sledding, cross-country skiing, and ice fishing with their pup. There is no admission fee to visit the park.

Hueston Woods State Park
6301 Park Office Road
College Corner, OH 45003
(513) 523-6347
www.bringfido.com/go/1DYX

Scioto Mile

Situated along the Scioto River in the shadow of the Columbus skyline, the **Scioto Mile** connects 145 acres of stunning parks, water features, and scenic lookouts that you and your four-legged friend are welcome to explore. The **Scioto Audubon Metro Park** is the most 'pupu-lar' of the attractions, with an on-site dog park equipped with agility stations and a digging area. Continuing north, you'll pass by the interactive Scioto Mile Fountain en route to **Battelle Riverfront Park**, a beautiful campus filled with monuments memorializing firefight-ers, war veterans, and historic moments. When your pup is ready for a break, stop for lunch at the nearby **BrewDog Franklinton** and sample a pint from one of the bar's 48 taps, while Fido hydrates with a bowl of water. Or, make your way to BrewDogs' **DogHouse Hotel & Brewery**, which boasts its very own craft beer museum and dog park.

Scioto Mile
W Rich Street
Columbus, OH 43215
(614) 645-3800
www.bringfido.com/go/1E75

Where to Stay:

You and your good boy won't mind spending a night in the doghouse at BrewDog's **DogHouse Hotel & Brewery** in Canal Winchester. IPA enthusi-asts and their furry sidekicks can experience an evening of beer bliss in guest rooms equipped with BrewDog draft beer taps, stocked mini fridges, and locally made craft beer soaps. Wake up in the morning to the aroma of barley and hops, grab a beer-paired breakfast, and then let Fido play in the on-site dog park. Up to two dogs of any size are welcome for no additional fee.

DogHouse Hotel & Brewery
100 Gender Road
Canal Winchester, OH 43110
(614) 908-3054
www.bringfido.com/go/1E76
Rates from $172/night

Where to Stay:

You'll have no trouble finding the **21c Museum Hotel Oklahoma City**. Just look for Woozy Blossom, the 16-foot steel tree outside the property. It's one of the many art installations found throughout the hotel and museum. During your stay, take Fido shopping for pet products and more at the 21c store. Food and water bowls and a cozy dog bed are available for your pup to use in your spacious guest room. Up to two dogs of any size are welcome for an additional fee of $75 per stay.

21c Museum Hotel Oklahoma City
900 W Main Street
Oklahoma City, OK 73106
(405) 982-6900
www.bringfido.com/go/1E4P
Rates from $152/night

Paseo Arts District

On your next visit to Oklahoma's capital city, bring your furry art connoisseur to the **Paseo Arts District**. This two-block street of Spanish-style buildings is home to more than 20 galleries, and your four-legged friend is welcome to visit many of them. Peruse the collections at **The Art Hall**, **Little D Gallery**, and **Prairie Arts Collective**. Shop for gifts at **Literati Press Bookshop** and **Little Market Paseo**. Then grab lunch at **Picasso Café** and order your hungry hound his own delectable dish from the doggy menu. After your art adventure, take your water-loving pooch to **Riversport OKC** in the Boathouse District. Snap on your pup's life jacket and paddle along the Oklahoma River in a flatwater kayak or stand-up paddleboard, admiring the art and architecture of downtown OKC. Rentals are offered for $20 per hour, and dog life jackets are required. Hours vary by season.

Paseo Arts District
3024 Paseo
Oklahoma City, OK 73103
(405) 525-2688
www.bringfido.com/go/1E4O

Myriad Botanical Gardens

Walk with your pup through a 15-acre natural escape in the heart of Oklahoma City at **Myriad Botanical Gardens**. Take a self-guided walking tour through ornamental landscapes in this interactive urban park, stopping to learn about plant species and admire the sculptures that are on display. Dogs are allowed everywhere except the Children's Garden and inside the Crystal Bridge Conservatory. Fido's favorite spot will be the **Myriad Botanical Gardens Dog Park**, where he can run off leash in a fenced area featuring turf-covered mounds, seating for humans, and doggy water stations. The outdoor grounds are open daily from 6:00 am to 11:00 pm and are free to visit. Before going back to your hotel, stop by **Bone Dog Boutique** for a self-service dog wash and delicious treat for your pooch.

Myriad Botanical Gardens
301 W Reno Avenue
Oklahoma City, OK 73102
(405) 445-7080
www.bringfido.com/go/1DZ1

Where to Stay:

Your furry traveling buddy will be impressed if you book a room at the **Aloft Oklahoma City Downtown Bricktown**. He'll love hanging out with you as you sip a cocktail in the hotel's W XYZ bar or play a game of pool in the Re:mix Lounge. He'll be even happier when he finds out about the fully fenced dog park located just behind the hotel. Up to two dogs of any size are welcome for no additional fee.

Aloft Oklahoma City Downtown Bricktown
209 N Walnut Avenue
Oklahoma City, OK 73104
(405) 605-2100
www.bringfido.com/go/1DZ2
Rates from $119/night

Secrets of Portlandia

With a reputation as one of the most dog-friendly cities in the country, Portland offers up a vacation's worth of things to do with Fido. Begin your visit to the City of Roses with the **Secrets of Portlandia** two-hour walking tour. Learn about the city's weird history and quirky subcultures while being treated to stand-up comedy from guide Erik Kennon. Free tours are available seven days a week from April through September (tips appreciated), and leashed dogs can join in the fun. Afterward, grab a bite to eat on the covered patio at **Tin Shed Garden Café**, where pups can dig into a plate of chicken or scarf a scoop of creamy peanut butter-banana ice cream. Head two miles south of downtown to **Sellwood Riverfront Park** to enjoy scenic views of the Willamette River while Fido romps in the 1.5-acre off-leash area, sniffs out the woodland trails, and plays fetch along the sandy shoreline.

Secrets of Portlandia
700 SW 6th Avenue
Portland, OR 97204
(503) 703-4282
www.bringfido.com/go/1DX0

Where to Stay:

Nestled on the banks of the Willamette River in an area known as 'Portland's Front Yard,' the **Kimpton RiverPlace Hotel** gives Fido easy access to a mile-long riverfront walking trail and huge lawn in downtown Portland. The property also provides complimentary bikes, a yoga mat in every room, and a hosted wine hour from 5:00 pm to 6:00 pm every evening. Dogs of any size are welcome for no additional fee.

Kimpton RiverPlace Hotel
1510 S Harbor Way
Portland, OR 97201
(503) 228-3233
www.bringfido.com/go/1DX1
Rates from $203/night

Where to Stay:

When planning a dog-friendly stay in central Oregon, look no further than **Bennington Properties**, which offers the largest assortment of canine-approved vacation homes in the Sunriver community. With weekly yappy hours in July and August, an on-site dog wash, and a fenced off-leash play area, the company headquarters also serves as a popular gathering spot for dog owners. Pups of any size stay in Bennington rentals for an additional fee of $20 per pet, per night (treats included).

Bennington Properties
56842 Venture Lane
Sunriver, OR 97707
(541) 705-2267
www.bringfido.com/go/1DX5
Rates from $85/night

Sunriver Resort

Located at the base of the Cascade Mountains in central Oregon, the 3,300-acre resort community of **Sunriver** is a vacation destination that Fido is sure to love. Walk or jog more than 30 miles of paved pathways or cycle around the village with a dog trailer rental from **Village Bike & Ski**. Explore hundreds of off-leash trails in the surrounding **Deschutes National Forest** or drive 30 minutes to **Mt. Bachelor Ski Resort**. Experienced hikers can climb all the way to the top of the 9,065-foot mountain, or for $24 per person, take a dog-friendly chairlift to the mid-mountain level at 7,775 feet and hike to the summit from there. While dogs aren't allowed on Mount Bachelor in the winter, **Wanoga Sno-Park** has a pooch-friendly trail and tubing hill nearby with entry for just $3 per vehicle. And, of course, the dozens of miles of trails back at Sunriver allow dogs year-round!

Sunriver Resort
17600 Center Drive
Sunriver, OR 97707
(800) 801-8765
www.bringfido.com/go/1DX4

Spinreel Dune Buggy

Bring Fido on a fur-flying adventure at the Oregon dunes with an off-road vehicle rental from **Spinreel Dune Buggy** in North Bend. Located across the street from Oregon's largest dune-riding area, the company has two-seater buggies with plenty of room in the back for your four-legged friend. After a quick lesson and safety briefing, you'll be ready to ride. Drive at your own pace as you enjoy panoramic views of the Pacific Ocean from the top of the majestic dunes. Rates start at $115 for a 30-minute ride. If you prefer having someone else at the wheel, head 30 miles north to **Sand Dunes Frontier** for a Big Buggy Tour. Your leashed pup is welcome to join you on guided trips. Rates are $14 per person and free for dogs. After your ride, let Fido shake off the sand in his fur with a hike along the nearby **John Dellenback Dunes Trail**.

Spinreel Dune Buggy
67045 Spinreel Road
North Bend, OR 97459
(541) 759-3313
www.bringfido.com/go/1DPW

Where to Stay:

After your dune-riding adventure, spend the night in one of eight pet-friendly yurts at **William M. Tugman State Park**. These rustic, rounded tent-like dwellings feature beds, wood flooring, heaters and electricity, but you'll need to bring your own sleeping bags and towels. Shared bathroom facilities are available on-site, and the park is located less than three miles from the John Dellenback Dunes Trail. Up to two dogs of any size are welcome for an optional fee of $10 per night.

William M. Tugman State Park
72549 Highway 101
Lakeside, OR 97449
(501) 759-3604
www.bringfido.com/go/1DPX
Rates from $39/night

Where to Stay:

After a day of adventure on the water, relax in a luxuriously appointed room at the **Oxford Hotel Bend**. The boutique property features modern, eco-friendly accommodations, nightly turn-down service, and a sauna and steam room. The hotel's pet package includes a bed, two pet bowls (one to take home), and organic dog treats. Pet massages, grooming, and walking services can also be arranged. Up to two dogs of any size are welcome for an additional fee of $59 per pet, per stay.

Oxford Hotel Bend
10 NW Minnesota Avenue
Bend, OR 97703
(541) 382-8436
www.bringfido.com/go/1DWW
Rates from $245/night

Tumalo Creek Kayak & Canoe

Floating down the slow-moving Deschutes River is one of the best ways to spend a hot summer day in Bend. Fortunately for Fido, dogs are welcome to swim in the river and join in the fun too! Bring your own inner tube, or rent a kayak, stand-up paddleboard, or canoe from **Tumalo Creek Kayak & Canoe**, which also outfits visitors with life jackets and other accessories. Conveniently located on the banks of the river near the Old Mill District, the company offers two-hour rentals starting at $40 for kayaks and paddleboards and $50 for canoes. Dogs are allowed for $15. After your relaxing float, give Fido a chance to stretch his legs during off-leash playtime at **Riverbend Beach Dog Park**. With separate small and large dog areas, pups of any size can enjoy splashing in the water and playing fetch in this fully fenced riverfront park.

Tumalo Creek Kayak & Canoe
805 SW Industrial Way
Bend, OR 97702
(541) 317-9407
www.bringfido.com/go/1DWV

Cannon Beach

Spend a few memorable days with your dog discovering the wonderful towns, beaches, scenic vistas and attractions along the majestic Oregon coast. When planning your journey, allow for plenty of time to explore the pet-friendly seaside town of Cannon Beach. Start your day with an early morning walk along the beach near **Haystack Rock**, a designated bird and marine sanctuary that rises 235 feet above the sand and sea. In the tide pools, you will see a variety of marine life, and the rock itself is home to cormorants, tufted puffins, and seagulls. Dogs are welcome to roam leash-free, provided they remain under voice command. After a stroll along the streets of downtown, spend an afternoon at **Ecola State Park**. Enjoy miles of hiking along the Oregon Coast Trail, following in the footsteps of Lewis and Clark. Day use admission to the park is $5 per vehicle, and dogs must remain on leash.

Haystack Rock
Hemlock Street & Gower Avenue
Cannon Beach, OR 97110
(503) 436-2623
www.bringfido.com/go/1DP5

Where to Stay:

The oceanfront **Surfsand Resort** in Cannon Beach offers sweeping views of Haystack Rock and the Tillamook Head Lighthouse. Fido can sneak a biscuit from the cookie jar at check-in. The resort also provides a dog bed and basket filled with extra sheets, towels, placemat, and feeding bowls for their canine guests. There's even a paw wash station near the beach! Up to two dogs of any size are welcome for an additional fee of $25 per pet, per night.

Surfsand Resort
148 W Gower Avenue
Cannon Beach, OR 97110
(503) 436-2274
www.bringfido.com/go/1DP6
Rates from $129/night

Where to Stay:

Stay in the heart of the Willamette Valley at the historic **McMenamins Hotel Oregon** in McMinnville. The handsome, red-brick building was built in 1905 and retains many original fixtures and accents, including porcelain sinks in the guestrooms and period furnishings. Food bowls and waste bags are available at the front desk, and Fido can join you for a craft brew at the hotel's pub or rooftop bar. Dogs of any size are welcome for an additional fee of $15 per pet, per night.

McMenamins Hotel Oregon
310 NE Evans Street
McMinnville, OR 97128
(503) 472-8427
www.bringfido.com/go/1DWZ
Rates from $69/night

Tour DeVine

Give Fido a bird's-eye view of the picturesque Willamette Valley on an aerial journey across Oregon wine country. **Tour DeVine**'s VIP experience begins in McMinnville with a pre-flight breakfast and glass of bubbly. You and your pooch will then be whisked away by helicopter to begin your winery-hopping adventure. The tour includes two or three winery visits and three or four helicopter flights. Along the way, you can sample some of the region's famous Pinot Noirs, while your pooch explores the winery grounds. A gourmet picnic lunch is provided during your second stop. Choose from one of three popular tour options, or customize the tour to visit the dog-friendly wineries of your choice. Tour DeVine operates from May to October. Prices start at $1,436 per tour, which includes all transportation and tasting fees for up to four adults. There is no additional fee for four-legged passengers.

Tour DeVine
3800 NE Three Mile Lane
McMinnville, OR 97128
(503) 687-3816
www.bringfido.com/go/1DWY

Dog Mountain Trail

Enjoy breathtaking scenic vistas, abundant wildlife, and a variety of terrains and ecosystems in the picturesque Columbia River Gorge area. Located on the border of Oregon and Washington, this canyon created by the Columbia River offers countless recreational opportunities, including the popular **Dog Mountain Trail**. The 6.9-mile modified loop trail with a 2,800-foot elevation gain is best suited to experienced hikers and well-conditioned dogs, but those reaching the summit are rewarded with amazing views of the gorge below, as well as Mount Saint Helens to the northwest and Mount Hood to the south. Plan a visit in May or June when the wildflowers are in peak bloom. For less experienced hikers, a visit to **Multnomah Falls** is in order. Park near the base of the falls for easy access to the 611-foot cascading waterfall, or hike up the paved trail to Benson Bridge for a closer view of the water.

Dog Mountain Trail
WA-14 at Milepost 53
Cook, WA 98605
(541) 308-1700
www.bringfido.com/go/1DU6

Where to Stay:

Nestled on the banks of the Columbia River, the **Best Western Plus Hood River Inn** offers comfortable guest rooms with private balconies or pet-friendly patios. The property boasts an assortment of amenities, including a private beach, pool, and spa. Fido will appreciate the large grassy lawn and riverside walking path. Up to two dogs of any size are welcome for an additional fee of $15 per night.

Best Western Plus Hood River Inn
1108 E Marina Way
Hood River, OR 97031
(541) 386-2200
www.bringfido.com/go/1DU5
Rates from $129/night

Three Sisters Wilderness

With nearly 260 miles of hiking trails, the **Three Sisters Wilderness** area of the Willamette National Forest is a nature lover's delight. Start off your adventure by stocking up on supplies in Sisters, a western-themed town dotted with unique shops. Next, take a scenic hour-long drive to the **Proxy Falls** trailhead, where you and your pooch can enjoy an easy-to-moderate 1.5-mile loop hike. Trek over open lava fields and dense evergreen forests on your way to see two magnificent waterfalls, each offering excellent photo opportunities. After hiking to the falls, make your way back to Sisters, or continue on the McKenzie Highway to hike **Sahalie and Koosah Falls**. Plan a visit in summer to ensure that you won't encounter any road closures due to snow, which can blanket McKenzie Pass for much of the year. Day use access is $5 per vehicle. Dogs should remain leashed in the Three Sisters Wilderness.

Three Sisters Wilderness
57600 McKenzie Highway
McKenzie Bridge, OR 97413
(541) 822-3381
www.bringfido.com/go/1DX9

Where to Stay:

After exploring the Three Sisters Wilderness, enjoy the comforts of home at **FivePine Lodge** in Sisters. Their pet-friendly cabins feature private patios, fireplaces, luxury bedding, and soaking tubs. Unwind at the nightly wine reception, or head next door to share a meal with Fido on the patio at **Three Creeks Brewing**. In the morning, Fido can stretch his legs on the adjacent walking trail. Two dogs of any size are welcome for an additional fee of $25 per night.

FivePine Lodge
1021 E Desperado Trail
Sisters, OR 97759
(541) 549-5900
www.bringfido.com/go/1DXA
Rates from $181/night

Where to Stay:

Housed in a 1907 landmark building next to Independence Park, the Kimpton Hotel Monaco in Philadelphia is a great base for exploring the City of Brotherly Love. Canine guests will also feel the love at check-in when they receive a special treat, along with comfy pet beds, bowls, and waste bags for use during their stay. Pet sitting, dog walking, and grooming arrangements can be made through the hotel concierge. Dogs of any size are welcome for no additional fee.

Kimpton Hotel Monaco
433 Chestnut Street
Philadelphia, PA 19106
(215) 925-2111
www.bringfido.com/go/1DZD
Rates from $201/night

Constitutional Walking Tour

Bring Fido on a journey to 18th century Philadelphia with **The Constitutional Walking Tour**. These two-hour guided tours highlight over 20 popular historical and cultural attractions around downtown Philadelphia. Trace the footsteps of the Founding Fathers by visiting the sites where American democracy was born, including the Liberty Bell, Independence Hall, Franklin Court, Betsy Ross House, and Congress Hall. Tours are available April through November, and tickets are $19 for adults and $12 for children. Four-legged 'pawtriots' are permitted free of charge as long as they remain leashed. If all the walking has left you and your pup hungry, head to the corner of 9th Street and Passyunk Avenue, where you can choose a favorite in the longtime cheesesteak war between **Pat's** and **Geno's**. Walk-up windows and outdoor seating make it easy to enjoy the Philly classic with your hound.

The Constitutional Walking Tour
525 Arch Street
Philadelphia, PA 19106
(215) 525-1776
www.bringfido.com/go/1DZC

Lehigh Gorge Scenic Railway

Nicknamed 'The Switzerland of America,' Jim Thorpe is a great weekend getaway for you and your canine companion. Walk your pup along the streets of the charming downtown village, hike the **D&L Trail at Lehigh Gorge State Park**, or head straight to the town's main attraction—the **Lehigh Gorge Scenic Railway**. Climb aboard an enclosed or open-air coach from the 1920s for a 16-mile journey through the beautiful Pennsylvania wilderness. On the one-hour narrated train ride, you'll learn about anthracite coal's role in the industrial revolution and enjoy stunning views of the Lehigh Gorge. The train operates on weekends and holidays from late May to late December. Tours typically depart at 11:00 am, 1:00 pm, and 3:00 pm, but additional trips are added in the busy fall foliage and summer seasons. Coach fares start at $17 for adults and $9 for children. Dogs ride for free.

Lehigh Gorge Scenic Railway
1 Susquehanna Street
Jim Thorpe, PA 18229
(570) 325-8485
www.bringfido.com/go/1DUH

Where to Stay:

Your tired pooch can take off his conductor's hat and spend the night just a few minutes from Jim Thorpe at the **Country Inn & Suites by Radisson Lehighton**. While Fido relaxes in your cozy guest room, you can get in a quick workout at the hotel's fitness center or take a refreshing swim in the heated indoor pool. A complimentary breakfast is offered daily. Up to two dogs of any size are welcome for an additional fee of $25 per night.

Country Inn & Suites
by Radisson Lehighton
1619 Interchange Road
Lehighton, PA 18235
(610) 379-5066
www.bringfido.com/go/1DUI
Rates from $90/night

Where to Stay:

After exploring Bushkill Falls, join the ranks of famous Americans such as Teddy Roosevelt, Henry Ford, John F. Kennedy, Mae West, and Robert Frost, who have been guests at the luxurious **Hotel Fauchere** in Milford. Relax in the beautifully appointed rooms, wander through the manicured garden, take Fido on a stroll through charming Milford, and enjoy an intimate dinner at the Delmonico Room. Up to two dogs of any size are welcome for an additional fee of $25 per pet, per night.

Hotel Fauchere
401 Broad Street
Milford, PA 18337
(570) 409-1212
www.bringfido.com/go/1DWU
Rates from $202/night

Bushkill Falls

Spanning 300 acres in the scenic Pocono Mountains, Pennsylvania's **Bushkill Falls** is a nature lover's delight. With eight waterfalls accessible from just over two miles of walking trails, the park is an excellent spot to explore with your pup. Open April through November, the park offers four trails of varying degrees of difficulty, making the falls accessible to visitors of all ability levels. Choose the Green Trail for a short 15-minute walk to the Main Falls. Allow at least two hours to hike the Red Trail, which offers a glimpse of all eight waterfalls. Family-friendly attractions, including miniature golf and paddleboat rides, are also available. Pack a picnic lunch or barbecue on the charcoal grills at the pavilion. Anglers can bring a tackle box and fish in one of the ponds. Admission is $18 for adults and $9 for children. Dogs are free, but remember to keep Fido leashed at all times in the park.

Bushkill Falls
138 Bushkill Falls Trail
Bushkill, PA 18324
(570) 588-6682
www.bringfido.com/go/1DWT

Gettysburg Battlefield

American history buffs won't want to miss a trip to the **Gettysburg National Military Park**. Walk through the battlefield with Fido or take a driving tour of the historic sites commemorating the battle that became a major turning point in the Civil War. Although dogs are not permitted in park buildings, they can join you at most of the outdoor memorials. Be sure to visit the Irish Brigade monument, which depicts a loyal Irish Wolfhound mourning the loss of his masters. The park is open year-round from 6:00 am to 7:00 pm, with extended evening hours from April through October. There is no admission fee. After the park closes, you and your furry friend can continue exploring Gettysburg on a guided walk with **Haunted Gettysburg Tours**. Tours depart at 7:30 pm and 9:00 pm each evening and cost $12 per person. Children under 8 and dogs attend for free.

Gettysburg National Military Park
1195 Baltimore Pike
Gettysburg, PA 17325
(717) 334-1124
www.bringfido.com/go/1DP8

Where to Stay:

The **Battlefield Bed and Breakfast** is a real Civil War-era farmhouse with a 30-acre nature preserve on the Gettysburg Battlefield. The B&B is said to be haunted, but don't be scared when you see a soldier in the morning—that's just a Civil War reenactor arriving for the daily history program. Where else can you try your hand at firing a musket before enjoying a hearty breakfast in the morning? Dogs of any size are welcome for no additional fee.

Battlefield Bed and Breakfast
2264 Emmitsburg Road
Gettysburg, PA 17325
(717) 334-8804
www.bringfido.com/go/1DP9
Rates from $179/night

IF YOU'RE AS TALL AS
MY MEASURING TAPE
You will need a
REGULAR HANDSTAMP
48"
To ride the
Phoenix
YOU MUST BE AS TALL
AS MY LADDER

Knoebels Amusement Resort

A day of family fun at the theme park doesn't have to mean leaving Fido at home. At **Knoebels Amusement Resort** in Elysburg, you can bring your furry family members to enjoy the carnival-like atmosphere of America's largest free amusement park. While the kids are off riding the thrill rides, you and your pooch can savor the delicious confections that fill the air with mouth-watering aromas. Test your skills at one of the many carnival games or visit one of three on-site museums, including the famous carousel museum. Your dog will enjoy riding the 1.5-mile pioneer train that circles the park, going through the Twister roller coaster and into the woods before returning to the depot. The park features more than 57 rides and attractions. Admission and parking are free, and ride tickets are available for purchase at the ticket booths. Dogs must be well-socialized and leashed at all times.

Knoebels Amusement Resort
391 Knoebels Boulevard
Elysburg, PA 17824
(570) 672-2572
www.bringfido.com/go/1DPB

Where to Stay:

RV owners and tent campers can stay overnight with their canine companions at **Knoebels Campground**. Those who prefer more pampered accommodations should drive an hour northwest to the **Genetti Hotel** in Williamsport. Choose from tastefully decorated European-style rooms with city, mountain, and river views. Other amenities include an outdoor swimming pool, fitness center, and picnic area. Two dogs up to 80 lbs are welcome for an additional fee of $15 per pet, per night.

Genetti Hotel
200 W Fourth Street
Williamsport, PA 17701
(570) 326-6600
www.bringfido.com/go/1DPC
Rates from $107/night

Where to Stay:

After witnessing the simplic-
ity of Amish life, you and Fido
can enjoy the comforts of the **La
Quinta Inn & Suites** in neighboring Ronks. Relax in rooms
equipped with modern amenities,
including Wi-Fi, a fitness center,
and heated pool. Although the
hotel's grassy area is fine for
Fido's morning walk, he would
prefer spending some off-leash
time at nearby **Beau's Dream
Dog Park at Buchanan Park**. The
park features doggy splash pads
and a tree that launches tennis
balls. Two dogs of any size are
welcome for an additional fee of
$20 per night.

La Quinta Inn & Suites
by Wyndham Lancaster
25 Eastbrook Road
Ronks, PA 17572
(717) 208-2453
www.bringfido.com/go/1DZ8
Rates from $72/night

Abe's Buggy Rides

Learn about Amish and Mennonite cultures
as you and Fido are carried in an authentic
Amish buggy on a private tour with **Abe's
Buggy Rides**. Your driver will provide historical facts and stories about the area during
your horse-drawn carriage ride along country roads. Choose a 20-minute tour for a quick
jaunt through the Lancaster County countryside.
A leisurely hour-long ride will give you time to
see many Amish homes, businesses and attractions, and includes a stop at a Mennonite craft
store and bake shop. Custom tours are available, and leashed dogs are welcome on all
trips. Prices start at $15 for adults and $7 for
children. Accepted payment forms are cash or
check only. While in the area, swing by **The
Amish Farm and House** for a guided tour of an
historic Amish home and 15-acre working farm.
Rates are $11 for adults and $8 for children.
Leashed dogs are allowed free of charge.

Abe's Buggy Rides
2596 Old Philadelphia Pike
Bird in Hand, PA 17505
(717) 392-1794
www.bringfido.com/go/1DZ7

Block Island

Get away from the mainland for a day or two and visit Block Island with your pooch. Hop on the **Block Island Ferry** for a 55-minute ride from Point Judith to the scenic island. Roundtrip rates start at $22 for adults and $10 for children. Dogs ride free of charge. After docking, make your way to the **Mohegan Bluffs**, a strip of secluded beach sandwiched between impressive clay cliffs and the Atlantic Ocean. You can walk the four-mile roundtrip distance by foot, or rent a bike and trailer from **Beach Rose Bicycles**. If you want to get there quickly, hail a taxi (both **McAloon's Taxi** and **Block Island Taxi and Tours** are dog friendly). After enjoying your time at the beach, stroll around the Southeast Lighthouse before taking a leisurely walk back to Old Harbor, or head in the opposite direction to complete a 13-mile bike ride around the island.

Block Island Ferry
304 Great Island Road
Narragansett, RI 02882
(401) 783-7996
www.bringfido.com/go/1DPK

Where to Stay:

Nestled on pristine Crescent Beach, the **Blue Dory Inn** offers close proximity to the ferry, charming Victorian-style guest rooms, and fresh-baked cookies served daily. Pet-friendly accommodations feature porches with stunning ocean views. After a good night's sleep, take Fido for a morning walk on the beach. Dogs can run free on the north and south beaches of Block Island but should remain leashed on the eastern shore. Dogs of any size are welcome for an additional fee of $50 per pet, per stay.

Blue Dory Inn
61 Dodge Street
New Shoreham, RI 02807
(401) 466-5891
www.bringfido.com/go/1DPL
Rates from $224/night

Where to Stay:

Just a few blocks from Bowen's Wharf in Newport's Historic Hill neighborhood, you'll find **Paws on Pelham**, an inn created specifically with pets in mind. All 13 rooms welcome four-legged guests, feature dog decor, and include a whimsical dog bed just for Fido. He'll also receive bowls, a pet mat, and treats at check-in. A delicious grab-and-go human breakfast is provided each morning. Two dogs of any size are welcome for no additional fee.

Paws on Pelham
96 Pelham Street
Newport, RI 02840
(401) 845-9400
www.bringfido.com/go/1DNC
Rates from $179/night

Cliff Walk

Visitors to pet-friendly Newport will want to include a stroll along the majestic **Cliff Walk** on their itinerary. This 3.5-mile oceanfront pathway is a designated National Recreation Trail that stretches from Easton's Beach (just south of Memorial Boulevard) to Bailey's Beach at the south end of Bellevue Avenue. The trek will offer you and your pup some of New England's most breathtaking views and a peek into the backyards of stately mansions constructed during the country's Gilded Age. Most of the path is paved, but navigation over a rocky shoreline is required to reach the trail's end. Cliff Walk is open year-round from sunrise to sunset, and dogs must remain leashed. For a view of Newport from the sea, set sail with Fido on a private boat charter with **Antique Yacht Collection**. Take a morning mimosa cruise, an evening sunset sail, or a half- or full-day charter. Sailing times vary, and rates start at $290 per journey.

Cliff Walk
175 Memorial Boulevard
Newport, RI 02840
(401) 845-5300
www.bringfido.com/go/1DNB

Magnolia Plantation & Gardens

Step back in time at **Magnolia Plantation & Gardens**, a Charleston estate that survived both the Revolutionary and Civil Wars. You and your pup can explore the beautiful grounds and trails on your own, or hop on the Nature Tram for a 45-minute tour of the plantation's wetlands, lakes, forests, and marshes. If your furry friend can be carried, he is even welcome to accompany you on a tour inside the home. Basic admission is $20 for adults and $10 for children. Add $8 for the tram or home tours. Dogs are welcome for free. If you have time, head to nearby **Drayton Hall**, which dates back to 1738 and is considered one of the finest examples of Georgian-Palladian architecture in the US. Although dogs are not allowed inside the home, they are welcome to tour the estate's gardens on two self-guided nature walks. Admission is $32 for adults and $10 for children. Dogs are admitted for no extra fee.

Magnolia Plantation & Gardens
3550 Ashley River Road
Charleston, SC 29414
(843) 571-1266
www.bringfido.com/go/1DZI

Where to Stay:

Just a short walk from the dog-friendly shops and eateries along King Street, you'll find Charleston's **Wentworth Mansion**. You'll be spoiled during your stay with a complimentary full breakfast each morning, afternoon wine and hors d'oeuvres, and evening turndown service with housemade chocolates. Your pooch won't feel left out, either. Delicious treats are always available at the front desk. Dogs of any size are welcome for an additional fee of $40 per pet, per night.

Wentworth Mansion
149 Wentworth Street
Charleston, SC 29401
(843) 853-1886
www.bringfido.com/go/1DZJ
Rates from $349/night

Where to Stay:

Spoil your furry first mate with an overnight stay at the **Montage Palmetto Bluff**, a luxury resort nestled on the shores of the May River in Bluffton. The hotel's canine ambassadors will be on hand to greet Fido and present him with an assortment of amenities, including delicious treats, feeding bowls, and a fluffy pet bed. For dinner, he can even choose a tasty meal from the doggy room service menu. Up to two dogs of any size are welcome for an additional fee of $100 per stay.

Montage Palmetto Bluff
477 Mount Pelia Road
Bluffton, SC 29910
(843) 706-6500
www.bringfido.com/go/1DZH
Rates from $396/night

Captain Buddy's

Join a boat tour with **Captain Buddy's** in Bluffton to explore the scenic waterways of South Carolina's Lowcountry. If you and your pup want an active day on the water, consider an off-shore fishing adventure to reel in some mackerel, grouper, or snapper. Or, motor out to the beaches of Disappearing Island during low tide to unearth colorful seashells and sand dollar skeletons. Captain Buddy can also take you on an expedition to Shark Tooth Island to search for megalodon teeth while your pooch gets some exercise on the beach. For a more laidback experience, choose a relaxing bird-watching or sunset cruise to snap photos of native birds gliding across saltwater marshes and watch bottlenose dolphins frolic in the water. Rates start at $225 for a two-hour trip for up to six people. Dogs are welcome aboard for no extra charge.

Captain Buddy's
Calhoun Street Fishing Pier
Bluffton, SC 29910
(843) 473-7733
www.bringfido.com/go/1DZG

Swamp Rabbit Trail

Bring your furry friend to Greenville for a hop along the **Swamp Rabbit Trail**, a 22-mile recreation path that winds through the vibrant city. At its epicenter, you'll find beautiful **Falls Park**. Explore the manicured landscape as you meander along the Reedy River with your four-legged companion. Cross the Liberty Bridge and admire the dramatic waterfall from above. Browse the art galleries at River-Place, and do some retail shopping at many of the dog-friendly stores along Main Street. When Fido has worked up an appetite, stop for a meal on the piazza at **Limoncello**. If the weather doesn't cooperate, head indoors to **Pour Taproom**, where your pooch is welcome to join you inside for a pint from one of dozens of self-service taps. If your pup still has energy to burn after his trail walk, bring him to the **Lake Conestee Nature Preserve** for a hike and some off-leash fun at the **Conestee Dog Park**.

Swamp Rabbit Trail
601 S Main Street
Greenville, SC 29601
(864) 232-2273
www.bringfido.com/go/1E4Y

Where to Stay:

After exploring Greenville with your pup, stay overnight at the **Aloft Greenville Downtown**, where canine guests are greeted with treats, bowls, beds, and toys upon arrival. Fido can people-watch from the hotel's second-floor balcony, while you enjoy a cocktail from the W XYZ bar. Go next door to do some shopping at the pet-friendly **Mast General Store**. Up to two dogs of any size are welcome at the hotel for no extra fee.

Aloft Greenville Downtown
5 N Laurens Street
Greenville, SC 29601
(864) 297-6100
www.bringfido.com/go/1E4Z
Rates from $139/night

Reptile Gardens

If you like scales and tails, bring Fido to **Reptile Gardens** in Rapid City. The world's largest reptile zoo welcomes you and your four-legged companion to explore the grounds and observe 225 species of snakes, crocodiles, frogs, lizards, tortoises, and other reptiles. Catch a glimpse of the rare Komodo dragon before visiting the menagerie of cold-blooded creatures in the famous Sky Dome. Need a break from the creepy-crawlies? Visit the park's prairie dog exhibit, where Fido can get up close and personal with these cute critters from an underground bubble. Reptile Gardens is open daily from March through November. Admission is $12 for adults, $7 for children, and free for dogs. For more animal adventures, head to nearby **Bear Country USA**. At this drive-thru wildlife park, you'll see dozens of bears, wolves, sheep, and elk. Admission is $18 per vehicle, and the park is open from May through November.

Reptile Gardens
8955 S Highway 16
Rapid City, SD 57702
(605) 342-5873
www.bringfido.com/go/1DPH

Where to Stay:

After getting acquainted with reptiles and bears, rest up at the **Hart Ranch Camping Resort**. Spread out across 195 acres of beautiful Black Hills countryside, Hart Ranch features full RV hook-up sites, a spacious tent area for campers, and modern pet-friendly cabins equipped with kitchens, heat and air conditioning, and private bathrooms. Pups are restricted to the south side of the resort near the dog run and hiking trail. Up to two dogs of any size are welcome for no additional fee.

Hart Ranch Camping Resort
23756 Arena Drive
Rapid City, SD 57702
(605) 399-2582
www.bringfido.com/go/1DPI
Rates from $55/night

Where to Stay:

After a bumpy ride on the trails, you won't have to travel far to enjoy a good night's sleep. **Mystic Hills Hideaway** offers private cabins that have everything you and your nature-loving pup need, including kitchenettes, refrigerators, outdoor grills, picnic tables, and fire pits. Standard cabins feature two Queen beds and a sleeper sofa, so the whole pack can vacation together. Dogs of any size are welcome for an additional fee of $20 per pet, per night.

Mystic Hills Hideaway
21766 Custer Peak Road
Deadwood, SD 57732
(605) 584-4794
www.bringfido.com/go/1E56
Rates from $80/night

Mystic Hills Hideaway

Hop in an ATV from **Mystic Hills Hideaway** and explore the South Dakota backcountry on four wheels with your furry co-pilot riding shotgun. The outfitter's ATVs can accommodate up to four passengers and are street legal, but you'll want to spend most of your time exploring some of the 650 miles of trails of the **Black Hills National Forest**. Discover rugged rock formations, canyons, gulches, open grassland parks, streams, and lakes on your adventure. Half-day and full-day rentals are available. Rates start at $320 per vehicle (which can accommodate up to four passengers), and dogs ride for no additional fee. When you need a rest from your day of exploring, make your way into downtown Deadwood to give Fido a taste of the Old West. He can belly up to the bar alongside you at **Saloon No. 10**, where you can sample one of more than 150 varieties of whiskey.

Mystic Hills Hideaway
21766 Custer Peak Road
Deadwood, SD 57732
(605) 584-4794
www.bringfido.com/go/1E55

Custer State Park

If your dog likes to walk on the wild side, he will definitely enjoy hiking the trails carved out by early pioneers at **Custer State Park** in the Black Hills of South Dakota. You're likely to encounter prairie dogs, elk, bighorn sheep, mountain goats, and deer on the trails, but the park is most famous for being home to one of the nation's largest free roaming bison herds. The best way to see them is by driving the 18-mile Wildlife Loop Road in the early morning or late evening, just before sunset. The drive usually takes about 45 minutes, but allow plenty of time for traffic delays due to wildlife crossings. If you do encounter a herd of the 2,000-pound animals on the road, it is important for everyone, including Fido, to remain in the vehicle. Custer State Park is open year-round. Admission is $20 per vehicle. Afterward, strap on the old feed bag for some hearty eats on the **Blue Bell Lodge** dining patio.

Custer State Park
Wildlife Loop Road
Custer, SD 57730
(605) 255-4515
www.bringfido.com/go/1DR9

Where to Stay:

Tucked among the ponderosa pines beside Grace Coolidge Creek, you'll find the **State Game Lodge**, which once served as the 'Summer White House' during President Calvin Coolidge's administration. Now, you and your pup can be a guest of the lodge in one of the property's 19 pet-friendly cabins. After a restful night's sleep, take Fido for a morning walk on the adjacent Creekside Trail, then feast on Buffalo Benedict in the lodge's main dining room. Dogs of any size are welcome for an additional fee of $10 per pet, per night.

State Game Lodge
13389 US Highway 16A
Custer, SD 57730
(605) 255-4541
www.bringfido.com/go/1DR8
Rates from $145/night

Where to Stay:

The Hermitage Hotel became Nashville's first pet-friendly hotel in 1941 when movie star Gene Autry and his horse, Champion, checked in for a week-long stay. To this day, the hotel continues to welcome four-legged guests with a dose of good old-fashioned Southern hospitality. Fido can sleep on a custom dog bed, order from the pet room service menu, and even schedule a daily walk through the concierge. Dogs of any size are welcome for an additional fee of $75 per pet, per stay.

The Hermitage Hotel
231 6th Avenue N
Nashville, TN 37219
(615) 244-3121
www.bringfido.com/go/1DQ6
Rates from $260/night

Walkin' Nashville

Country music lovers will enjoy learning about the golden era of their favorite genre on a tour with **Walkin' Nashville**. Grammy-nominated music journalist Bill DeMain takes visitors on a two-hour stroll through downtown Nashville on his Music City Legends Tour. The tour starts at the corner of Fifth Avenue and Union Street and visits sites including the Ernest Tubb Record Shop, Castle Recording Studio, and Sho-Bud Steel Guitar Company. Fans of Dolly Parton, Willie Nelson, Loretta Lynn, and Johnny Cash will hear fascinating stories about their favorite music stars' careers as they walk through the heart of Music City. Tours depart at 10:30 am on Tuesdays, Thursdays, Fridays and Saturdays from April through November. They are offered on Fridays and Saturdays from December through March. Tickets are $30 for adults and $15 for children. Well-behaved dogs can join for free with prior notice.

Walkin' Nashville
414 Union Street
Nashville, TN 37219
(615) 499-5159
www.bringfido.com/go/1DQ5

Backbeat Tours

Put on Fido's leash and go walking in Memphis with **Backbeat Tours**. Hear the story of how the city became the 'Home of the Blues' on an hour-long historic walking tour of Beale Street. Departure times vary by season, and tickets are $15 per person. Dogs tag along for free. After your tour, make your way to the **National Civil Rights Museum** located at the former Lorraine Motel, where civil rights leader Dr. Martin Luther King, Jr. was assassinated on April 4, 1968. Dogs aren't allowed inside the museum, but the grounds outside are worth a visit. The motel's sign and façade have been preserved as they appeared in 1968, and two vintage replica cars are parked beneath the balcony where Dr. King was shot. Signage memorializing his life and the events of that fateful day are also located outside. There is no entry fee to access the exterior of the museum.

Backbeat Tours
197 Beale Street
Memphis, TN 38103
(901) 527-9415
www.bringfido.com/go/1DZL

Where to Stay:

After a day of sightseeing, spend a night with your pup at **The Peabody Memphis**. During your stay, don't miss the famous Mallard ducks march down the red carpet to the hotel lobby fountain. Ceremonial processions take place daily at 11:00 am and 5:00 pm. Your pup will also get the red carpet treatment during his stay. He'll be greeted with a duck-shaped treat at check-in, and he can order room service from the special pet menu. Dogs up to 75 lbs are welcome for an additional fee of $100 per stay.

The Peabody Memphis
149 Union Avenue
Memphis, TN 38103
(901) 529-4000
www.bringfido.com/go/1DZM
Rates from $219/night

Cades Cove Loop Road

Even though dogs aren't allowed on most trails at **Great Smoky Mountains National Park**, you can still enjoy the park's most popular attraction with Fido in tow. Take a scenic drive on the 11-mile loop around Cades Cove, and you'll easily spot dozens of white-tailed deer, black bears, and other animals roaming the open fields that were once farmed by pioneers. Depending on traffic conditions, motorists should allow two to four hours to drive the entire loop. If you'd prefer to take Fido on a walk instead, plan to visit on a Wednesday between June and September. **Cades Cove Loop Road** is closed to vehicular traffic during that time to give bicyclists and pedestrians an opportunity to enjoy the awe-inspiring scenery. After navigating the loop, head to nearby **River Rat Tubing** for some fun on the water. Dogs up to 60 lbs can join you on a float trip down the Little River. Day passes are $18 for adults and free for dogs.

Cades Cove Loop Road
Great Smoky Mountains National Park
Townsend, TN 37882
(865) 436-1200
www.bringfido.com/go/1DZO

Where to Stay:

After a day of exploring the Smokies, you and your pup can kick back in a cozy cabin at the **Dancing Bear Lodge** in Townsend. All cabins feature luxurious feather beds, wood-burning fireplaces, and private porches with hot tubs. Enjoy a glass of wine and a delicious meal as your pooch sits tableside on the outdoor deck of the on-site Appalachian Bistro. A complimentary breakfast is served daily. Dogs of any size are welcome for an additional fee of $50 per stay.

Dancing Bear Lodge
7140 E Lamar Alexander Parkway
Townsend, TN 37882
(865) 448-6000
www.bringfido.com/go/1DZP
Rates from $210/night

Where to Stay:

After a fun-filled day exploring Austin, recharge at **Hotel Saint Cecilia**. Every suite, studio, and bungalow in this secluded estate pays homage to the great writers, musicians, and artists of the decades. You and your pup can enjoy the sounds of the greats on the in-room Geneva sound systems with turntables. Other amenities include mini-bars stocked with unusual treats, made-to-order breakfasts, and an outdoor pool. Furry guests also receive treats, bowls, and toys. Dogs of any size are welcome for an additional fee of $25 per pet, per night.

Hotel Saint Cecilia
112 Academy Drive
Austin, TX 78704
(512) 852-2400
www.bringfido.com/go/1DZS
Rates from $295/night

Zilker Park Boat Rentals

On your next visit to Austin, make a bee line for Lady Bird Lake. You and your pup can enjoy the serenity of the water with a canoe or kayak rental from **Zilker Park Boat Rentals**. Located just 10 minutes from downtown, a scenic float on the lake will provide you with magnificent views of the Austin skyline and a glimpse of the famous bat colony that resides under the Congress Avenue Bridge. Rental rates start at $18 per hour. When you're back on dry land, head to **Zilker Botanical Garden** to explore over 30 acres of lush gardens with Fido. The garden is open daily from 9:00 am to 5:00 pm. Admission is $8 for adults and $4 for children. Dogs are free. If your pup needs to cool off, nearby **Red Bud Isle** is the perfect spot to swim and play in the waters of the Colorado River. When you get hungry, check out Austin's **Yard Bar**, an outdoor restaurant and bar with its own dog park ($20 membership required).

Zilker Park Boat Rentals
2101 Andrew Zilker Road
Austin, TX 78746
(512) 478-3852
www.bringfido.com/go/1DZR

San Antonio Ghost Tours

Is your pooch willing to brave the spirits still defending the Alamo? If so, sign up for a Haunted History Ghost Walk with **Sisters Grimm Ghost Tours** in San Antonio. Your guide will take human and canine visitors on a 90-minute stroll past three of the most haunted spots in the city—the Alamo, the Spanish Governor's Mansion, and the Menger Hotel. Double up your pup's paranormal fun by booking a dog-friendly San Antonio Ghost Walk with **Bad Wolf Ghost Tours**. On this tour, you will get to explore historic downtown and the **River Walk** district. Both tours are conducted nightly, and tickets are $20 for adults, $15 for children, and free for dogs. When you've had your fill of ghost stories, head back to River Walk, where many of the outdoor restaurants and shops welcome furry guests. Enjoy the colorful patio and authentic Mexican fare at **Casa Rio**.

Sisters Grimm Ghost Tours
204 Alamo Plaza, Suite #T
San Antonio, TX 78205
(210) 638-1338
www.bringfido.com/go/1E6P

Where to Stay:

For a frightfully fun stay near River Walk, book a dog-friendly room at the **Emily Morgan Hotel**. Although the hotel is rumored to be haunted, canine guests will be greeted with treats, not tricks. Dogs up to 50 lbs are welcome for an additional fee of $50 per pet, per stay. If your pooch is on the larger side, opt for a room at the **Hotel Havana**, where pups receive a comfy dog bed and food dishes to use during their visit. Dogs of any size are permitted for an additional fee of $25 per pet, per stay.

Emily Morgan Hotel
705 E Houston Street
San Antonio, TX 78205
(210) 225-5100
www.bringfido.com/go/1E6Q
Rates from $103/night

Where to Stay:

After spending some quality time in the great outdoors, savor the beauty of Texas from a relaxing rocking chair on the veranda at the **Best Western Plus Fredericksburg**. Deluxe rooms are equipped with free high-speed internet, work desks, and mini refrigerators. Fuel up in the morning with a complimentary hot breakfast and catch some rays on a lounge chair at the outdoor swimming pool. Dogs up to 80 lbs are welcome for an additional fee of $30 per night.

Best Western Plus Fredericksburg
314 E Highway Street
Fredericksburg, TX 78624
(830) 992-2929
www.bringfido.com/go/1DTZ
Rates from $80/night

Texas Hill Country

The town of Fredericksburg serves as a central hub for exploring Texas Hill Country's numerous dog-friendly state parks. Start your tour at **Enchanted Rock State Natural Area**. Situated 20 miles north of Fredericksburg, the 1,643-acre park is popular among hikers and rock-climbers. Drive an hour west to **South Llano River State Park**, where you can rent kayaks and canoes or go tubing with your pup down the scenic river. In nearby Johnson City, **Pedernales Falls State Park** offers excellent family-friendly hiking and wildlife viewing opportunities. Travel north to **Inks Lake State Park** in Burnet to fish for bass or catfish with your four-legged friend. Primitive camping and backpacking are available at the **Hill Country State Natural Area**, located 60 miles away in Bandera. Entrance fees and hours vary by location. As you enjoy the parks, be sure to keep Fido on a leash at all times.

Hill Country State Natural Area
10600 Bandera Creek Road
Bandera, TX 78003
(830) 796-4413
www.bringfido.com/go/1DTY

Galveston Island State Park

Galveston is home to some of the best dog-friendly fresh and saltwater fishing spots in the South. Try your luck on the bay at **Galveston Island State Park**, where your canine angler can help you reel in speckled trout, redfish, and flounder. Stretch your pup's legs with a hike along the bayside trails and boardwalks, or bring a canoe or kayak to enter paddling trails that provide access to beautiful dune hiking. Admission is $5 for adults and free for children and dogs. If you prefer a guided fishing trip, book an inshore or deep sea excursion with **Get Hooked Charters**. Tour prices start at $450 for up to three adults, and dogs ride for free. After Fido has reeled in the big one, reward him with dinner at **Marina Bar & Grill**, where he can order something from the dog menu. If your pup still has energy to burn, take him on an evening walk at dog-friendly **East Beach** or **Stewart Beach Park**.

Galveston Island State Park
14901 FM3005
Galveston, TX 77554
(409) 737-1222
www.bringfido.com/go/1E00

Where to Stay:

Located just one block from the beach, the **Red Roof PLUS Galveston Beachfront** is a convenient, budget-friendly option for an overnight visit to Galveston Island. There is ample green space around the hotel for your pup's potty breaks, and pet-friendly shops and dining options are within walking distance. Humans can enjoy a dip in the hotel pool while Fido rests after a fun day in the sand. One dog up to 70 lbs is welcome for no additional fee.

Red Roof PLUS
Galveston Beachfront
3924 Avenue U
Galveston, TX 77550
(409) 750-9400
www.bringfido.com/go/1E01
Rates from $54/night

Where to Stay:

Continue Fido's aquatic adventures at the **La Quinta Inn & Suites South Padre Beach**. The oceanfront property offers human amenities that include an outdoor pool, fitness center, and complimentary daily breakfast. But the best part for your pooch is that he can sleep just steps away from the dog-friendly beach. Up to two dogs of any size are welcome for an additional fee of $20 per pet, per night.

La Quinta Inn & Suites South Padre Beach
7000 Padre Boulevard
South Padre Island, TX 78597
(956) 772-7000
www.bringfido.com/go/1E07
Rates from $60/night

Sea Turtle, Inc.

Even if your furry friend is afraid of the water, he can still get up close and personal with marine life at **Sea Turtle, Inc.**, a nonprofit sea turtle rescue in South Padre Island. Well-behaved pups are invited to tag along as you visit the center's permanent turtle residents, tour the museum, and browse the gift shop. Presentations are made throughout the day to educate visitors on the importance of protecting endangered sea life. Be sure to catch a 'Turtle Talk' in the education complex before stopping by the sea turtle hospital to observe the rehabilitation process. The facility is open daily (except Mondays) from 10:00 am to 4:00 pm, and admission is $10 for adults and $4 for children. Dogs are welcome for free. If Fido is ready for some lunch after his turtle encounter, make your way to nearby **Lobo Del Mar Café** for dog-friendly waterside dining.

Sea Turtle, Inc.
6617 Padre Boulevard
South Padre Island, TX 78597
(956) 761-4511
www.bringfido.com/go/1E06

Houston Arboretum

Escape the congestion of the city and bring Fido to the **Houston Arboretum & Nature Center**, a 155-acre urban sanctuary on the western edge of **Memorial Park**. Visitors are invited to explore five miles of walking trails that wind through a variety of habitats. Guide your pup through the arboretum's prairie on a loop around Meadow Pond. Meander along an elevated boardwalk through the savanna grasses. Take a 1.7-mile woodland hike to reach views of the Buffalo Bayou. The arboretum is open daily from 7:00 am until dusk. Admission is free. When it's time for lunch, head over to the food truck hub in the Eastern Glades area of Memorial Park, which offers relaxing picnic areas next to Hines Lake. After exploring the parks, head to the **Hobbit Café**, where four-legged 'hobbits' and humans alike can enjoy Houston's best patio and original mead bar, and Fido can rest up under the shade of a giant oak tree.

Houston Arboretum & Nature Center
4501 Woodway Drive
Houston, TX 77024
(713) 681-8433
www.bringfido.com/go/1E5J

Where to Stay:

Located just one mile south of the Houston Arboretum's west entrance, the **La Quinta Inn & Suites Houston Galleria** is a comfortable and budget-friendly place to put your paws up for the night. Four-legged guests will enjoy the secluded courtyard area with a walking path and gazebo, while the humans will appreciate the complimentary breakfast and outdoor pool. Up to two dogs of any size are welcome for no additional fee.

La Quinta Inn & Suites Houston Galleria
1625 W Loop South
Houston, TX 77027
(713) 355-3440
www.bringfido.com/go/1E5K
Rates from $69/night

Palo Duro Creek Ranch

Mosey along with Fido to **Palo Duro Creek Ranch**—a working cattle ranch in the Texas Panhandle—where you can tour the nation's second largest canyon. Travel back in time to the fascinating Old West as your guide regales you with vivid history and delightful folklore of the area. Enjoy spectacular views of Palo Duro Canyon as you travel over rugged terrain in a customized Jeep that's well-equipped for the trip. Dogs of any size are allowed on the one- or two-hour tours, which are offered daily. Rates start at $38 per person, and pups ride for free. After your tour, visit the world-famous **Cadillac Ranch**. At this public art installation, Fido can pose for a photo next to 10 graffiti-covered Cadillacs that have been half-buried into the ground. The public is invited to leave their mark on the vehicles, so be sure to bring a can of spray paint.

Palo Duro Creek Ranch
11301 TX-217
Canyon, TX 79015
(806) 488-2100
www.bringfido.com/go/1DZW

Where to Stay:

If you and your canine companion need a nice place to crash after a long day of exploring Palo Duro Canyon State Park, stay in the conveniently located Holiday Inn Express Canyon. Enjoy a clean, comfortable room, complimentary daily breakfast, and evening snacks. The hotel also offers many amenities, including a fitness center, indoor pool, and hot tub. Two dogs of any size are welcome for an additional fee of $25 per pet, per night.

Holiday Inn Express Canyon
2901 4th Avenue
Canyon, TX 79015
(806) 655-4445
www.bringfido.com/go/1DZX
Rates from $95/night

Where to Stay:

Hit the roaring rapids and then go glamping at **Under Canvas Moab**. From March to October, pups can join you beneath the desert skies in a luxury tent outfitted with a wood-burning stove, private bathroom, and hot shower. Nestled in the shadow of the towering redstone plateaus of **Arches National Park**, it's the perfect spot to relax and stargaze in solitude. Up to three dogs of any size are welcome for an additional fee of $25 per pet, per night.

Under Canvas Moab
13784 US-191
Moab, UT 84532
(888) 496-1148
www.bringfido.com/go/1E0G
Rates from $209/night

Moab Rafting & Canoe

Let your dog paddle the Colorado River with **Moab Rafting & Canoe Company**. Whether you and your canine compadre plan to paddle the rapids to the edge of Arches National Park in a single afternoon or set off on a multi-day adventure with overnight camping, the staff at Moab Rafting & Canoe Company will help you design the perfect trip. Choose from a variety of self-guided excursions and outfit your canoe with everything you need for the trip. Camping gear rentals include coolers, sleeping bags, tents, dry bags, water jugs, and more. You can even rent a 'Full Kitchen Box' with everything you'll need to prepare meals along the river (except the food). Overnight trips are suitable for humans with moderate wilderness skills and pups with some camping experience. Rates for self-guided trips vary based on the length of your expedition.

Moab Rafting & Canoe Company
2480 S Highway 191
Moab, UT 84532
(435) 259-7722
www.bringfido.com/go/1E0F

Best Friends Animal Sanctuary

Best Friends Animal Sanctuary, located in Kanab's scenic Angel Canyon, is the largest lifetime care animal sanctuary in the nation. Driving through Angel Canyon, you'll immediately feel the peace and tranquility of a place where so many animals have been loved and healed from their hard journeys in life. Any day of the week you and your well-behaved pooch can take a free 90-minute guided tour of the nonprofit's facilities. In addition to the tour, you and Fido can relax at the wishing garden, visit Angel's Rest, and hike on ancient Indian trails in and around the beautiful scenery at the Sanctuary. Just bring plenty of water and sunscreen. If a 90-minute tour just isn't enough, you can also sign up to volunteer at Best Friends for a day, a weekend, or as long as you'd like. There really is nowhere else like it on earth.

Best Friends Animal Sanctuary
5001 Angel Canyon Road
Kanab, UT 84741
(435) 644-2001
www.bringfido.com/go/1E09

Where to Stay:

Just five miles south of the Best Friends Animal Sanctuary, you'll find the non-profit's newest addition—the **Best Friends Roadhouse & Mercantile**. Designed with furry guests in mind, the property features 40 rooms with some unique pet-centric features like pull-out dog beds and pet cubbies. Other perks include a fenced pet park with splash zone and dog-washing stations. Breakfast is served in the Mercantile building, where you can stock up on pet supplies. A complimentary shuttle to the Sanctuary is also offered. Up to four dogs of any size are welcome for no additional fee.

Best Friends Roadhouse
& Mercantile
30 N 300 W
Kanab, UT 84741
(435) 644-3400
www.bringfido.com/go/1E0A
Rates from $129/night

Where to Stay:

After your four-legged ornithologist puts away his binoculars, drive three miles to the **Best Western Brigham City Inn & Suites** for a restful night's stay. The hotel features modern rooms with separate sitting areas, refrigerators, and complimentary Wi-Fi. You can take a dip in the indoor pool, enjoy a soothing soak in the on-site hot tub, and fill up each morning at the complimentary breakfast buffet. Two dogs up to 80 lbs are welcome for an additional fee of $15 per night.

Best Western Brigham City
Inn & Suites
480 Westland Drive
Brigham City, UT 84302
(435) 723-0440
www.bringfido.com/go/1DQ3
Rates from $80/night

Bear River Migratory Bird Refuge

You and your canine companion can witness all the beauty and wonder nature has to offer at the **Bear River Migratory Bird Refuge**, located just west of Brigham City on the northeastern arm of the Great Salt Lake. Established in 1928, this 74,000-acre National Wildlife Refuge is the permanent and winter home to over 270 species of birds. Pack your camera and take the 12-mile Auto Tour that loops through the refuge's native wetlands to observe and photograph countless feathered friends in their natural habitat, including American White Pelicans, Black-necked Stilts, and Tundra Swans. Although not allowed inside the refuge's Wildlife Education Center, Fido can stretch his legs on the 1.5-mile walking trail located behind the facility. The Auto Tour Loop is open year-round sunrise to sunset, road conditions and weather permitting. There is no admission fee.

Bear River Migratory Bird Refuge
2155 W Forest Street
Brigham City, UT 84302
(435) 723-5887
www.bringfido.com/go/1DQ2

Dreamland Safari Tours

With so many natural wonders in the Kanab area, choosing the best way to spend your time there can be challenging. Let the team at **Dreamland Safari Tours** help you plan the best adventure for you and your pup. The company offers more than 30 different day tour options and can customize a trip that suits your interests. Where else can you hike through a mystical slot canyon, hunt for petroglyphs, and walk in the footsteps of a dinosaur? If you're lucky enough to get your paws on a permit to hike to the famous 'Wave' in the **Paria Canyon Wilderness**, Dreamland Safari Tours can guide you there. If not, your furkids will love playing at **Coral Pink Sand Dunes State Park**. Just be prepared for a bumpy offroad 4x4 adventure through deep sand. Two-hour tours start at $99 for adults and $50 for children. Well-socialized dogs ride for free and are welcome on all excursions except the Toroweap Tour.

Dreamland Safari Tours
4350 E Mountain View Drive
Kanab, UT 84741
(435) 644-5506
www.bringfido.com/go/1E0B

Where to Stay:

Steeped in retro 1960s era charm, the **Quail Park Lodge** in Kanab has the vibe of a traditional roadside motel but offers some upscale amenities you'd only expect in a higher end hotel. All rooms include plush bedding, spa-quality bath products, and pillow-top mattresses with triple-sheeted bedding. Pet blankets are provided, and there is an on-site pet relief area. Up to two dogs of any size are welcome for an additional fee of $10 per pet, per night.

Quail Park Lodge
125 N 300 W (Highway 89)
Kanab, UT 84741
(435) 215-1447
www.bringfido.com/go/1E0C
Rates from $89/night

Mad Tom Orchard

Vermont offers year-round outdoor fun for humans and their furry friends. But Fido's 'pick' for the perfect time to visit is early fall. In addition to being prime leaf peeping season, the months of September and October are great for harvesting some fall favorites. More than 150 varieties of apples are grown in the state, and you can find many of them at **Mad Tom Orchard** in East Dorset. The farm invites you and your pooch to pick apples and then have a picnic with fresh cider and donuts from the farm shop. If you miss apple season, there's still time to pick the perfect fall pumpkin at **Winslow Farms** in Pittsford. After you've scoured the five-acre pumpkin patch, stop by the dairy barn to sample more autumnal treats. The farm also welcomes visitors and their pups to choose and cut their own Christmas tree each holiday season.

Mad Tom Orchard
2615 Mad Tom Road
East Dorset, VT 05253
(802) 366-8107
www.bringfido.com/go/1E7F

Where to Stay:

Unwind from your adventures in one of **The Paw House Inn**'s uniquely furnished, canine-themed rooms. In addition to cozy accommodations, this dog-centric property in West Rutland offers a wide variety of activities to keep you and your pup entertained. Go for a hike through wildflower fields, spend time together picking berries, or let Fido run off leash at the Inn's fully fenced on-site dog park. Up to two dogs of any size are welcome for no additional fee. Add $25 for a third dog.

The Paw House Inn
1376 Clarendon Avenue
West Rutland, VT 05777
(802) 558-2661
www.bringfido.com/go/1E7G
Rates from $225/night

Where to Stay:

After exploring Stowe, you and your pup can unwind at **The Lodge at Spruce Peak**. Located at the base of Mount Mansfield, the alpine-style lodge offers exquisite accommodations with goose-down feather beds, stone fireplaces, and floor-to-ceiling windows in most rooms. Canine guests receive a plush dog bed and chew toy upon arrival. The property's 'Dog Sanctuary' is great for morning walks. Dogs of any size are welcome for an additional fee of $125 per stay.

The Lodge at Spruce Peak
7412 Mountain Road
Stowe, VT 05672
(802) 760-4700
www.bringfido.com/go/1DOP
Rates from $254/night

Gondola SkyRide

Although Stowe is best known for its winter activities, you and Fido will find plenty to do there when it's not snowing. In the spring, catch the **Gondola SkyRide** to access pet-friendly hiking trails and a sweet treat from The Waffle at the summit of Mount Mansfield. Roundtrip tickets are $30 for adults and $21 for kids. **Smugglers' Notch State Park** is the place to enjoy cool air on a hot summer day. After a quick 20-minute hike to Bingham Falls, Fido can wade in the swimming hole at the base of the 25-foot waterfall. Finally, zigzag your way to the top of Vermont's highest mountain on the **Stowe Scenic Auto Road** for a brilliant display of New England's famous fall foliage. For $25 per vehicle and $9 per passenger, you'll get a 360-degree view of the Adirondack Mountains ablaze in hues of red, orange, gold, and yellow. Dogs are welcome for no extra fee.

Gondola SkyRide
7416 Mountain Road
Stowe, VT 05672
(802) 253-3500
www.bringfido.com/go/1DOO

Dog Mountain

Dog lovers come to St. Johnsbury from all around the world to celebrate and remember their beloved furry friends that have crossed over the Rainbow Bridge. Sit on one of the hand-carved pews inside the chapel at **Dog Mountain**, surrounded by photos of passed dogs and handwritten messages their families tacked onto the walls in memoriam. 'You were the best co-pilot, Rocco. I'll always miss you.' Post a message in the Dog Chapel yourself, or hug your canine companion a little tighter and stay awhile. Either way, leave plenty of time to explore the beautiful grounds. Dogs are free to run, play, and swim wherever they'd like in this 150-acre doggy paradise. The only rule is to leave your leash at the door! Dog Mountain was the creation of the late Stephen Huneck, a talented artist whose love for dogs is obvious in his works on display in the on-site gallery.

Dog Mountain
143 Parks Road
St. Johnsbury, VT 05819
(800) 449-2580
www.bringfido.com/go/1E0J

Where to Stay:

Located just 13 miles from Dog Mountain, the **Wildflower Inn** is situated on 570 acres of bucolic Vermont farmland in Lyndonville. After enjoying the innkeepers' signature buttermilk pancakes topped with fresh-from-the-orchard maple syrup, you and your pooch can work off your meal by exploring the vast woods and meadows surrounding the quaint, pet-friendly bed-and-breakfast. Up to two dogs of any size are allowed in Carriage House rooms on the first floor for an additional fee of $100 per pet, per stay.

Wildflower Inn
2059 Darling Hill Road
Lyndonville, VT 05851
(802) 626-8310
www.bringfido.com/go/1E0I
Rates from $215/night

Where to Stay:

Stay in the heart of Williamsburg at **Kingsmill Resort**, situated along the picturesque James River. The golf resort's guest rooms offer plenty of space for your pooch to stretch all four legs. Fido is free to explore the walking trails or join you on the water in a kayak or pontoon boat rental from the resort's marina. Fishing gear is also available. Two dogs up to 75 lbs are welcome for an additional fee of $75 per night.

Kingsmill Resort
1010 Kingsmill Road
Williamsburg, VA 23185
(866) 371-6732
www.bringfido.com/go/1DNP
Rates from $189/night

Colonial Williamsburg

Take Fido on a revolutionary vacation with a visit to **Colonial Williamsburg**. As you explore the nation's largest living history museum, you'll meet dozens of costumed interpreters in period dress. Walk your pooch down the pedestrian-friendly streets lined with nearly 100 original buildings from the 18th century. Although dogs are not allowed to enter the historic buildings, they are welcome throughout the exterior grounds of Colonial Williamsburg. After working up an appetite, grab a bite to eat at **The Cheese Shop** on D.O.G. Street, where your pup can sample some Virginia ham on the outdoor patio. After lunch, make the trip to nearby **Historic Jamestowne**, site of the 1607 James Fort. There, you can witness ongoing excavation work and view artifacts recovered by the Jamestown Rediscovery archaeologists. Tickets are $10 per person, and doggos are free.

Colonial Williamsburg
101 Visitor Center Drive
Williamsburg, VA 23185
(888) 974-7926
www.bringfido.com/go/1DNO

Torpedo Factory Art Center

Unleash your inner artist at the **Torpedo Factory Art Center** in Alexandria. Take a leisurely stroll along the Potomac River waterfront and wander through this hub of artists' studios with your pooch. See the creative process and resulting artistic works of over 165 vendors in the open studio space. Purchase an original work of art, chat with your favorite artist about their methods and inspiration, or sign up for a class at The Art League School. Ten galleries offer exhibition space for photography, fiber arts, enamel work, pottery and ceramic art. Leashed dogs are always welcome, and there is no admission fee. Guided tours are available upon request. The Torpedo Factory is located next to Alexandria's City Marina, where the Potomac River boat Company embarks on a 'Canine Cruise' several times a year. The 45-minute cruise costs $30 for adults and $15 for children. Dogs float for free.

Torpedo Factory Art Center
105 N Union Street
Alexandria, VA 22314
(703) 746-4570
www.bringfido.com/go/1DNE

Where to Stay:

Located on buzzing King Street, **The Alexandrian** is a perfect spot to relax and unwind after a day of sightseeing. This historic property features a dog-friendly interior courtyard where you can enjoy a glass of wine while your pup munches on a treat from nearby boutique pet store **The Dog Park**. The hotel offers a 24-hour fitness center for the humans, as well as complimentary bike rentals. Up to two dogs of any size are welcome for an additional fee of $25 per stay.

The Alexandrian
480 King Street
Alexandria, VA 22314
(703) 549-6080
www.bringfido.com/go/1DNF
Rates from $97/night

Where to Stay:

You and your four-legged friend can look forward to incredible waterfront vistas and spectacular sunsets during your stay at **Snug Harbor Marina** on Chincoteague Island. Relax in the beach chairs outside your cottage, plan a family cookout, or take Fido for a stroll down to the beachfront Tiki Bar. You can even rent a skiff or pontoon boat to explore more of the island together. Dogs of any size are welcome for an additional fee of $40 per pet, per night.

Snug Harbor Marina & Resort
7536 East Side Road
Chincoteague, VA 23336
(757) 336-6176
www.bringfido.com/go/1DUE
Rates from $149/night

Assateague Explorer

You and your pup can discover hidden Assateague on a Pony Express Nature Cruise with **Assateague Explorer**. Departing from the Assateague Nature Centre on Chincoteague Island, Captain Mark will welcome you aboard the *Misty* and take you on a two-hour boat tour offering a glimpse of Virginia's wild pony population. Along the way, you'll also have the chance to see dolphins, bald eagles, and other wildlife. Want to really immerse yourself in this wonderful ecosystem? Bring your pup's life jacket and opt for the three-hour guided kayak tour to get eye to eye with even more of the animals inhabiting these beautiful islands. Tours depart several times a day, but advance reservations are recommended. Tickets are $47 for the boat tour and $62 for the kayak tour. Dogs can join either excursion for no additional fee.

Assateague Explorer
Curtis Merritt Harbor
2246 Curtis Merritt Harbor Drive
Chincoteague, VA 23336
(757) 336-5956
www.bringfido.com/go/1DUD

Virginia Wine Country

Spend a weekend exploring some of Virginia's finest and most dog-friendly wineries with a trio of stops in Delaplane. Begin your tour at **Barrel Oak Winery & Farm Taphouse**. Reserve a hillside picnic table, play Frisbee with Fido, and schedule a tasting to sample their delicious 'Chocolate Lab' dessert wine. Outside seating with wine bottle service is available daily. Next, head over to **Three Fox Vineyards**. Find a cozy spot on the heated patio or at a creekside picnic table to enjoy the winery's offerings. Your pooch might even be crowned 'Dog of the Month' and have his picture featured on the winery's website. Finally, make your way to **Aspen Dale Winery at the Barn** to savor food pairings with a wine flight. Dogs are welcome inside the tasting room located in a converted 200-year-old barn. Explore the 50-acre property with your pup and meet the resident miniature horses, thoroughbreds, and goats.

Barrel Oak Winery & Farm Taphouse
3623 Grove Lane
Delaplane, VA 20144
(540) 364-6402
www.bringfido.com/go/1E7I

Where to Stay:

Salamander Resort & Spa in Middleburg is the perfect place to kick up your paws after a day of wine tasting in the foothills of the Blue Ridge Mountains. You and your pup will enjoy exploring this beautiful 340-acre country estate. Dog-friendly rooms are located on the terrace level for easy access to the grounds, and all furry guests receive a pet amenity kit at check-in. Up to two dogs of any size are welcome for an additional fee of $130 per stay.

Salamander Resort & Spa
500 N Pendleton Street
Middleburg, VA 20117
(540) 751-3160
www.bringfido.com/go/1E7J
Rates from $495/night

Skyline Drive

Spanning the entire length of **Shenandoah National Park** from Front Royal to Waynesboro, the 105-mile **Skyline Drive National Scenic Byway** will give your dog a bird's-eye view of the Blue Ridge Mountains in Virginia. The picturesque three-hour drive is wildly popular in the fall when the leaves are changing colors, but roadside rhododendron, trillium, azaleas, and buttercups put on a cheerful show throughout the year. Stop along the way at one of 75 scenic overlooks. Most have trailheads that will provide a relatively easy hiking break for your four-legged friend. Of the 500 miles of trails in Shenandoah National Park, all but 20 miles are dog friendly. The entrance fee is $30 per vehicle. Dog paddling is also an option with **Downriver Canoe Company**, which allows dogs of any size on their paddling, hiking, and camping outings in the park. Short trips start at $54 per canoe.

Skyline Drive
US 340 & Skyline Drive
Front Royal, VA 22630
(540) 999-3500
www.bringfido.com/go/1DNI

Where to Stay:

For a true cabin-in-the-woods getaway with sweeping views and unparalleled serenity, Shenandoah National Park offers a trio of pet-friendly properties: **Big Meadows Lodge, Skyland,** and **Lewis Mountain Cabins**. Guests with pets can choose to 'ruff it' in a rustic cabin at Lewis Mountain or opt for a modern suite at Big Meadows Lodge and Skyland. All three locations operate from April to November and allow two dogs of any size for an additional fee of $30 per pet, per night.

Big Meadows Lodge
Shenandoah National Park
Mile 51.2 Skyline Drive
Luray, VA 22851
(877) 847-1919
www.bringfido.com/go/1DNJ
Rates from $80/night

Where to Stay:

Make the short drive north from Mount Vernon to the **Kimpton Lorien Hotel & Spa**. Located in the heart of Old Town Alexandria, this elegant property prides itself on pampering guests of both the two- and four-legged variety. Your pup will be provided a plush dog bed, food and water bowls, and mats for use during his visit. Relax alongside Fido with a glass of Chardonnay at the nightly hosted wine hour. Dogs of any size are welcome for no additional fee.

Kimpton Lorien Hotel & Spa
1600 King Street
Alexandria, VA 22314
(703) 894-3434
www.bringfido.com/go/1DUG
Rates from $239/night

Mount Vernon

During George Washington's lifetime, many beloved dogs lived with him and Martha at **Mount Vernon** in Alexandria. While your pooch is not able to venture inside the historic mansion today, there is still plenty to keep both of you busy on this 50-acre estate. Spend time in the gardens, visit George Washington's tomb, and enjoy breathtaking views of the Potomac River from the piazza. On select Saturdays in the spring and fall, bring your dog for the All the President's Pups Tour. This 1.25-mile walking tour explores canine life at the estate. Along the way, learn about George Washington's love for man's best friend and his efforts to improve the quality of his hunting dogs through breeding. Admission to Mount Vernon is $21 for adults and $10 for children. Add $10 for the walking tour. Dogs are welcome for no additional fee but must remain leashed at all times.

Mount Vernon
3200 Mount Vernon Memorial Highway
Alexandria, VA 22121
(703) 780-2000
www.bringfido.com/go/1DUF

Discovery Trail

Make the trek to the Long Beach Peninsula for some fun in the sand and surf on over 28 miles of uninterrupted beach. Spend a day walking Fido in the footsteps of Lewis and Clark on the 8.5-mile **Discovery Trail**, a paved oceanfront pathway stretching from North Long Beach to Ilwaco. If you're there during winter, bring your binoculars for some great whale watching opportunities. The North Head Lighthouse at **Cape Disappointment State Park** is the area's best viewing spot. With over 6.5 miles of hiking trails and a popular dog beach, the park is a great place to play fetch with your furry friend. Day passes cost $10 per vehicle, and the park is open daily from 6:30 am to dusk. After working up an appetite, drop by **The Cove Restaurant** for lunch or dinner. The Patio Pup menu offers tasty morsels such as crumbled beef patties and salmon filet.

Discovery Trail
210 26th Street NW
Long Beach, WA 98631
(360) 642-2400
www.bringfido.com/go/1E0W

Where to Stay:

Extend your trip to Long Beach with a stay at the **Lighthouse Oceanfront Resort**. The property's one-, two-, and three-bedroom townhouses are just steps from the pet-friendly beach. All units feature separate living areas, full kitchens, fireplaces, and private balconies. On-site amenities include an indoor pool, hot tub, fitness center, grill stations, and indoor tennis courts. Treats and pet towels are available in the lobby. Dogs of any size are welcome for an additional fee of $15 per pet, per night.

Lighthouse Oceanfront Resort
12417 Pacific Way
Long Beach, WA 98631
(360) 642-3622
www.bringfido.com/go/1E0X
Rates from $92/night

Where to Stay:

If one day on Friday Harbor isn't enough, spend the night at **Earthbox Inn & Spa**. Located just four blocks from the Friday Harbor Ferry Landing, the property offers clean, modern accommodations in an ideal location. Enjoy complimentary use of the hotel's beach cruiser bikes to explore the charming island, schedule a hot beach stone massage, or relax in the heated indoor pool. Two dogs up to 75 lbs are welcome for an additional fee of $25 per pet, per night.

Earthbox Inn & Spa
410 Spring Street
Friday Harbor, WA 98250
(360) 378-4000
www.bringfido.com/go/1E0L
Rates from $147/night

San Juan Island

Hop on board a **Washington State Ferry** in Anacortes for a trip to San Juan Island. When you arrive at Friday Harbor, ditch the car in favor of a 'Scoot Coupe' from **Susie's Mopeds**, which will serve as your transportation for the day. Two miles away, you'll find **Jackson Beach**, where your dog will enjoy running in the sand. Continue on to **San Juan Island National Historical Park** to learn about the history of the island and the Pig War. Make a pit stop at **Pelindaba Lavender Farm** to let Fido roam the purple fields and try a lavender-flavored dog biscuit. Lastly, head over to **Lime Kiln Point State Park**—a 36-acre park where whales are commonly spotted between May and September. When you complete your loop around the island, refuel with 'Your New Favorite Turkey Sandwich' from **The Market Chef**. There'll be enough to share with your hungry hound!

Washington State Ferry
2100 Ferry Terminal Road
Anacortes, WA 98221
(206) 464-6400
www.bringfido.com/go/1E0K

Warehouse Wine District

With more than 100 wineries and tasting rooms that showcase the fine wines produced in Washington's Columbia Valley, the town of Woodinville is a must-visit for dog-loving vinophiles! Though you won't find any picturesque vineyards near the **Warehouse Wine District**, this industrial area of town has the largest concentration of tasting rooms in the state. Most are open on weekends from noon to 5:00 pm, but plan ahead to guarantee a tasting reservation. Enjoy a rich Tempranillo while Fido gets ear scratches at **J&A's Winery**, or sip on a seasonal Rosé as you and your pup enjoy the seven-acre private arboretum and walking trails at **JM Cellars**. Your furry companion is also welcome to join you at the 'Wine Walk' events held throughout the year when the vitners roll up their bay doors for an evening of small-batch wine tastings. Event schedules and admission prices vary, but dogs are always free.

Warehouse Wine District
14700 148th Avenue NE
Woodinville, WA 98072
(425) 287-6820
www.bringfido.com/go/1DNS

Where to Stay:

Foodies and vinophiles will love spending a relaxing weekend at the **Willows Lodge**. Located a stone's throw from some of Washington's finest vineyards, this luxurious Woodinville hotel also features world-class fine dining. In the morning, you'll see chefs from the Barking Frog restaurant harvesting ingredients from the herb garden for their evening tasting menu. Two dogs of any size are welcome for an additional fee of $75 per stay.

Willows Lodge
14580 NE 145th Street
Woodinville, WA 98072
(425) 424-3900
www.bringfido.com/go/1DNT
Rates from $224/night

Iron Springs Resort

One of the lasting traditions at **Iron Springs Resort** in Copalis Beach is digging for razor clams with the family. Located in one of the best clam-digging areas along the Washington Coast, the resort offers easy access to these tasty bivalves in the fall, winter, and early spring. All you need is a clamming shovel, container, and clamming license for each digger over the age of 15. Pick up all three at the resort's General Store, and let Fido help dig up your quota of these delicious shellfish at the beach. When your buckets are full, the resort's cleaning station and beachside fire pits make it easy to prepare your family's evening clambake. The following day, Fido can paddle through a 'Ghost Forest' at **Griffiths-Priday State Park** in Ocean Shores, or venture a bit farther to see some of the world's largest trees—topping 300 feet—in the **Quinault Rain Forest**.

Iron Springs Resort
3707 Highway 109
Copalis Beach, WA 98535
(360) 276-4230
www.bringfido.com/go/1E0S

Where to Stay:

Your overnight stay at **Iron Springs Resort** includes a well-appointed cabin, complete with a kitchen, fireplace or wood-burning stove, grill, deck, and wireless internet. Your pup will receive a tennis ball and special treat at check-in before having his picture snapped for the doggy display in the General Store. Dog bowls, towels, and a washing station are available in each cabin. Up to three dogs of any size are welcome for an additional fee of $20 per pet, per night.

Iron Springs Resort
3707 Highway 109
Copalis Beach, WA 98536
(360) 276-4230
www.bringfido.com/go/1E0T
Rates from $189/night

Where to Stay:

When your four-legged rustler is finished herding sheep, head to the **Prairie Hotel** in nearby Yelm to get a night's worth of shut-eye. Sleep in a comfy dog-friendly room equipped with complimentary Wi-Fi. You can also load up on sweet and savory snacks in the lobby market. The large grassy yard surrounding the property is ideal for walking Fido. Up to two dogs of any size are welcome for an additional fee of $15 per pet, per night.

Prairie Hotel
701 Prairie Park Lane SE
Yelm, WA 98597
(360) 458-8300
www.bringfido.com/go/1DQC
Rates from $120/night

Ewe-topia Herd Dog Training

Your dog will think he's died and gone to heaven at **Ewe-topia Herd Dog Training** in Roy. Located near Seattle, Ewe-topia allows dogs of all shapes and sizes to try their paws at sheep herding. The owners, Joe and Linda, are animal behavior experts who can quickly assess your pooch's temperament and match him up to the appropriate livestock—typically three sheep or five ducks. When Fido steps into the ring for the first time, he'll have the time of his life chasing the furry or feathered animals around the ring. But this challenging exercise actually provides an important lesson in socialization as well. You may even notice a difference in your dog's manners after the first visit! All lessons are by appointment only and must be booked by phone. The price is $17 per session. All students are required to bring a collar and leash and dress in weather-appropriate clothing.

Ewe-topia Herd Dog Training
6311 288th Street S
Roy, WA 98580
(253) 843-2929
www.bringfido.com/go/1DQB

Methow Trails

If you and your pup are avid outdoor adventurers, you will love a trip to **Methow Trails** near Winthrop at any time of year. In spring, summer and fall, you can hike the trail system for breathtaking scenery, bird-watching, and wildlife viewing. But the real fun starts with the winter's first snow! Fido is welcome to join you off leash as you explore 25 miles of superb Nordic ski trails, including Gunn Ranch Trailhead, Cub Creek Trailhead, Winthrop Fish Hatchery, Lunachik, and Big Valley. Practice your skills to prepare for the 'Doggie Dash' event held every February, where dogs and their humans ski a short loop together in costume. Come to the trails for a day, or stay overnight in one of three dog-friendly **Rendezvous Huts**. All Rendezvous ski trails require the purchase of a day use pass at the Methow Trails office. Passes cost $25 for adults and $10 for dogs.

Methow Trails
309 Riverside Avenue
Winthrop, WA 98862
(509) 996-3287
www.bringfido.com/go/1E15

Where to Stay:

After a full day of cross-country skiing, Fido can relax in one of three dog-friendly **Rendezvous Huts**. Located along the groomed trails, these huts offer ski-in, ski-out access along with full kitchens, cooking utensils, wood stove heaters, sleeping pads, propane lights, and outhouses. Freight haulers will supply your hut with personal items for an additional $95 fee. Each hut can accommodate up to eight people. Dogs get their own bed and are welcome for no extra fee.

Rendezvous Huts
Cub Creek Road
Winthrop, WA 98862
(509) 996-8100
www.bringfido.com/go/1E17
Rates from $175/night

Where to Stay:

Your well-traveled pooch will be a VIP guest at the **Ace Hotel Seattle**, a trendy crash pad located in the heart of the Belltown District. Once a hotel for maritime workers, this minimalist property features loft-style rooms adorned with local artwork. Before settling in for the night, explore the neighborhood with your pup on an evening walk to nearby **Olympic Sculpture Park**. The hotel welcomes up to two dogs of any size for no additional fee.

Ace Hotel Seattle
2423 1st Avenue
Seattle, WA 98121
(206) 448-4721
www.bringfido.com/go/1E10
Rates from $79/night

Kenmore Air

For a bird's-eye view of the Emerald City, take a 'Seattle Scenic Seaplane Tour' with **Kenmore Air**. You and your furry flying ace will enjoy stunning views of the Seattle skyline, Elliot Bay, and Lake Union on this 20-minute flightseeing adventure. Tours are offered several times daily (Thursday to Monday) and start at $99 per person. Lap dogs are welcome for no additional fee, but a seat must be purchased for dogs over 25 lbs. Advance reservations are required. If your pup prefers boats over floatplanes, you can take a self-guided tour of Lake Union in a classic wooden row boat rental from the **Center for Wooden Boats**. Rates vary depending on the equipment rented. Hours of operation are Wednesday through Sunday from 10:00 am to 4:00 pm. For a sweet treat after rowing, hop on board the **Seattle Ferry Service**'s 45-minute 'Sunday Ice Cream Cruise.' Tickets are $12 for adults, $8 for children, and free for dogs.

Kenmore Air
950 Westlake Avenue N
Seattle, WA 98109
(866) 435-9524
www.bringfido.com/go/1E13

Discovery Bay Golf Club

Play a round of golf with your pup at the dog-friendly **Discovery Bay Golf Club** in Port Townsend. Located on the shores of beautiful Discovery Bay, this 18-hole marvel is Washington's oldest public golf course. Tee off and enjoy the day in the company of your furry friend surrounded by magnificent views of the Olympic and Cascade mountain ranges. Just make sure your well-mannered pooch stays on a leash. Green fees for 18 holes are $38 for adults and $12 for children. Twilight rates are also available. After your round, make your way to the **Port Ludlow Inn** for a delicious farm-to-table meal on the pet-friendly verandah of The Fireside Restaurant. Stretch your legs on one of the resort's pet-friendly hiking trails or rent a kayak or paddleboard for a day on the water. Dogs must be leashed at all times when exploring the resort's outdoor areas.

Discovery Bay Golf Club
7401 Cape George Road
Port Townsend, WA 98368
(360) 385-0704
www.bringfido.com/go/1DQD

Where to Stay:

Port Ludlow Inn is a boutique waterfront inn with 37 rooms and suites overlooking pictur-esque Ludlow Bay. The inn's staff members love dogs, and Fido is sure to be greeted with a warm welcome (and locally-made biscuit) at check-in. Guests with pets are provided a map of recommended hiking trails in the area. Other amenities include a dog-friendly beach, restaurant, and marina located on the prem-ises. Up to two dogs of any size are welcome for an additional fee of $50 per stay. Add $30 for a third pet.

Port Ludlow Inn
1 Heron Road
Port Ludlow, WA 98365
(360) 437-7000
www.bringfido.com/go/1DQE
Rates from $179/night

Trans-Allegheny Lunatic Asylum

You'll be glad to have Fido by your side as you take a spine-chilling tour of the historic **Trans-Allegheny Lunatic Asylum** in Weston. A working facility from 1864 to 1994, the asylum was intended as a sanctuary for those suffering from mental illness. However, ever-changing definitions of 'humane treatment' led to a number of experimental procedures being performed here over the years. A costumed guide will tell you all about them as she escorts your group around the expansive building. Your well-behaved, leashed pooch is welcome to join you on the daytime History & Heritage Tour. The asylum is open annually from late March to early November. Tours are offered several times daily (except Mondays). Rates start at $10 per person for first floor tours. If you want to view all four floors, the admission fee is $30 per person. Dogs visit for free.

Trans-Allegheny Lunatic Asylum
71 Asylum Drive
Weston, WV 26452
(304) 269-5070
www.bringfido.com/go/1DNW

Where to Stay:

Located on the shores of Stonewall Jackson Lake, **Stonewall Resort** is a charming Adirondack-style lodge in Roanoke. Enjoy spectacular lake, mountain, or golf course views as you relax in your oversized room, or head outdoors to explore 1,900 acres of woodlands with your pooch. The surrounding state park has 16 miles of dog-friendly hiking trails, and kayak rentals are only $15 per day. Up to two dogs of any size are welcome for an additional fee of $25 per pet, per night.

Stonewall Resort
940 Resort Drive
Roanoke, WV 26447
(304) 269-7400
www.bringfido.com/go/1DNX
Rates from $89/night

Where to Stay:

Located just a few blocks from the ferry, **The Blennerhassett Hotel** is your home for the night. This Gaslight Era hotel greets Fido with complimentary dog treats in the lobby, as well as food bowls and waste bags. One dog of any size is welcome for an additional fee of $50 per stay. Add $25 for a second pet. After getting settled in your room, explore charming downtown Parkersburg and stop for dinner at the dog-friendly **Parkersburg Brewing Co.**

The Blennerhassett Hotel
320 Market Street
Parkersburg, WV 26101
(304) 422-3131
www.bringfido.com/go/1E19
Rates from $96/night

Blennerhassett Island

Escape to **Blennerhassett Island State Park** for a special day out with your pup. Located in the middle of the Ohio River on the border between West Virginia and Ohio, the park is home to numerous trails, manicured grounds, and a reconstructed Palladian mansion that offers visitors a historical glimpse at colonial plantation life. To reach the island, head to Point Park in downtown Parkersburg and climb aboard the *Island Belle* sternwheeler for a short 20-minute riverboat journey. Upon arrival, stretch Fido's legs on a self-guided walking tour. Along the way, you will see volunteers in period costume, as well as horse-drawn covered wagons carting visitors around the island. The park is open from early May through mid-November, with ferry service offered daily (except Mondays). Admission includes transportation and is $12 for adults, $8 for children, and free for dogs.

Blennerhassett Island State Park
137 Juliana Street
Parkersburg, WV 26101
(304) 420-4800
www.bringfido.com/go/1E18

Northern Sky Theater

Door County's **Northern Sky Theater** brings original musical theater to the dogs! All summer long, the professional nonprofit theater company performs a variety of Wisconsin-centric, family-friendly musicals in the outdoor amphitheater at Peninsula State Park in Fish Creek. Your pup is welcome to take in one of the shows, which are offered nightly (except Sundays) from mid-June through August. Dogs aren't allowed to sing along with the show, so guests with pets are simply asked to find a spot for Spot at the back of the amphitheater (in case you need to make a quick exit). Bring a picnic to enjoy during the show, or purchase snacks and beverages at the concession stand. Average temperatures can dip into the 50s at night, so wear layers and bring a blanket for your pooch. Ticket prices are $30 for adults, $15 for children, and free for dogs.

Northern Sky Theater
Peninsula State Park
10169 Shore Road
Fish Creek, WI 54212
(920) 854-6117
www.bringfido.com/go/1DNY

Where to Stay:

Located just a short drive from Peninsula State Park, the **Edgewater Resort** is nestled on a private shoreline overlooking Wisconsin's beautiful Eagle Harbor in Ephraim. Choose a one- or two-bedroom cottage with a kitchenette, gas fireplace, and private entry for a cozy and relaxing stay. Dogs of any size are welcome for an additional fee of $25 per pet, per night. When the sun goes down, bring Fido to the nightly 'Fish Boil' (reservations required) at the resort's **Old Post Office Restaurant**.

Edgewater Resort
10040 Water Street
Ephraim, WI 54211
(920) 854-2734
www.bringfido.com/go/1DNZ
Rates from $110/night

Where to Stay:

Motorcycle enthusiasts will be in hog heaven at **The Iron Horse Hotel**, a boutique property geared toward bikers and their furry friends. Guests arriving in Milwaukee on two wheels will appreciate the covered motorcycle parking, self-service bike wash, and industrial loft-style guest rooms designed with boot benches and custom hooks for hanging leathers. Up to two dogs of any size are welcome for an additional fee of $100 per stay.

The Iron Horse Hotel
500 W Florida Street
Milwaukee, WI 53204
(414) 374-4766
www.bringfido.com/go/1DQG
Rates from $188/night

Milwaukee Boat Line

The **Milwaukee Boat Line** invites canines to join its crew for a 90-minute cruise down the Milwaukee River to Lake Michigan. Departing from the **Milwaukee RiverWalk** in the historic Third Ward district, the company's popular sightseeing tour combines history and trivia with gorgeous views of the city. Live narration is provided by entertaining tour guides and the captain. Snacks, soft drinks, beer, and cocktails are available for purchase on board. Tours are offered several times a day from early May through the end of September. There's also a 'Happy Hour' cruise at sundown with lively music and drink specials on the menu. Prices start at $20 for adults and $10 for children. Well-behaved dogs are welcome aboard for no additional fee. After the tour, take a leisurely stroll along the scenic three-mile RiverWalk or head straight to **Estabrook Beer Garden** to enjoy a beer and bratwurst with your pooch.

Milwaukee Boat Line
101 W Michigan Street
Milwaukee, WI 53203
(414) 294-9450
www.bringfido.com/go/1DQF

Dells Boat Tours

Shaped by an ancient glacier, the Wisconsin Dells is a five-mile-long gorge on the Wisconsin River with incredible sandstone cliffs towering as high as 100 feet in the air. These magnificent rock formations are best seen from the water on a two-hour scenic river cruise with **Dells Boat Tours**. The company offers tours of both the Upper and Lower Dells, but dog lovers should definitely choose the Upper Dells Boat Tour. Fido will have a chance to stretch his legs at the mysterious Witches Gulch and witness a specially trained dog leap over a five-foot chasm between two cliffs at Stand Rock. The demonstration is a tribute to the world's first stop-action photo taken by famous Dells photographer H.H. Bennett in 1888. Tickets are $32 for adults and $16 for children. Dogs of all sizes ride for free, provided there is room on the boat. Tours depart several times daily from April through October.

Dells Boat Tours
107 Broadway
Wisconsin Dells, WI 53965
(608) 254-8555
www.bringfido.com/go/1E1B

Where to Stay:

After watching a fellow dog leap through the air at Standing Rock, Fido will be glad to have all four paws on the ground at **Baker's Sunset Bay Resort** in Wisconsin Dells. Treats are provided at check-in at this family-friendly resort on Lake Delton, which features a sandy beach, indoor and outdoor pools, and a nightly bonfire. Rowboats and kayaks are available free of charge. Up to two dogs of any size are welcome for an additional fee of $15 per pet, per night.

Baker's Sunset Bay Resort
921 Canyon Road
Wisconsin Dells, WI 53965
(608) 254-8406
www.bringfido.com/go/1E1C
Rates from $88/night

Where to Stay:

With accommodations ranging from primitive campsites to deluxe cabins with full kitchens, **Justin Trails Resort** offers a lodging option for everyone's budget. Rates include most on-site activities and a hearty four-course breakfast featuring organic eggs, pancakes, and Donna's famous homemade granola. Pups are free to explore the resort's fields and forests off leash, but they must be leashed around the main lodge and cabins. Dogs of any size are welcome for an additional fee of $39 per pet, per night.

Justin Trails Resort
7452 Kathryn Avenue
Sparta, WI 54656
(608) 269-4522
www.bringfido.com/go/1DUA
Rates from $149/night

Justin Trails Resort

With over 200 acres of open fields and forests, your pooch will have plenty of space for off-leash frolicking at the **Justin Trails Resort** in Sparta. Fido can fetch Frisbees on one of the two 18-basket championship disc golf courses or go for a hike on the property's 10-mile trail system with resident Siberian husky, Heidi. In the winter, the same trails can be enjoyed on a snow tubing, snowshoeing, or skijoring adventure. Not sure how to skijor? The owners, Don and Donna Justin, can give your dog a private lesson. In less than an hour, he'll be pulling you along the 3/4-mile groomed 'Dog Loop' on skis! Sparta is also home to the nation's first Rails-to-Trails bicycle path. To ride the 32-mile **Elroy-Sparta State Trail** with your pup, rent a bike and dog cart from the **Tunnel Trail Campground** for $20 per day. A $5 trail pass is also required for all bikers over 16 years old.

Justin Trails Resort
7452 Kathryn Avenue
Sparta, WI 54656
(608) 269-4522
www.bringfido.com/go/1DU9

Cody Wyoming Adventures

Begin your exploration of America's Wild West with **Cody Wyoming Adventures**. On the company's Red Canyon Wild Mustang Tour, you and your pup can venture deep into the McCullough Peaks area to see wild mustangs run free. Keep your eyes open for free-ranging prairie dogs, antelope, and the occasional coyote. These 2.5-hour guided bus trips are $40 per adult and $38 per child. Dogs are welcome to join for free but must be approved in advance. After returning to Cody, continue your sightseeing with **Cody Trolley Tours**, where Fido can accompany you on a 60-minute, 22-mile loop around Buffalo Bill's namesake town. Tours cost $27 for adults and $15 for children. Dogs ride for free. Top off your day in the Rodeo Capital of the World by sharing a prime rib with your pup at **Buffalo Bill's Restaurant & Saloon**, located at the famous Irma Hotel, built by Buffalo Bill in 1902.

Cody Wyoming Adventures
1119 12th Street
Cody, WY 82414
(307) 587-6988
www.bringfido.com/go/1E1D

Where to Stay:

Following a full day of activities in cowboy country, **The Cody** is a great place to unwind. The hotel's friendly staff will welcome both you and Fido with cookies upon arrival. Enjoy them by the fireplace, or retreat to the jetted tub in your guest room. Want s'more? You'll find marshmallows, chocolate bars, and graham crackers outside by the fire pit too! Up to two dogs of any size are welcome in the hotel's ground floor rooms for no additional fee.

The Cody Hotel
232 W Yellowstone Avenue
Cody, WY 82414
(307) 587-5915
www.bringfido.com/go/1E1E
Rates from $120/night

Black Dog Raft Company

Explore the winding Snake River on a rafting trip with **Black Dog Raft Company**. Dogs are welcome to join their owners on a 13-mile scenic float where you'll likely spot bald eagles and osprey, as well as otters, beavers, deer, elk, and moose. Let your guide work the oars while you and your pup relax and take in the views of the snow-capped Teton Mountain Range. Trips depart three times daily between May and September, and rates start at $300 for two adults and a dog. If you are visiting Jackson in the winter, stop by the **National Elk Refuge**. From mid-December through early April, you and your pooch can spot a herd of elk grazing their winter habitat. Wrap up your exciting day with a walk around Jackson Square Park for photos in front of the famous antler arches before grabbing dinner at **Cafe Genevieve**, a Jackson Hole favorite of dogs and humans alike.

Black Dog Raft Company
529 No Name Alley
Jackson, WY 83001
(307) 699-4110
www.bringfido.com/go/1E1H

Where to Stay:

After an adventurous day in Jackson, saddle up and ride over to **Cowboy Village Resort** to rest up. This authentic log cabin property is located in downtown Jackson and close to many pet-friendly shops and restaurants. You and your pup will feel right at home with a kitchenette in each room and free Wi-Fi to keep you connected. Guests also have access to an on-site indoor pool and fitness center. Two dogs of any size are welcome for no additional fee.

Cowboy Village Resort
120 S Flatcreek Drive
Jackson, WY 83001
(307) 733-3121
www.bringfido.com/go/1E1I
Rates from $99/night

DIRECTORY

ALABAMA
ATTRACTIONS

Audubon Bird Sanctuary
211 Bienville Boulevard
Dauphin Island, AL 36528
(251) 861-3607
www.bringfido.com/go/1DIM
pg. 8

Dauphin Island Beach
1501 Bienville Boulevard
Dauphin Island, AL 36528
(251) 861-3607
www.bringfido.com/go/1DIO
pg. 8

The Flying Harpoon
112 Windmill Ridge Road
Gulf Shores, AL 36542
(251) 948-4645
www.bringfido.com/go/1DSC
pg. 62

Fort Gaines
51 Bienville Boulevard
Dauphin Island, AL 36528
(251) 861-6992
www.bringfido.com/go/1DIN
pg. 8

International Motorsports Hall of Fame
3198 Speedway Boulevard
Lincoln, AL 35096
(256) 362-5002
www.bringfido.com/go/1DQS
pg. 9

Islander's Restaurant
1504 Bienville Boulevard
Dauphin Island, AL 36528
(251) 861-2225
www.bringfido.com/go/1DIP
pg. 8

HOTELS

Best Western Plus Bass Hotel & Suites
1949 Village Drive
Leeds, AL 35094
(205) 640-5300
www.bringfido.com/go/1DQT
pg. 9

Dauphin Island Harbor House
730 Cadillac Avenue
Dauphin Island, AL 36528
(251) 861-2119
www.bringfido.com/go/1DIY
pg. 8

Staybridge Suites Gulf Shores
3947 Gulf Shores Parkway
Gulf Shores, AL 36542
(251) 975-1030
www.bringfido.com/go/1DSA
pg. 62

ALASKA
ATTRACTIONS

Alaska Railroad
411 W 1st Avenue
Anchorage, AK, 99501
(800) 544-0552
www.bringfido.com/go/1DIK
pg. 11

Chugach Adventures
1553 Alyeska Highway
Girdwood, AK 99587
(907) 783-1860
www.bringfido.com/go/1DII
pg. 11

North Pole
125 Snowman Lane
North Pole, AK 99705
(907) 488-2281
www.bringfido.com/go/1DFZ
pg.12

North Pole Dog Park
159 E 3rd Avenue
North Pole, AK 99705
(907) 388-7002
www.bringfido.com/go/1DG2
pg. 12

Winner Creek Trail
601 Crow Creek Road
Girdwood, AK 99587
(907) 277-4321
www.bringfido.com/go/1DIL
pg. 11

HOTELS

Hotel North Pole
449 N Santa Claus Lane
North Pole, AK 99705
(907) 488-4800
www.bringfido.com/go/1DFQ
pg. 12

Ski Inn
189 Hightower Road
Girdwood, AK 99587
(907) 783-0002
www.bringfido.com/go/1DIJ
pg. 11

ARIZONA
ATTRACTIONS

A Day in the West
2900 W State Route 89A
Sedona, AZ 86336
(928) 282-4320
www.bringfido.com/go/1DFS
pg. 13

Butterfield Stage Coach
326 E Allen Street
Tombstone, AZ 85638
(520) 457-9317
www.bringfido.com/go/1DIS
pg. 16

Creekside American Bistro
251 AZ-179
Sedona, AZ 86336
(928) 282-1705
www.bringfido.com/go/1E3N
pg. 13

Glen Canyon National Recreation Area
691 Scenic View Road
Page, AZ 86040
(928) 608-6200
www.bringfido.com/go/1DIV
pg. 14

Good Enough Mine Tour
501 E Toughnut Street
Tombstone, AZ 85638
(520) 255-1353
www.bringfido.com/go/1DIQ
pg. 16

Good Enough Trolley
501 E Toughnut Street
Tombstone, AZ 85638
(520) 255 5553
www.bringfido.com/go/1E5G
pg. 16

Pima Air & Space Museum
6000 E Valencia Road
Tucson, AZ 85756
(520) 574-0462
www.bringfido.com/go/1DIG
pg. 15

Tombstone After Dark
501 E Toughnut Street
Tombstone, AZ 85638
(520) 255-5553
www.bringfido.com/go/1E5H
pg. 16

T. Miller's Tombstone Mercantile
530 E Allen Street
Tombstone, AZ 85638
(520) 457-2405
www.bringfido.com/go/1E3O
pg. 16

Wahweap Marina
100 Lake Shore Drive
Page, AZ 86040
(928) 645-2433
www.bringfido.com/go/1DIT
pg. 14

HOTELS

El Portal Sedona
95 Portal Lane
Sedona, AZ 86336
(800) 313-0017
www.bringfido.com/go/1DFT
pg. 13

Katie's Cozy Cabins
16 W Allen Street
Tombstone, AZ 85638
(520) 559-0464
www.bringfido.com/go/1DIR
pg. 16

Lake Powell Resort
100 Lake Shore Drive
Page, AZ 86040
(928) 645-2433
www.bringfido.com/go/1DIU
pg. 14

Loews Ventana Canyon Resort
7000 N Resort Drive
Tucson, AZ 85750
(520) 299-2020
www.bringfido.com/go/1DIH
pg. 15

ARKANSAS

ATTRACTIONS

Belle of Hot Springs Riverboat
5200 Central Avenue
Hot Springs, AR 71913
(501) 525-4438
www.bringfido.com/go/1E3P
pg. 17

Crater of Diamonds State Park
209 State Park Road
Murfreesboro, AR 71958
(870) 285-3113
www.bringfido.com/go/1DID
pg. 19

Garvan Woodland Gardens
550 Arkridge Road
Hot Springs, AR 71913
(501) 262-9300
www.bringfido.com/go/1DFU
pg. 17

HOTELS

Crater of Diamonds State Park Campground
209 State Park Road
Murfreesboro, AR 71958
(870) 285-3113
www.bringfido.com/go/1DIF
pg. 19

Lookout Point Lakeside Inn
104 Lookout Circle
Hot Springs, AR 71913
(501) 525-6155
www.bringfido.com/go/1DFV
pg. 17

Parker Creek Bend Cabins
89 Parker Creek Road
Murfreesboro, AR 71958
(844) 712-2246
www.bringfido.com/go/1DIE
pg. 19

CALIFORNIA

ATTRACTIONS

17-Mile Drive
1700 17-Mile Drive
Pebble Beach, CA 93953
(831) 622-8307
www.bringfido.com/go/1DG3
pg. 35

Abalonetti Bar & Grill
57 Fisherman's Wharf
Monterey, CA 93940
(831) 373-1851
www.bringfido.com/go/1DHK
pg. 31

Aqua Adventures
1548 Quivira Way
San Diego, CA 92109
(619) 523-9577
www.bringfido.com/go/1DH1
pg. 21

Arroyo Burro Beach
2981 Cliff Drive
Santa Barbara, CA 93109
(805) 687-3714
www.bringfido.com/go/1DN1
pg. 25

Asilomar State Beach
Sunset Drive
Pacific Grove, CA 93950
(831) 646-6440
www.bringfido.com/go/1DH4
pg. 35

Baker Beach
1504 Pershing Drive
San Francisco, CA 94129
(415) 561-4323
www.bringfido.com/go/1DUU
pg. 39

Bay Cruisers
845 Embarcadero
Morro Bay, CA 93442
(805) 771-9339
www.bringfido.com/go/1DJH
pg. 29

Blue & Gold Fleet
Pier 41
San Francisco, CA 94133
(415) 705-8203
www.bringfido.com/go/1DJ6
pg. 38

Boathouse at Hendry's Beach
2981 Cliff Drive
Santa Barbara, CA 93109
(805) 898-2628
www.bringfido.com/go/1DN4
pg. 25

Bronson Canyon Trail
3200 Canyon Drive
Los Angeles, CA 90068
(323) 666-5046
www.bringfido.com/go/1DM2
pg. 23

Cannery Row
649 Cannery Row
Monterey, CA 93940
(831) 649-6690
www.bringfido.com/go/1DHL
pg. 31

Carivintas Winery
476 1st Street
Solvang, CA 93463
(805) 693-4331
www.bringfido.com/go/1DIB
pg. 22

Carmel Beach
Ocean Avenue & Scenic Road
Carmel, CA 93923
(831) 624-2522
www.bringfido.com/go/1DH5
pg. 35

Catch a Canoe & Bicycles Too
1 S Big River Road
Mendocino, CA 95460
(707) 937-0273
www.bringfido.com/go/1DHG
pg. 41

The Cliff
577 S Coast Highway
Laguna Beach, CA 92651
(949) 494-1956
www.bringfido.com/go/1E5E
pg. 28

Crissy Field
1199 East Beach
San Francisco, CA 94129
(415) 561-4323
www.bringfido.com/go/1DUX
pg. 39

DeeTours of Santa Barbara
1 Garden Street
Santa Barbara, CA 93101
(805) 448-8425
www.bringfido.com/go/1DIW
pg. 24

Degnan's Deli
9015 Village Drive
Yosemite Valley, CA 95389
(888) 413-8869
www.bringfido.com/go/1DTW
pg. 36

Devils Postpile National Monument
Devils Postpile Access Road
Mammoth Lakes, CA 93546
(760) 934-2289
www.bringfido.com/go/1DGK
pg. 30

Dirty Dog Wash
504 Main Street
Huntington Beach, CA 92648
(714) 960-7002
www.bringfido.com/go/1DHA
pg. 20

Dog Beach Dog Wash
4933 Voltaire Street
San Diego, CA
(619) 523-1700
www.bringfido.com/go/1DLY
pg. 27

Douglas Family Preserve
Medcliff Road & Selrose Lane
Santa Barbara, CA 93101
(805) 564-5418
www.bringfido.com/go/1DN3
pg. 25

Eleven53 Café
Gondola Building on Summit
Mammoth Lakes, CA 93546
(760) 934-0745
www.bringfido.com/go/1DHF
pg. 30

Fiesta Island Park
1590 E Mission Bay Drive
San Diego, CA 92109
(619) 525-8213
www.bringfido.com/go/1DH3
pg. 21

The Forge
Junipero Street & 5th Avenue
Carmel, CA 93921
(831) 624-2233
www.bringfido.com/go/1DH8
pg. 35

Fountain of Woof
Carmel Plaza
Ocean Avenue & Mission Street
Carmel, CA 93921
(831) 624-0138
www.bringfido.com/go/1DH6
pg. 35

Fresco Valley Café
442 Atterdag Road
Solvang, CA 93463
(805) 688-8857
www.bringfido.com/go/1DIA
pg. 22

Fun Zone Boat Company
700 Edgewater Place
Newport Beach, CA 92661
(949) 673-0240
www.bringfido.com/go/1DG0
pg. 28

Heisler Park
375 Cliff Drive
Laguna Beach, CA 92651
(949) 497-9229
www.bringfido.com/go/1E5C
pg. 28

Hog Island Oyster Co.
20215 Shoreline Highway
Marshall, CA 94940
(415) 663-9218
www.bringfido.com/go/1DUZ
pg. 32

Hollywood Walk of Fame
7018 Hollywood Boulevard
Los Angeles, California 90028
(323) 469-8311
www.bringfido.com/go/1DM4
pg. 23

Huntington Dog Beach
100 Goldenwest Street
Huntington Beach, CA 92647
(714) 841-8644
www.bringfido.com/go/1DGC
pg. 20

Kiva Beach
35 Visitor Center Road
South Lake Tahoe, CA 96150
(530) 543-2674
www.bringfido.com/go/1DUN
pg. 37

Lake Hollywood Park
3160 Canyon Lake Drive
Los Angeles, CA 90068
(818) 243-1145
www.bringfido.com/go/1DM3
pg. 23

Mad Dogs & Englishmen
Ocean Avenue & Mission Street
Carmel, CA 93921
(831) 250-7687
www.bringfido.com/go/1DH7
pg. 29

Mammoth Adventure Center
10001 Minaret Road
Mammoth Lakes, CA 93546
(800) 626-6684
www.bringfido.com/go/1DHD
pg. 30

Mammoth Mountain Scenic Gondola
10001 Minaret Road
Mammoth Lakes, CA 93546
(760) 934-2571
www.bringfido.com/go/1DHE
pg. 30

The Marshall Store
19225 State Route 1
Marshall, CA 94940
(415) 663-1339
www.bringfido.com/go/1DV1
pg. 32

Mendocino Coast Botanical Gardens
18220 N Highway One
Fort Bragg, CA 95437
(707) 964-4352
www.bringfido.com/go/1DH9
pg. 33

Monterey Bay Whale Watch
84 Fisherman's Wharf
Monterey, CA 93940
(831) 375-4658
www.bringfido.com/go/1DHI
pg. 31

Morro Bay State Park
60 State Park Road
Morro Bay, CA 93442
(805) 772-2560
www.bringfido.com/go/1DJJ
pg. 29

Murray Circle
602 Murray Circle
Sausalito, CA 94965
(415) 339-4750
www.bringfido.com/go/1DJ8
pg. 38

Naked Dog Bistro
424 Forest Avenue
Laguna Beach, CA 92651
(949) 715-9900
www.bringfido.com/go/1E5D
pg. 28

Nick's Cove Restaurant
23240 Highway 1
Marshall, CA 94940
(415) 663-1033
www.bringfido.com/go/1DV3
pg. 32

The Original Dog Beach
5156 W Point Loma Boulevard
San Diego, CA 92107
(619) 236-5555
www.bringfido.com/go/1DLW
pg. 27

OstrichLand USA
610 E Highway 246
Solvang, CA 93463
(805) 686-9696
www.bringfido.com/go/1DI8
pg. 22

Pacific Hideaway
500 Pacific Coast Highway
Huntington Beach, CA 92648
(714) 963-4448
www.bringfido.com/go/1DHC
pg. 20

Point Reyes National Seashore
1 Bear Valley Road
Point Reyes Station, CA 94956
(415) 464-5100
www.bringfido.com/go/1DV2
pg. 32

Presidio Café
300 Finley Road
San Francisco, CA 94129
(415) 561-4600
www.bringfido.com/go/1DUW
pg. 39

Presidio Ecology Trail
Arguello Boulevard
San Francisco, CA 94129
(415) 561-5300
www.bringfido.com/go/1DUV
pg. 39

Presidio of San Francisco
103 Montgomery Street
San Francisco, CA 94129
(415) 561-5300
www.bringfido.com/go/1DUS
pg. 39

Runyon Canyon Park
2000 N Fuller Avenue
Los Angeles, CA 90046
(323) 666-5046
www.bringfido.com/go/1DM0
pg. 23

Russian River Adventures
20 Healdsburg Avenue
Healdsburg, CA 95448
(707) 433-5599
www.bringfido.com/go/1DG9
pg. 40

Sally's Fish House & Bar
1 Market Place
San Diego, CA 92101
(619) 358-6740
www.bringfido.com/go/1DLZ
pg. 27

SeaQuake Brewing
400 Front Street
Crescent City, CA 95531
(707) 465-4444
www.bringfido.com/go/1DJ5
pg. 43

Skunk Train
100 W Laurel Street
Fort Bragg, CA 95437
(707) 964-6371
www.bringfido.com/go/1DG6
pg. 33

Tahoe City Winter Sports Park
251 N Lake Boulevard
Tahoe City, CA 96145
(530) 583-1516
www.bringfido.com/go/1DUK
pg. 37

Tahoe Sport Fishing
900 Ski Run Boulevard
South Lake Tahoe, CA 96150
(530) 541-5448
www.bringfido.com/go/1DUM
pg. 37

Top Dog Barkery
21010 Pacific Coast Highway
Huntington Beach, CA 92648
(714) 960-3647
www.bringfido.com/go/1DHB
pg. 20

Trees of Mystery
15500 US-101
Klamath, CA 95548
(800) 638-3389
www.bringfido.com/go/1DJ3
pg. 43

Yosemite National Park
9035 Village Drive
Yosemite National Park,
CA 95389
(209) 372-0200
www.bringfido.com/go/1DTU
pg. 36

HOTELS

Anchor Beach Inn
880 Highway 101 S
Crescent City, CA 95531
(707) 464-2600
www.bringfido.com/go/1DJ4
pg. 43

AutoCamp Yosemite
6323 CA-140
Midpines, CA 95345
(888) 405-7553
www.bringfido.com/go/1DTV
pg. 36

Bayfront Inn
1150 Embarcadero
Morro Bay, CA 93442
(805) 772-5607
www.bringfido.com/go/1DJI
pg. 29

Beach House Inn
320 W Yanonali Street
Santa Barbara, CA 93101
(805) 966-1126
www.bringfido.com/go/1DN2
pg. 25

Belmond El Encanto
800 Alvarado Place
Santa Barbara, CA 93103
(805) 845-5800
www.bringfido.com/go/1DIX
pg. 24

Best Western Dry Creek Inn
198 Dry Creek Road
Healdsburg, CA 95448
(707) 433-0300
www.bringfido.com/go/1DGB
pg. 40

Cavallo Point
601 Murray Circle
Sausalito, CA 94965
(415) 339-4700
www.bringfido.com/go/1DJ7
pg. 38

Convict Lake Resort
2000 Convict Lake Road
Mammoth Lakes, CA 93546
(760) 934-3800
www.bringfido.com/go/1DGL
pg. 30

Cypress Inn
Lincoln Street & 7th Avenue
Carmel, CA 93921
(831) 624-3871
www.bringfido.com/go/1DG4
pg. 35

Fireside Lodge
515 Emerald Bay Road
South Lake Tahoe, CA 96150
(530) 544-5515
www.bringfido.com/go/1DUL
pg. 37

Flying Flags RV Resort
& Campground
180 Avenue Of The Flags
Buellton, CA 93427
(805) 688-3716
www.bringfido.com/go/1DI9
pg. 22

Healdsburg Inn on the Plaza
112 Matheson Street
Healdsburg, CA 95448
(707) 433-6991
www.bringfido.com/go/1DGA
pg. 40

Hotel Solamar
435 6th Avenue
San Diego, CA 92101
(619) 819-9500
www.bringfido.com/go/1DH2
pg. 21

The Inn at Schoolhouse Creek
7051 N Highway One
Little River, CA 95456
(707) 937-5525
www.bringfido.com/go/1DG7
pg. 33

Inn at the Presidio
42 Moraga Avenue
San Francisco, CA 94129
(415) 800-7356
www.bringfido.com/go/1DUT
pg. 39

The Kimpton Everly Hotel
1800 Argyle Avenue
Los Angeles, CA 90028
(213) 279-3532
www.bringfido.com/go/1DM1
pg. 23

**Kimpton Shorebreak
Huntington Beach Resort**
500 Pacific Coast Highway
Huntington Beach, CA 92648
(714) 861-4470
www.bringfido.com/go/1DGD
pg. 20

Little River Inn
7901 N Highway One
Little River, CA 95456
(707) 937-5942
www.bringfido.com/go/1DG8
pg. 33

Lodge at the Presidio
105 Montgomery Street
San Francisco, CA 94129
(415) 561-1234
www.bringfido.com/go/1DUY
pg. 39

Narrow Gauge Inn
48571 Highway 41
Fish Camp, CA 93623
(559) 683-7720
www.bringfido.com/go/1DTX
pg. 36

Nick's Cove
23240 Highway 1
Marshall, CA 94940
(415) 663-1033
www.bringfido.com/go/1DV0
pg. 32

Ocean Villa Inn
5142 W Point Loma Boulevard
San Diego, CA 92107
(619) 224-3481
www.bringfido.com/go/1DLX
pg. 27

Portola Hotel & Spa
2 Portola Plaza
Monterey, CA 93940
(800) 342-4295
www.bringfido.com/go/1DHJ
pg. 31

Royal Copenhagen Inn
1579 Mission Drive
Solvang, CA 93463
(805) 688-5561
www.bringfido.com/go/1DIC
pg. 22

The Stanford Inn by the Sea
44850 Comptche Ukiah Road
Mendocino, CA 95460
(707) 937-5615
www.bringfido.com/go/1DHH
pg. 41

Svendsgaard's Inn
San Carlos Street & 4th Avenue
Carmel, CA 93923
(831) 624-1511
www.bringfido.com/go/1DG5
pg. 35

The Tides Laguna Beach
460 N Coast Highway
Laguna Beach, CA 92651
(949) 494-2494
www.bringfido.com/go/1DG1
pg. 28

COLORADO

ATTRACTIONS

Colorado River Runs
43 County Highway 111
Bond, Colorado 80423
(970) 653-4292
www.bringfido.com/go/1DJ1
pg. 49

Edwards Freedom Park
450 Miller Ranch Road
Edwards, CO 81632
(970) 766-5555
www.bringfido.com/go/1E3W
pg. 49

Galloping Goose
W San Juan Avenue
Telluride, CO 81435
(970) 728-2168
www.bringfido.com/go/1DHO
pg. 47

Garden of the Gods
1805 N 30th Street
Colorado Springs, CO 80904
(719) 634-6666
www.bringfido.com/go/1DGM
pg. 45

High Country Dogs
3530 County Road 83
Tabernash, CO 80478
(970) 406-0158
www.bringfido.com/go/1DHR
pg. 44

**Leadville Colorado & Southern
Railroad**
326 E 7th Street
Leadville, CO 80461
(719) 486-3936
www.bringfido.com/go/1DIZ
pg. 51

Manitou Cliff Dwellings
10 Cliff Dwellings Road
Manitou Springs, CO 80829
(719) 685-5242
www.bringfido.com/go/1E3V
pg. 45

Pub Dog Colorado
2207 Bott Avenue
Colorado Springs, CO 80904
(719) 375-0771
www.bringfido.com/go/1E3U
pg. 45

Telluride Gondola
300 W San Juan Avenue
Telluride, CO 81435
(970) 728-3041
www.bringfido.com/go/1DHM
pg. 47

HOTELS

The Broadmoor
1 Lake Avenue
Colorado Springs, CO 80906
(719) 577-5775
www.bringfido.com/go/1DGN
pg. 45

Devil's Thumb Ranch
3530 County Road 83
Tabernash, CO 80478
(970) 726-5632
www.bringfido.com/go/1E3T
pg. 44

The Inn at Riverwalk
27 Main Street
Edwards, CO 81632
(970) 926-0606
www.bringfido.com/go/1DJ2
pg. 49

Mountain Lodge at Telluride
457 Mountain Village Boulevard
Telluride, CO 81435
(970) 369-5000
www.bringfido.com/go/1DHN
pg. 47

The Ritz-Carlton, Bachelor Gulch
0130 Daybreak Ridge
Avon, CO 81620
(970) 748-6200
www.bringfido.com/go/1DJ0
pg. 51

Sundance Trail Guest Ranch
17931 W County Road 74E
Red Feather Lakes, CO 80545
(970) 224-1222
www.bringfido.com/go/1DHQ
pg. 48

CONNECTICUT
ATTRACTIONS
Devil's Hopyard State Park
366 Hopyard Road
East Haddam, CT 06423
(860) 526-2336
www.bringfido.com/go/1DM8
pg. 52

Hop Culture Farms & Brewing Co.
144 Cato Corner Road
Colchester, CT 06415
(860) 305-9556
www.bringfido.com/go/1DM5
pg. 52

Mystic Seaport
75 Greenmanville Avenue
Mystic, CT 06355
(860) 572-0711
www.bringfido.com/go/1DHI
pg. 53

Mystic Yacht Charter
101 Greenmanville Avenue
Mystic, CT 06355
(401) 678-6740
www.bringfido.com/go/1E42
pg. 53

Sea View Snack Bar
145 Greenmanville Avenue
(860) 572-0096
Mystic, CT 06355
www.bringfido.com/go/1E43
pg. 53

Yankee Cider Company
23 Petticoat Lane
East Haddam, CT 06423
(860) 873-2433
www.bringfido.com/go/1DM7
pg. 52

HOTELS
Hampton Inn & Suites Mystic
6 Hendel Drive
Mystic, CT 06355
(860) 536-2536
www.bringfido.com/go/1DHU
pg. 53

Saybrook Point Resort & Marina
2 Bridge Street
Old Saybrook, CT 06475
(860) 395-2000
www.bringfido.com/go/1DM6
pg. 52

DELAWARE
ATTRACTIONS
Anglers Fishing Center
213 Anglers Road
Lewes, DE 19958
(302) 644-4533
www.bringfido.com/go/1DJ9
pg. 54

Fenwick Island State Park
36840 Coastal Highway
Fenwick Island, DE 19971
(302) 227-2800
www.bringfido.com/go/1DQU
pg. 55

Irish Eyes Pub & Restaurant
213 Anglers Road
Lewes, DE 19958
(302) 645-8888
www.bringfido.com/go/1DJB
pg. 54

Island Watersports
39084 Harpoon Road
Fenwick Island, DE 19944
(302) 537-2628
www.bringfido.com/go/1DQW
pg. 55

Just Hooked
1500 Coastal Highway
Fenwick Island, DE 19944
(302) 581-0098
www.bringfido.com/go/1DQZ
pg. 55

Seaside Country Store
1208 Coastal Highway
Fenwick Island, DE 19944
(302) 539-6110
www.bringfido.com/go/1DQY
pg. 55

Viking Golf
38960 Island Street
Fenwick Island, DE 19944
(302) 539-1644
www.bringfido.com/go/1DQX
pg. 55

HOTELS
**Homestead Bed & Breakfast
at Rehoboth Beach**
35060 Warrington Road
Rehoboth Beach, DE 19971
(302) 226-7625
www.bringfido.com/go/1DJA
pg. 54

Seaside Inn
1401 Coastal Highway
Fenwick Island, DE 19944
(302) 251-5000
www.bringfido.com/go/1DQV
pg. 55

DISTRICT OF COLUMBIA
ATTRACTIONS
Adventure DC Tricycle Tours
1440 G Street NW
Washington, DC 20005
(202) 669-7274
www.bringfido.com/go/1DR0
pg. 56

Art and Soul
415 New Jersey Avenue NW
Washington, DC 20001
(202) 393-7777
www.bringfido.com/go/1DR5
pg. 57

Boating in DC
Potomac Avenue SE
& 1st Street SE
Washington, DC 20003
(202) 337-9642
www.bringfido.com/go/1DR3
pg. 57

DC Ghosts
Lafayette Park at The Marquis
De Lafayette Statue
Washington, DC 20001
(202) 810-0709
www.bringfido.com/go/1DR2
pg. 56

HOTELS

The Jefferson
1200 16th Street NW
Washington, DC 20036
(202) 448-2300
www.bringfido.com/go/1DR1
pg. 56

The River Inn
924 25th Street NW
Washington, DC 20037
(202) 337-7600
www.bringfido.com/go/1DR4
pg. 57

FLORIDA

ATTRACTIONS

Captain Gill's River Cruises
501 Bay City Road
Apalachicola, FL 32320
(850) 370-0075
www.bringfido.com/go/1DMF
pg. 60

Coopertown Airboats
22700 SW 8th Street
Miami, FL 33194
(305) 226-6048
www.bringfido.com/go/1DO1
pg. 69

Crystal River Archaeological State Park
3400 N Museum Point
Crystal River, FL 34428
(352) 795-3817
www.bringfido.com/go/1DMQ
pg. 64

De Leon Springs State Park
601 Ponce de Leon Boulevard
De Leon Springs, FL 32130
(386) 985-4212
www.bringfido.com/go/1DV9
pg. 63

Dog Bar
1627 Euclid Avenue
Miami Beach, FL 33139
(305) 532-5654
www.bringfido.com/go/1DO4
pg. 69

Dolphin Research Center
58901 Overseas Highway
Grassy Key, FL 33050
(305) 289-1121
www.bringfido.com/go/1DMM
pg. 68

Florida Manatee Adventures
2880 N Seabreeze Point
Crystal River, FL 34429
(352) 476-7556
www.bringfido.com/go/1DMO
pg. 64

Fountain of Youth Archaeological Park
11 Magnolia Avenue
St. Augustine, FL 32084
(904) 829-3168
www.bringfido.com/go/1DQM
pg. 65

Fountain of Youth Eco/ History Tours
601 Ponce de Leon Boulevard
De Leon Springs, FL 32130
(386) 837-5537
www.bringfido.com/go/1DVB
pg. 63

Gulfside City Park
2001 Algiers Lane
Sanibel, FL 33957
(239) 472-1080
www.bringfido.com/go/1DV7
pg. 59

High Tide
1717 Collins Avenue
Miami Beach, FL 33139
(305) 200-0377
www.bringfido.com/go/1DO5
pg. 69

Hurricane Café
14050 U.S. Highway 1
Juno Beach, FL 33408
(561) 630 2012
www.bringfido.com/go/1DRQ
pg. 67

The Island Cow
2163 Periwinkle Way
Sanibel, FL 33957
(239) 472-0606
www.bringfido.com/go/1DV8
pg. 59

J.N. Ding Darling National Wildlife Refuge
1 Wildlife Drive
Sanibel, FL 33957
(239) 472-1100
www.bringfido.com/go/1DV6
pg. 59

Jupiter Dog Beach
2188 Marcinski Road
Jupiter, FL 33477
(561) 748-8140
www.bringfido.com/go/1DRP
pg. 67

Key West Aquarium
1 Whitehead Street
Key West, FL 33040
(305) 296-2051
www.bringfido.com/go/1DMU
pg. 70

Lazy Dog Adventures
5114 Overseas Highway
Key West, FL 33040
(305) 295-9898
www.bringfido.com/go/1DMR
pg. 70

Lincoln Road Mall
1610 Lenox Avenue
Miami Beach, FL 33139
(305) 389-3767
www.bringfido.com/go/1DO3
pg. 69

Littleheads Kayak Rentals
14140 River Road
Pensacola, FL 32507
(251) 284-5107
www.bringfido.com/go/1DS9
pg. 62

O.C. White's Restaurant
118 Avenida Menendez
St. Augustine, FL 32084
(904) 824-0808
www.bringfido.com/go/1DMJ
pg. 61

The Old Spanish Sugar Mill
601 Ponce de Leon Boulevard
De Leon Springs, FL 32130
(386) 985-5644
www.bringfido.com/go/1DVC
pg. 63

Palm Beach Bicycle Trail Shop
50 Cocoanut Row, Suite 117
Palm Beach, FL 33480
(561) 659-4583
www.bringfido.com/go/1DRV
pg. 67

Palm Beach Lake Trail
1 Whitehall Way
Palm Beach, FL 33480
(800) 554-7256
www.bringfido.com/go/1DRN
pg. 67

St. Augustine Eco Tours
111 Avenida Menendez
St. Augustine, FL 32084
(904) 377-7245
www.bringfido.com/go/1DMH
pg. 61

Tarkiln Bayou Preserve State Park
2401 Bauer Road
Pensacola, FL 32507
(850) 492-1595
www.bringfido.com/go/1DSB
pg. 62

Tarpon Bay Explorers
900 Tarpon Bay Road
Sanibel, FL 33957
(239) 472-8900
www.bringfido.com/go/1DV4
pg. 59

Theater of the Sea
84721 Overseas Highway
Islamorada, FL 33036
(305) 664-2431
www.bringfido.com/go/1DMK
pg. 68

Tides Beachside Bar & Grill
82100 Overseas Highway
Islamorada, FL 33036
(305) 307-3732
www.bringfido.com/go/1DMN
pg. 68

Vilano Beach
2750 Anahma Drive
St. Augustine, FL 32085
(904) 209-0752
www.bringfido.com/go/1DQO
pg. 65

HOTELS

Alling House
215 E French Avenue
Orange City, FL 32763
(386) 775-7648
www.bringfido.com/go/1DVA
pg. 63

Ambrosia Key West
622 Fleming Street
Key West, FL 33040
(305) 296-9838
www.bringfido.com/go/1DMS
pg. 70

Bayfront Marin House
142 Avenida Menendez
St. Augustine, FL 32084
(904) 824-4301
www.bringfido.com/go/1DMI
pg. 61

Best Western Crystal River Resort
614 NW US Highway 19
Crystal River, FL 34428
(352) 795-3171
www.bringfido.com/go/1DMP
pg. 64

Holiday Inn Express North Palm Beach Oceanview
13950 U.S. Highway 1
Juno Beach, FL 33408
(561) 622-4366
www.bringfido.com/go/1DRO
pg. 67

Islander Resort
82100 Overseas Highway
Islamorada, FL 33036
(305) 664-2031
www.bringfido.com/go/1DML
pg. 68

Kimpton Surfcomber Hotel
1717 Collins Avenue
Miami Beach, FL 33139
(305) 532-7715
www.bringfido.com/go/1DO2
pg. 69

Saint Augustine Beach House
10 Vilano Road
St. Augustine, FL 32084
(904) 217-3765
www.bringfido.com/go/1DQN
pg. 65

Signal Inn
1811 Olde Middle Gulf Drive
Sanibel, FL 33957
(239) 472-4690
www.bringfido.com/go/1DV5
pp. 59

Water Street Hotel and Marina
329 Water Street
Apalachicola, FL 32320
(850) 653-3700
www.bringfido.com/go/1DMG
pg. 60

GEORGIA

ATTRACTIONS

Anna Ruby Falls
3455 Anna Ruby Falls Road
Helen, GA 30545
(706) 878-1448
www.bringfido.com/go/1DT6
pg. 77

Barnsley Gardens
597 Barnsley Gardens Road
Adairsville, GA 30103
(770) 773-7480
www.bringfido.com/go/1DHY
pg. 73

Bonaventure Cemetery
330 Bonaventure Road
Thunderbolt, GA 31404
(912) 412-4687
www.bringfido.com/go/1DJC
pg. 75

Cool River Tubing
590 Edelweiss Strasse
Helen, GA 30545
(706) 878-2665
www.bringfido.com/go/1DT2
pg. 77

Driftwood Beach
North Beachview Drive
Jekyll Island, GA 31527
(912) 635-3636
www.bringfido.com/go/1DTC
pg. 78

Ghost City Tours
100 Bull Street, #200
Savannah, GA 31401
(855) 999-9026
www.bringfido.com/go/1DJE
pg. 75

Hearse Ghost Tours
412 E Duffy Street
Savannah, GA 31401
(912) 695-1578
www.bringfido.com/go/1DJF
pg. 75

Hofbrauhaus Restaurant
9001 N Main Street
Helen, GA 30545
(706) 878-2248
www.bringfido.com/go/1DT7
pg. 77

Jekyll Island Dolphin Tours
366 N Riverview Drive
Jekyll Island, GA 31527
(912) 635-3152
www.bringfido.com/go/1DT8
pg. 78

Mosaic Jekyll Island Museum
100 Stable Road
Jekyll Island, GA 31527
(912) 635-4036
www.bringfido.com/go/1DTB
pg. 78

North Loop Trail
Along Beachview and Riverview
Drives
Jekyll Island, GA 31527
(912) 638-9014
www.bringfido.com/go/1DTD
pg. 78

Ocean View Trail
Along North Beachview Drive
Jekyll Island, GA 31527
(912) 638-9014
www.bringfido.com/go/1DTE
pg. 78

Old Savannah Tours
250 Martin Luther King Jr
Boulevard
Savannah, GA 31401
(912) 234-8128
www.bringfido.com/go/1DI3
pg. 71

Oliver Bentleys
Oglethorpe Square
127 Abercorn Street
Savannah, GA 31401
(912) 201-1688
www.bringfido.com/go/1DI0
pg. 71

Rock City
1400 Patten Road
Lookout Mountain, GA 30750
(706) 820-2531
www.bringfido.com/go/1DHV
pg. 72

Savannah Pedicab
635 E Broughton Street
Savannah, GA 31401
(912) 232-7900
www.bringfido.com/go/1DI4
pg. 71

Unicoi State Park
1788 GA-356
Helen, GA 30545
(706) 878-2201
www.bringfido.com/go/1DT4
pg. 77

Unicoi to Helen Trail
1788 GA-356
Helen, GA 30545
(706) 878-2201
www.bringfido.com/go/1DT5
pg. 77

**The Wharf at Jekyll Island
Club Resort**
370 Riverview Drive
Jekyll Island, GA 31527
(912) 635-3612
www.bringfido.com/go/1DTA
pg. 78

HOTELS

Barnsley Resort
597 Barnsley Gardens Road
Adairsville, GA 30103
(770) 773-7480
www.bringfido.com/go/1DHZ
pg. 73

Bear Creek Lodge & Cabins
219 Escowee Drive
Helen, GA 30545
(706) 773-1040
www.bringfido.com/go/1DT3
pg. 77

Foley House Inn
14 W Hull Street
Savannah, GA 31401
(912) 232-6622
www.bringfido.com/go/1DI1
pg. 71

Holiday Inn Resort Jekyll Island
701 N Beachview Drive
Jekyll Island, GA 31527
(912) 635-2211
www.bringfido.com/go/1DT9
pg. 78

Kimpton Brice Hotel
601 E Bay Street
Savannah, GA 31401
(912) 238-1200
www.bringfido.com/go/1DI2
pg. 71

Olde Harbour Inn
508 E Factors Walk
Savannah, GA 31401
(912) 234-4100
www.bringfido.com/go/1DJD
pg. 75

Seventy-Four Ranch
9205 Highway 53 W
Jasper, GA 30143
(770) 547-8580
www.bringfido.com/go/1DJG
pg. 76

HAWAII

ATTRACTIONS

Barefoot Beach Café
2699 Kalakaua Avenue
Honolulu, HI 96815
(808) 924-2233
www.bringfido.com/go/1DPG
pg. 80

Creative Soul Scavenger Hunts
5-5161 Kuhio Highway F
Hanalei, HI 96714
(505) 692-0644
www.bringfido.com/go/1DTH
pg. 79

Gone Surfing Hawaii
330 Saratoga Road
Honolulu, HI 96815
(808) 429-6404
www.bringfido.com/go/1DPD
pg. 80

JoJo's Shave Ice
5-5190 Kuhio Highway
Hanalei, HI 96714
(808) 378-4612
www.bringfido.com/go/1DTK
pg. 79

Kauai North Shore Dog Park
5445 Kahiliholo Road
Kilauea, HI 96754
(808) 240-2670
www.bringfido.com/go/1DTJ
pg. 79

The Public Pet
3422 Waialae Avenue
Honolulu, HI 96816
(808) 737-8887
www.bringfido.com/go/1DPF
pg. 80

HOTELS

Ko'a Kea Hotel & Resort
2251 Poipu Road
Koloa, HI 96756
(844) 236-3817
www.bringfido.com/go/1E6V
pg. 79

The Surfjack Hotel & Swim Club
412 Lewers Street
Honolulu, HI 96815
(808) 923-8882
www.bringfido.com/go/1DPE
Rates from $96/night
pg. 80

IDAHO

ATTRACTIONS

Dog Beach Park
Serenity Lee Trail
Sandpoint, ID 83864
(208) 263-3613
www.bringfido.com/go/1DRC
pg. 81

Laughing Dog Brewing
805 Schweitzer Plaza Drive
Ponderay, ID 83852
(208) 263-9222
www.bringfido.com/go/1DRD
pg. 81

Long Drift Outfitters
Kootenai River
Sandpoint, ID 83864
(303) 917-2822
www.bringfido.com/go/1DRA
pg. 81

HOTELS

Dog Bark Park Inn
2421 Business Loop 95
Cottonwood, ID 83522
(208) 962-3647
www.bringfido.com/go/1DN5
pg. 83

La Quinta Inn by Wyndham Sandpoint
415 Cedar Street
Sandpoint, ID 83864
(208) 263-9581
www.bringfido.com/go/1DRB
pg. 81

ILLINOIS

ATTRACTIONS

Allerton Park & Retreat Center
515 Old Timber Road
Monticello, IL 61856
(217) 333-3287
www.bringfido.com/go/1DVH
pg. 88

Garden of the Gods Recreation Area
Garden of the Gods Road
Herod, IL 62947
(618) 253-7114
www.bringfido.com/go/1DVG
pg. 85

Greenhouse Café
515 Old Timber Road
Monticello, IL 61856
(217) 333-3287
www.bringfido.com/go/1DVJ
pg. 88

Houlihan's Restaurant
1902 S 1st Street
Champaign, IL 61820
(217) 819-5005
www.bringfido.com/go/1DVK
pg. 88

Mercury Cruises
112 E Wacker Drive
Chicago, IL 60601
(312) 332-1353
www.bringfido.com/go/1DOU
pg. 87

Naperville Riverwalk
500 Jackson Avenue
Naperville, IL 60540
(630) 848-5000
www.bringfido.com/go/1DJM
pg. 84

Quigley's Irish Pub
43 E Jefferson Avenue
Naperville, IL 60540
(630) 428-4774
www.bringfido.com/go/1DJO
pg. 84

Rim Rock National Recreation Trail
Karbers Ridge Road
Junction, IL 62954
(618) 253-7114
www.bringfido.com/go/1DVF
pg. 85

Seadog Cruises
600 E Grand Avenue
Chicago, IL 60611
(312) 321-7600
www.bringfido.com/go/1DOS
pg. 87

Shawnee National Forest
Karbers Ridge Road
Junction, IL 62954
(618) 253-7114
www.bringfido.com/go/1DVD
pg. 85

Two Bostons
103 W Jefferson Avenue
Naperville, IL 60540
(630) 357-7621
www.bringfido.com/go/1DJN
pg. 84

Wag 'N Paddle
1847 W Jefferson Avenue
Naperville, IL 60540
(331) 229-8660
www.bringfido.com/go/1DJK
pg. 84

HOTELS

**Best Western Plus Champaign
Urbana Inn**
516 W Marketview Drive
Champaign, IL 61822
(217) 355-5566
www.bringfido.com/go/1DVI
pg. 88

**Hotel Indigo Naperville
Riverwalk**
120 Water Street
Naperville, IL 60540
(630) 778-9676
www.bringfido.com/go/1DJL
pg. 84

Kimpton Hotel Palomar
505 N State Street
Chicago, IL 60654
(312) 755-9703
www.bringfido.com/go/1DOT
pg. 87

Rim Rock's Dogwood Cabins
798 Karbers Ridge Road
Elizabethtown, IL 62931
(618) 264-6036
www.bringfido.com/go/1DVE
pg. 85

INDIANA
ATTRACTIONS

100 Acres at Newfields
4000 N Michigan Road
Indianapolis, IN 46208
(317) 923-1331
www.bringfido.com/go/1E6G
pg. 90

Central Canal Towpath
E Westfield Boulevard and
N College Avenue
Indianapolis, IN 46220
(317) 327-7431
www.bringfido.com/go/1E6J
pg. 90

Flatwater
832 E Westfield Boulevard
Indianapolis, IN 46220
(317) 257-5466
www.bringfido.com/go/1E6L
pg. 90

Indiana Dunes National Park
1215 N State Road 49
Porter, IN 46304
(219) 395-1882
www.bringfido.com/go/1DVN
pg. 89

Indiana Dunes State Park
1600 N 25 E
Chesterton, IN 46304
(219) 926-1952
www.bringfido.com/go/1DVL
pg. 89

Indianapolis Art Center ArtsPark
820 E 67th Street
Indianapolis, IN 46220
(317) 255-2464
www.bringfido.com/go/1E6I
pg. 90

Monon Trail
1430 E 96th Street
Indianapolis, IN 46240
(317) 327-7431
www.bringfido.com/go/1E6K
pg. 90

**RV Motorhome Hall of Fame
& Museum**
21565 Executive Parkway
Elkhart, IN 46514
(574) 293-2344
www.bringfido.com/go/1DMV
pg. 91

HOTELS

Elkhart Campground
25608 County Road 4
Elkhart, IN 46514
(574) 264-2914
www.bringfido.com/go/1DMW
pg. 91

Ironworks Hotel
2721 E 86th Street
Indianapolis, IN 46240
(463) 221-2200
www.bringfido.com/go/1E6H
pg. 90

Riley's Railhouse
123 N 4th Street
Chesterton, IN 46304
(219) 395-9999
www.bringfido.com/go/1DVM
pg. 89

IOWA
ATTRACTIONS

Iowa Arboretum
1875 Peach Avenue
Madrid, IA 50156
(515) 795-3216
www.bringfido.com/go/1DVO
pg. 92

Living History Farms
11121 Hickman Road
Urbandale, IA 50322
(515) 278-5286
www.bringfido.com/go/1DVR
pg. 93

The Mucky Duck Pub
3100 S Duff Avenue
Ames, IA 50010
(515) 598-5127
www.bringfido.com/go/1DVQ
pg. 92

HOTELS

Best Western Plus Des Moines West Inn & Suites
1450 NW 118th Street
Clive, IA 50325
(515) 221-2345
www.bringfido.com/go/1DVT
pg. 93

GrandStay Hotel & Suites Ames
1606 S Kellogg Avenue
Ames, IA 50010
(515) 232-8363
www.bringfido.com/go/1DVP
pg. 92

Stoney Creek Hotel and Conference Center
5291 Stoney Creek Court
Johnston, IA 50131
(515) 334-9000
www.bringfido.com/go/1DVS
pg. 93

KANSAS
ATTRACTIONS

Dorothy's House & Land of Oz
567 Yellow Brick Road
Liberal, KS 67901
(620) 624-7624
www.bringfido.com/go/1DVU
pg. 95

Shawnee Mission Park
7900 Renner Road
Shawnee, KS 66219
(913) 438-7275
www.bringfido.com/go/1DVW
pg. 94

HOTELS

Holiday Inn Express & Suites Liberal
412 Ziegler Avenue
Liberal, KS 67901
(620) 624-2485
www.bringfido.com/go/1DVV
pg. 95

Hyatt Place Kansas City Lenexa City Center
8741 Ryckert Street
Lenexa, KS 66219
(913) 742-7777
www.bringfido.com/go/1DVX
pg. 94

KENTUCKY
ATTRACTIONS

Buffalo Trace Distillery
113 Great Buffalo Trace
Frankfort, KY 40601
(502) 696-5926
www.bringfido.com/go/1DMX
pg. 97

Coldstream Dog Park
1850 Piscano Drive
Lexington, KY 40511
(859) 288-2900
www.bringfido.com/go/1DK3
pg. 99

Dinosaur World
711 Mammoth Cave Road
Cave City, KY 42127
(270) 773-4345
www.bringfido.com/go/1DJV
pg. 98

Kentucky Horse Park
4089 Iron Works Parkway
Lexington, KY 40511
(800) 678-8812
www.bringfido.com/go/1DK1
pg. 99

HOTELS

21c Museum Hotel Lexington
167 W Main Street
Lexington, KY 40507
(859) 899-6800
www.bringfido.com/go/1DN0
pg. 97

21c Museum Hotel Louisville
700 W Main Street
Louisville, KY 40202
(502) 217-6300
www.bringfido.com/go/1DMY
pg. 97

Big Bone Lick State Historic Site Campground
3380 Beaver Road
Union, KY 41091
(859) 384-3522
www.bringfido.com/go/1DJZ
pg. 98

Embassy Suites by Hilton Lexington UK Coldstream
1801 Newtown Pike
Lexington, KY 40511
(859) 455-5000
www.bringfido.com/go/1DK2
pg. 99

Yogi Bear's Jellystone Park
1002 Mammoth Cave Road
Cave City, KY 42127
(270) 773-3840
www.bringfido.com/go/1DJY
pg. 98

LOUISIANA
ATTRACTIONS

Algiers Ferry
1 Canal Street
New Orleans, LA 70130
(504) 309-9789
www.bringfido.com/go/1DW3
pg. 101

Atchafalaya Experience
1908 Atchafalaya River Highway
Breaux Bridge, LA 70517
(337) 277-4726
www.bringfido.com/go/1DVY
pg. 100

Avery Island
329 Avery Island Road
Avery Island, LA 70513
(337) 373-6139
www.bringfido.com/go/1DW0
pg. 100

Bloody Mary's Tours
941 Bourbon Street
New Orleans, LA 70116
(504) 523-7684
www.bringfido.com/go/1DW1
pg. 101

The Crown & Anchor
200 Pelican Avenue
New Orleans, LA 70114
(504) 227-1007
www.bringfido.com/go/1DW4
pg. 101

HOTELS

Mouton Plantation
338 N Sterling Street
Lafayette, LA 70501
(337) 233-7816
www.bringfido.com/go/1DVZ
pg. 100

**The Old No. 77 Hotel
& Chandlery**
535 Tchoupitoulas Street
New Orleans, LA 70130
(504) 527-5271
www.bringfido.com/go/1DW2
pg. 101

MAINE

ATTRACTIONS

Acadia National Park
25 Visitor Center Road
Bar Harbor, ME 04609
(207) 288-3338
www.bringfido.com/go/1DOV
pg. 102

Boothbay Railway Village
586 Wiscasset Road
Boothbay, ME 04537
(207) 633-4727
www.bringfido.com/go/1DSF
pg. 106

Cape Pier Chowder House
79 Pier Road
Cape Porpoise, ME 04046
(207) 967-0123
www.bringfido.com/go/1DSM
pg. 103

Cap'n Fish's Cruises
42 Commercial Street
Boothbay Harbor, ME 04538
(207) 613-7339
www.bringfido.com/go/1DSD
pg. 106

Carriages of Acadia
21 Dane Farm Road
Mount Desert, ME 04730
(877) 276-3622
www.bringfido.com/go/1DOX
pg. 102

Casco Bay Lines
56 Commercial Street
Portland, ME 04101
(207) 774-7871
www.bringfido.com/go/1DSH
pg. 105

Island Explorer
19 Firefly Lane
Bar Harbor, ME 04609
(207) 288-4573
www.bringfido.com/go/1DP0
pg. 102

Jordan Pond House
2928 Park Loop Road
Seal Harbor, ME 04675
(207) 276-3316
www.bringfido.com/go/1DOY
pg. 102

Portland Lobster Company
180 Commercial Street
Portland, ME 04101
(207) 775-2112
www.bringfido.com/go/1DSJ
pg. 105

Sea Princess Cruises
26 Sea Street
Northeast Harbor, ME 04662
(207) 276-5352
www.bringfido.com/go/1DOZ
pg. 102

Seashore Trolley Museum
195 Log Cabin Road
Kennebunkport, ME 04046
(207) 967-2800
www.bringfido.com/go/1DSK
pg. 103

Two Salty Dogs Pet Outfitters
22 McKown Street
Boothbay Harbor, ME 04538
(207) 633-7387
www.bringfido.com/go/1DSG
pg. 106

HOTELS

**Canterbury Cottage Bed
& Breakfast**
12 Roberts Avenue
Bar Harbor, ME 04069
(207) 288-2112
www.bringfido.com/go/1DOW
pg. 102

The Colony Hotel
140 Ocean Avenue
Kennebunkport, ME 04046
(207) 967-3331
www.bringfido.com/go/1DSL
pg. 103

Inn by the Sea
40 Bowery Beach Road
Cape Elizabeth, ME 04107
(207) 799-3134
www.bringfido.com/go/1DSI
pg. 105

Spruce Point Inn Resort & Spa
88 Grandview Avenue
Boothbay Harbor, ME 04538
(207) 633-4152
www.bringfido.com/go/1DSE
pg. 106

MARYLAND

ATTRACTIONS

Ayers Creek Adventures
8628 Grey Fox Lane
Berlin, MD 21811
(443) 513-0889
www.bringfido.com/go/1DU7
pg. 108

Gathland State Park
900 Arnoldstown Road
Jefferson, MD 21755
(301) 791-4767
www.bringfido.com/go/1DK5
pg. 107

Quiet Waters Park
600 Quiet Waters Park Road
Annapolis, MD 21403
(410) 222-1777
www.bringfido.com/go/1DQR
pg. 109

River & Trail Outfitters
604 Valley Road
Knoxville, MD 21758
(301) 834-9950
www.bringfido.com/go/1DK6
pg. 107

Savage River State Forest
127 Headquarters Lane
Grantsville, MD 21536
(301) 895-5759
www.bringfido.com/go/1DN7
pg. 111

Watermark Cruises
1 Dock Street
Annapolis, MD 21401
(410) 268-7601
www.bringfido.com/go/1DQP
pg. 109

HOTELS

Castaways Campground
12550 Eagles Nest Road
Berlin, MD 21811
(410) 213-0097
www.bringfido.com/go/1DU8
pg. 108

Graduate Annapolis
126 West Street
Annapolis, MD 21401
(410) 263-7777
www.bringfido.com/go/1DQQ
pg. 109

Savage River Lodge
1600 Mount Aetna Road
Frostburg, MD 21532
(301) 689-3200
www.bringfido.com/go/1DN6
pg. 111

The Treehouse Camp
20716 Townsend Road
Rohrersville, MD 21779
(301) 432-5585
www.bringfido.com/go/1DK4
pg. 107

MASSACHUSETTS

ATTRACTIONS

Boston Common
139 Tremont Street
Boston, MA, 02111
(617) 635-4505
www.bringfido.com/go/1DOB
pg. 115

Boston Water Taxi
One Long Wharf
Boston, MA 02110
(617) 227-4320
www.bringfido.com/go/1DOD
pg. 115

Cape Air & Nantucket Airlines
660 Barnstable Road
Hyannis, MA 02601
(800) 227-3247
www.bringfido.com/go/1DOF
pg. 113

Captain John Boats
10 Town Wharf
Plymouth, MA 02360
(508) 746-2643
www.bringfido.com/go/1E4L
pg. 114

Cisco Brewers
5 Bartlett Farm Road
Nantucket, MA 02554
(508) 325-5929
www.bringfido.com/go/1DON
pg. 113

deCordova Sculpture Park
51 Sandy Pond Road
Lincoln, MA 01773
(781) 259-8355
www.bringfido.com/go/1DK7
pg. 117

Dog Gone Sailing Charters
10 MacMillan Pier
Provincetown, MA 02657
(508) 566-0410
www.bringfido.com/go/1DO6
pg. 112

Dolphin Fleet of Provincetown
307 Commercial Street
Provincetown, MA 02657
(508) 240-3636
www.bringfido.com/go/1DO8
pg. 112

Freedom Trail
139 Tremont Street
Boston, MA 02111
(617) 357-8300
www.bringfido.com/go/1DO9
pg. 115

Lobster Hut
25 Town Wharf
Plymouth, MA 02360
(508)746-2270
www.bringfido.com/go/1E4N
pg. 114

Myles Standish State Forest
194 Cranberry Road
Carver, MA 02330
(506) 866-2526
www.bringfido.com/go/1E4M
pg. 114

Nobadeer Beach
Nobadeer Avenue
Nantucket, MA 02554
(508) 228-0925
www.bringfido.com/go/1DOM
pg. 113

Pilgrim Memorial State Park
79 Water Street
Plymouth, MA 02360
(508) 747-5360
www.bringfido.com/go/1E4I
pg. 114

Public Garden
Charles Street & Beacon Street
Boston, MA 02116
(617) 723-8144
www.bringfido.com/go/1DOC
pg. 115

Sanford Farm
118 Madaket Road
Nantucket, MA 02554
(508) 228-2884
www.bringfido.com/go/1DOK
pg. 113

State Street Provisions
225 State Street
Boston, MA 02109
(617) 863-8363
www.bringfido.com/go/1DOE
pg. 115

Steamship Authority
141 School Street
Hyannis, MA 02601
(508) 477-8600
www.bringfido.com/go/1DOH
pg. 113

Tupancy Links
157 Cliff Road
Nantucket, MA 02554
(508) 228-2884
www.bringfido.com/go/1DOL
pg. 113

The Wave
20 S Water Street
Nantucket, MA 02554
(508) 228-7025
www.bringfido.com/go/1DOJ
pg. 113

Young's Bicycle Shop
6 Broad Street
Nantucket, MA 02554
(508) 228-1151
www.bringfido.com/go/1DOI
pg. 113

HOTELS

**The Cottages & Lofts
at Nantucket Boat Basin**
24 Old South Wharf
Nantucket, MA 02554
(508) 325-1499
www.bringfido.com/go/1DOG
pg. 113

Hampton Inn & Suites Plymouth
10 Plaza Way
Plymouth, MA 02360
(508) 747-5000
www.bringfido.com/go/1E4J
pg. 114

Provincetown Hotel at Gabriel's
102 Bradford Street
Provincetown, MA 02657
(508) 487-3232
www.bringfido.com/go/1DO7
pg. 112

Westin Waltham Boston
70 3rd Avenue
Waltham, MA 02451
(781) 290-5600
www.bringfido.com/go/1DK8
pg. 117

XV Beacon Hotel
15 Beacon Street
Boston, MA 02108
(617) 670-1500
www.bringfido.com/go/1DOA
pg. 115

MICHIGAN

ATTRACTIONS

Argo Park Canoe & Kayak
1055 Longshore Drive
Ann Arbor, MI 48105
(734) 794-6241
www.bringfido.com/go/1DK9
pg. 123

Bavarian Belle Riverboat
925 S Main Street
Frankenmuth, MI 48734
(866) 808-2628
www.bringfido.com/go/1DPQ
pg. 118

Broadway Park
800 Broadway Street
Ann Arbor, MI 48104
(734) 794-6230
www.bringfido.com/go/1DKB
pg. 123

Fuller Park
1519 Fuller Road
Ann Arbor, MI 48105
(734) 794-6230
www.bringfido.com/go/1DKC
pg. 123

Grizzly Peaks Brewing Company
120 W Washington Street
Ann Arbor, MI 48104
(734) 741-7325
www.bringfido.com/go/1DKE
pg. 123

Hart-Montague Trail State Park
Montague Trailhead Park
Spring Street & Water Street
Montague, MI 49437
(231) 873-3083
www.bringfido.com/go/1DRT
pg. 119

Hello Cats & Dogs
925 S Main Street, #H5
Frankenmuth, MI 48734
(989) 652-2005
www.bringfido.com/go/1DPT
pg. 118

Mackinac Island
7274 Main Street
Mackinac Island, MI 49757
(906) 847-3783
www.bringfido.com/go/1DUO
pg. 121

Mackinac Island Carriage Tours
7278 Main Street
Mackinac Island, MI 49757
(906) 847-3325
www.bringfido.com/go/1DUR
pg. 121

Nichols Arboretum
1610 Washington Heights
Ann Arbor, MI 48104
(734) 647-7600
www.bringfido.com/go/1DKD
pg. 123

River Place Shops
925 S Main Street
Frankenmuth, MI 48734
(800) 600-0105
www.bringfido.com/go/1DPS
pg. 118

Seney National Wildlife Refuge
1674 Refuge Entrance Road
Seney, MI 49883
(906) 586-9851
www.bringfido.com/go/1DKM
pg. 120

Shepler's Ferry
556 E Central Avenue
Mackinaw City, MI 49701
(800) 828-6157
www.bringfido.com/go/1DUQ
pg. 121

Silver Lake Buggy Rentals
8288 W Hazel Road
Mears, MI 49436
(231) 873-8833
www.bringfido.com/go/1DRR
pg. 119

Toonerville Trolley
7195 Co Road 381
Soo Junction, MI 49000
(888) 778-7246
www.bringfido.com/go/1DKK
pg. 120

WaterDog Outfitters
4464 Dowling Street
Montague, MI 49437
(231) 740-5673
www.bringfido.com/go/1DRU
pg. 119

HOTELS
Drury Inn & Suites Frankenmuth
260 S Main Street
Frankenmuth, MI 48734
(989) 652-2800
www.bringfido.com/go/1DPR
pg. 118

Graduate Ann Arbor
615 E Huron Street
Ann Arbor, MI 48104
(734) 769-2200
www.bringfido.com/go/1DKA
pg. 123

Mission Point Resort
6633 Main Street
Mackinac Island, MI 49757
(906) 847-3312
www.bringfido.com/go/1DUP
pg. 121

Northland Outfitters
8174 Highway M-77
Germfask, MI 49836
(906) 586-9801
www.bringfido.com/go/1DKL
pg. 120

The Weathervane Inn
4527 Dowling Street
Montague, MI 49437
(231) 292-9092
www.bringfido.com/go/1DRS
pg. 119

MINNESOTA
ATTRACTIONS
A Place for Fido
600 E Superior Street
Duluth, MN 55802
(218) 464-4484
www.bringfido.com/go/1DW7
pg. 125

Lake Country Air & Beaver
Air Tours
5000 Minnesota Avenue
Duluth, MN 55802
(612) 812-1223
www.bringfido.com/go/1DW5
pg. 125

The Lakewalk
Carlton Street to Brighton Beach
Duluth, MN 55802
(218) 730-5000
www.bringfido.com/go/1DW8
pg. 125

PortLand Malt Shoppe
716 E Superior Street
Duluth, MN 55802
(218) 723-5281
www.bringfido.com/go/1DW9
pg. 125

HOTELS
Fitger's Inn
600 E Superior Street
Duluth, MN 55802
(218) 722-8826
www.bringfido.com/go/1DW6
pg. 125

Gunflint Lodge
143 S Gunflint Lake Road
Grand Marais, MN 55604
(218) 388-2296
www.bringfido.com/go/1DKN
pg. 124

MISSISSIPPI
ATTRACTIONS
Biloxi Shrimping Trip
693 Beach Boulevard
Biloxi, MS 39530
(228) 392-8645
www.bringfido.com/go/1DWA
pg. 127

Cypress Swamp Trail
Natchez Trace Parkway
Canton, MS 39046
(800) 305-7417
www.bringfido.com/go/1DY3
pg. 126

Elvis Presley Birthplace
306 Elvis Presley Drive
Tupelo, MS 38801
(662) 841-1245
www.bringfido.com/go/1DY0
pg. 126

Jeff Busby Park
305 Estes Road
Ackerman, MS 39735
(800) 305-7417
www.bringfido.com/go/1DY1
pg. 126

Little Mountain Trail
305 Estes Road
Ackerman, MS 39735
(800) 305-7417
www.bringfido.com/go/1DY2
pg. 126

Natchez National Historical Park
210 State Street
Natchez, MS 39120
(601) 446-5790
www.bringfido.com/go/1DY4
pg. 126

Natchez Trace Parkway
Natchez, MS 39120
(800) 305-7417
www.bringfido.com/go/1DXY
pg. 126

Shaggy's Beach Bar & Grill
1763 Beach Boulevard
Biloxi, MS 39531
(228) 432-5005
www.bringfido.com/go/1DWC
pg. 127

HOTELS
Choctaw Hall
310 N Wall Street
Natchez, MS 39120
(601) 807-0196
www.bringfido.com/go/1DXZ
pg. 126

Hard Rock Hotel & Casino Biloxi
777 Beach Boulevard
Biloxi, MS 39530
(228) 374-7625
www.bringfido.com/go/1DWB
pg. 127

MISSOURI
ATTRACTIONS

The Doghaus
1800 S 10th Street
St. Louis, MO 63104
(314) 809-1817
www.bringfido.com/go/1DXX
pg. 129

Fantastic Caverns
4872 N Farm Road 125
Springfield, MO 65803
(417) 833-2010
www.bringfido.com/go/1E4G
pg. 131

Gateway Arch National Park
11 N 4th Street #1810
St. Louis, MO 63102
(314) 655-1600
www.bringfido.com/go/1DXV
pg. 129

Mount Pleasant Estates
5634 High Street
Augusta, MO 63332
(636) 482-9463
www.bringfido.com/go/1DWH
pg. 132

National Tiger Sanctuary
518 State Highway BB
Saddlebrooke, MO 65630
(417) 587-3633
www.bringfido.com/go/1DWD
pg. 128

Purina Farms
200 Checkerboard Drive
Gray Summit, MO 63039
(314) 982-3232
www.bringfido.com/go/1DWF
pg. 132

HOTELS

**Best Western Plus
Washington Hotel**
2621 E 5th Street
Washington, MO 63090
(636) 390-8877
www.bringfido.com/go/1DWG
pg. 132

Four Seasons Hotel St. Louis
999 N 2nd Street
St. Louis, MO 63102
(314) 881-5800
www.bringfido.com/go/1DXW
pg. 129

Hotel Vandivort
305 E Walnut Street
Springfield, MO 65806
(417) 832-1515
www.bringfido.com/go/1E4H
pg. 131

Lilleys' Landing Resort & Marina
367 River Lane
Branson, MO 65616
(417) 334-6380
www.bringfido.com/go/1DWE
pg. 128

MONTANA
ATTRACTIONS

Bonsai Brewing Company
549 Wisconsin Avenue
Whitefish, MT 59937
(406) 730-1717
www.bringfido.com/go/1DXU
pg. 133

Hugh Rogers WAG Park
1720 E 2nd Street
Whitefish, MT 59937
(406) 863-2470
www.bringfido.com/go/1DXS
pg. 133

Sweet Peaks Ice Cream
419 E 3rd Street
Whitefish, MT 59937
(406) 862-4668
www.bringfido.com/go/1DXT
pg. 133

Whitefish Tours & Shuttle
541 Spokane Avenue
Whitefish, MT 59937
(406) 212-0080
www.bringfido.com/go/1DXQ
pg. 133

Yellowstone National Park
30 Yellowstone Avenue
West Yellowstone, MT
(406) 646-7701
www.bringfido.com/go/1E4F
pg. 134

HOTELS

The Pine Lodge
920 Spokane Avenue
Whitefish, MT 59937
(406) 204-4519
www.bringfido.com/go/1DXR
Rates from $80/night
pg. 133

Under Canvas Yellowstone
890 Buttermilk Creek Road
West Yellowstone, MT 59758
(406) 219-0441
www.bringfido.com/go/1E4E
pg. 134

NEBRASKA
ATTRACTIONS

Bryson's Airboat Tours
839 County Road 19
Fremont, NE 68025
(402) 968-8534
www.bringfido.com/go/1DPU
pg. 136

HOTELS

**Element Omaha Midtown
Crossing**
3253 Dodge Street
Omaha, NE 68131
(402) 614-8080
www.bringfido.com/go/1DPV
pg. 136

Fort Robinson State Park Cabins
3200 Highway 20
Crawford, NE 69339
(308) 665-2900
www.bringfido.com/go/1DWJ
pg. 135

NEVADA
ATTRACTIONS

Foxtail Winter Snowplay Area
6725 Lee Canyon Road
Las Vegas, NV 89124
(702) 385-2754
www.bringfido.com/go/1DXH
pg. 139

Mount Charleston
2525 Kyle Canyon Road
Las Vegas, NV 89124
(702) 872-5486
www.bringfido.com/go/1DTF
pg. 139

**Red Rock Canyon National
Conservation Area**
1000 Scenic Loop Drive
Las Vegas, NV 89161
(702) 515-5350
www.bringfido.com/go/1DN8
pg. 137

Valley of Fire State Park
Valley of Fire Highway
Overton, NV 89040
(702) 397-2088
www.bringfido.com/go/1DNA
pg. 137

HOTELS

Delano Las Vegas
3970 Las Vegas Boulevard S
Las Vegas, NV 89119
(877) 632-5400
www.bringfido.com/go/1DN9
pg. 137

**Mount Charleston Lodge
& Cabins**
5355 Kyle Canyon Road
Las Vegas, NV 89124
(702) 872-5408
www.bringfido.com/go/1DTG
pg. 139

NEW HAMPSHIRE

ATTRACTIONS

Conway Scenic Railroad
38 Norcross Circle
North Conway, NH 03860
(603) 356-5251
www.bringfido.com/go/1DKO
pg. 141

Great Glen Trails
1 Mount Washington Auto Road
Gorham, NH 03581
(603) 466-3988
www.bringfido.com/go/1DXM
pg. 140

Kancamagus Highway
Kancamagus Highway & Main
Street
Conway, NH 03818
(800) 346-3687
www.bringfido.com/go/1DXK
pg. 140

Mt. Washington Auto Road
1 Mount Washington Auto Road
Gorham, NH 03581
(603) 466-3988
www.bringfido.com/go/1DXI
pg. 140

White Mountain National Forest
71 White Mountain Drive
Campton, NH 03223
(603) 536-6100
www.bringfido.com/go/1DXL
pg. 140

HOTELS

The Glen House
979 NH Route 16
Gorham, NH 03581
(603) 466-3420
www.bringfido.com/go/1DXJ
pg. 140

Whitney's Inn at Jackson
357 Black Mountain Road
Jackson, NH 03846
(603) 383-8916
www.bringfido.com/go/1DKP
pg. 141

NEW JERSEY

ATTRACTIONS

8th Avenue Dog Beach
8th Avenue & Ocean Avenue
Asbury Park, NJ 07712
(732) 616-0749
www.bringfido.com/go/1DKT
pg. 143

Cape May Whale Watcher
1218 Wilson Drive
Cape May, NJ 08204
(609) 884-5445
www.bringfido.com/go/1DKQ
pg. 142

Cape May Winery
711 Townbank Road
Cape May, NJ 08204
(609) 884-1169
www.bringfido.com/go/1DKS
pg. 142

The Dawg Joint
513 Bangs Avenue
Asbury Park, NJ 07712
www.bringfido.com/go/1DTL
pg. 143

Wonder Bar
1213 Ocean Avenue
Asbury Park, NJ 07712
(732) 455-3767
www.bringfido.com/go/1DKW
pg. 143

HOTELS

The Asbury
210 5th Avenue
Asbury Park, NJ 07712
(732) 774-7100
www.bringfido.com/go/1DKU
pg. 143

Highland House
131 N Broadway
Cape May, NJ 08204
(609) 898-1198
www.bringfido.com/go/1DKR
pg. 142

NEW MEXICO

ATTRACTIONS

ABQ Trolley Company
303 Romero Street NW
Albuquerque, NM 87104
(505) 200-2642
www.bringfido.com/go/1DY8
pg. 144

Alien Zone
216 N Main Street
Roswell, NM 88201
(575) 627-6982
www.bringfido.com/go/1DTQ
pg. 146

Highland Park
825 Silver Avenue SE
Albuquerque, NM 87102
(505) 768-5300
www.bringfido.com/go/1DYB
pg. 144

International UFO Museum
114 N Main Street
Roswell, NM 88203
(575) 625-9495
www.bringfido.com/go/1DTN
pg. 146

Petroglyph National Monument
6510 Western Trail NW
Albuquerque, NM 87120
(505) 899-0205
www.bringfido.com/go/1DYA
pg. 144

Roswell UFO Spacewalk
116 E 2nd Street
Roswell, NM 88201
(575) 910 2113
www.bringfido.com/go/1DTP
pg. 146

Santa Fe Mountain Adventures
Don Diego Court
Santa Fe, NM 87505
(505) 988-4000
www.bringfido.com/go/1DTS
pg. 145

Woof Bowl Dog Park
1600 N Grand Avenue
Roswell, NM 88201
(575) 624-6720
www.bringfido.com/go/1DTR
pg. 146

HOTELS

Hotel Parq Central
806 Central Avenue SE
Albuquerque, NM 87102
(505) 242-0040
www.bringfido.com/go/1DY9
pg. 144

Inn of the Turquoise Bear
342 E Buena Vista Street
Santa Fe, NM 87505
(505) 983 0798
www.bringfido.com/go/1DTT
pg. 145

The Roswell Inn
2101 N Main Street
Roswell, NM 88201
(575) 623-6050
www.bringfido.com/go/1DTO
pg. 146

NEW YORK

ATTRACTIONS

Atwater Estate Vineyards
5055 NY 414
Burdett, NY 14818
(800) 331-7323
www.bringfido.com/go/1DL4
pg. 151

The Battery
State Street & Battery Place
New York, NY 10004
(212) 344-3491
www.bringfido.com/go/1E5T
pg. 155

Brooklyn Bridge
Brooklyn Bridge, NY 10038
(212) 639-9675
www.bringfido.com/go/1E5P
pg. 155

Brooklyn Bridge Park
334 Furman Street
Brooklyn, NY 11201
(718) 222-9939
www.bringfido.com/go/1E7W
pg. 155

Buttermilk Falls State Park
116 E Buttermilk Falls Road
Ithaca, NY 14850
(607) 273-5761
www.bringfido.com/go/1DYF
pg. 147

Cayuga Lake Wine Trail
2770 Ernsberger Road
Romulus, NY 14541
(800) 684-5217
www.bringfido.com/go/1DL5
pg. 151

Central Park
59th Street & 5th Avenue
New York, NY 10022
(212) 310-6600
www.bringfido.com/go/1E5X
pg. 153

Charging Bull
Broadway & Morris Street
New York, NY 10004
www.bringfido.com/go/1E5S
pg. 155

The Classy Canine
375 County Road 39
Southampton, NY 11968
(631) 283-1306
www.bringfido.com/go/1DWQ
pg. 156

Claudia Matles Yoga
P.O. Box 2565
Southampton NY 11969
(631) 721-7511
www.bringfido.com/go/1DWR
pg. 156

East Hampton Main Beach
104 Ocean Avenue
East Hampton, NY 11937
(631) 324-0074
www.bringfido.com/go/1DWP
pg. 156

Hillside Dog Park
4 Vine Street
Brooklyn, NY 11201
(212) 639-9675
www.bringfido.com/go/1E5W
pg. 155

Ludovico Sculpture Trail
Bridge Street
Seneca Falls, NY 13148
(315) 568-8204
www.bringfido.com/go/1DL6
pg. 151

Luke's Lobster
11 Water Street
Brooklyn, NY 11201
(917) 882-7516
www.bringfido.com/go/1E5U
pg. 155

Montauk Point Lighthouse
2000 Montauk Highway
Montauk, NY 11954
(631) 668-2544
www.bringfido.com/go/1DWS
pg. 156

NYC Ferry
South Street & Gouverneur Lane
New York, NY 10005
(844) 469-3377
www.bringfido.com/go/1E5R
pg. 155

NYC Horse Carriage Rides
7th Avenue & 59th Street
Central Park South
New York, NY 10009
(516) 606-6212
www.bringfido.com/go/1E5Z
pg. 153

Oyster Bay Brewing Company
36 Audrey Avenue
Oyster Bay, NY 11771
(516) 802-5546
www.bringfido.com/go/1DYK
pg. 149

Penguin Bay Winery
6075 NY 414
Hector, NY 14841
(607) 546-5115
www.bringfido.com/go/1DL3
pg. 151

Ravines Wine Cellars
400 Barracks Road
Geneva, NY 14456
(315) 781-7007
www.bringfido.com/go/1DL2
pg. 151

Robert H. Treman State Park
105 Enfield Falls Road
Ithaca, NY 14850
(607) 273-3440
www.bringfido.com/go/1DYD
pg. 147

Sagamore Hill
20 Sagamore Hill Road
Oyster Bay, NY 11771
(516) 922-4788
www.bringfido.com/go/1DYH
pg. 149

Sag Harbor Charters
23 Marine Park Drive
Sag Harbor, NY 11963
(631) 459-1823
www.bringfido.com/go/1DWN
pg. 156

Sands Point Preserve
127 Middle Neck Road
Sands Point, NY 11050
(516) 571-7901
www.bringfido.com/go/1DYJ
pg. 149

Seneca Lake Wine Trail
2 N Franklin Street, Suite 320
Watkins Glen, NY 14891
(877) 536-2717
www.bringfido.com/go/1DL0
pg. 151

Shake Shack
366 Columbus Avenue
New York, NY 10024
(646) 747-8770
www.bringfido.com/go/1E60
pg. 153

Whiteface Mountain
5021 State Route 86
Wilmington, NY 12997
(518) 946-2223
www.bringfido.com/go/1DL7
pg. 152

Whiteface Veterans' Memorial Highway
NY-431 & Whiteface Memorial Highway
Wilmington, NY 12997
(518) 946-2223
www.bringfido.com/go/1DLA
pg. 152

Wilmington Trail
33 Reservoir Road
Wilmington, NY 12997
(518) 946-2223
www.bringfido.com/go/1DL9
pg. 152

HOTELS

1 Hotel Brooklyn Bridge
60 Furman Street
Brooklyn, NY 11201
(347) 696-2500
www.bringfido.com/go/1E5Q
pg. 155

Emerald Glen Getaway
217 Pegg Road
Morris, NY 13808
(510) 552-3500
www.bringfido.com/go/1DWM
pg. 150

Firelight Camps
1150 Danby Road
Ithaca, NY 14850
(607) 229-1644
www.bringfido.com/go/1DYG
pg. 147

The Gould Hotel
108 Falls Street
Seneca Falls, NY 13148
(315) 712-4000
www.bringfido.com/go/1DL1
pg. 151

High Peaks Resort
2384 Saranac Avenue
Lake Placid, NY 12946
(518) 523-4411
www.bringfido.com/go/1DL8
pg. 152

La Tourelle Hotel & Spa
1150 Danby Road
Ithaca, NY 14850
(607) 273-2734
www.bringfido.com/go/1DYE
pg. 147

Mill House Inn
31 N Main Street
East Hampton, NY 11937
(631) 324-9766
www.bringfido.com/go/1DWO
pg. 156

Oheka Castle
135 W Gate Drive
Huntington, NY 11743
(631) 659-1400
www.bringfido.com/go/1DYI
pg. 149

The Sherry-Netherland
781 5th Avenue
New York, NY 10022
(212) 355-2800
www.bringfido.com/go/1E5Y
pg. 153

NORTH CAROLINA

ATTRACTIONS

Bald Head Island
Deep Point Marina
1301 Ferry Road SE
Southport, NC 28461
(910) 457-5003
www.bringfido.com/go/1DLB
pg. 158

Biltmore Estate
1 Lodge Street
Asheville, NC 28803
(828) 225-1333
www.bringfido.com/go/1DLF
pg. 159

Cape Hatteras National Seashore
1401 National Park Drive
Manteo, NC 27954
(252) 473-2111
www.bringfido.com/go/1DRH
pg. 163

Cary Cart Company
1 Marina Wynd
Bald Head Island, NC 28461
(910) 457-7333
www.bringfido.com/go/1DLD
pg. 158

Chimney Rock State Park
431 Main Street
Chimney Rock, NC 28720
(828) 625-9611
www.bringfido.com/go/1DLQ
pg. 157

Corolla Cantina
1159 Austin Street
Corolla, NC 27927
(252) 597-1730
www.bringfido.com/go/1DRL
pg. 162

Corolla Outback Adventures
1150 Ocean Trail
Corolla, NC 27927
(252) 453-4484
www.bringfido.com/go/1DRJ
pg. 162

Deep Point Marina
1301 Ferry Road SE
Southport, NC 28461
(910) 269-2380
www.bringfido.com/go/1E80
pg. 158

French Broad Outfitters
230 Hominy Creek Road
Asheville, NC 28806
(828) 505-7371
www.bringfido.com/go/1DLH
pg. 159

Lake Lure Adventure Company
470 Memorial Highway
Lake Lure, NC 28746
(828) 625-8066
www.bringfido.com/go/1DLT
pg. 157

Lucky Dog Bark & Brew Charlotte
2220 Thrift Road
Charlotte, NC 28208
(704) 333-4114
www.bringfido.com/go/1DLO
pg. 161

Old Rock Café
431 Main Street
Chimney Rock, NC 28720
(828) 625-2329
www.bringfido.com/go/1DLS
pg. 157

Outer Banks Airlines
410 Airport Road
Manteo, NC 27954
(252) 256-2322
www.bringfido.com/go/1DRG
pg. 163

Riverside Adventure Company
10 Marina Wynd
Bald Head Island, NC 28461
(910) 457-4944
www.bringfido.com/go/1DLE
pg. 158

Sierra Nevada Brewing Co.
100 Sierra Nevada Way
Mills River, NC 28732
(828) 681-5300
www.bringfido.com/go/1E4B
pg. 157

Surfin' Spoon
2408 S Virginia Dare Trail
Nags Head, NC 27959
(252) 441-7873
www.bringfido.com/go/1E9L
pg. 163

US National Whitewater Center
5000 Whitewater Center Parkway
Charlotte, NC 28214
(704) 391-3900
www.bringfido.com/go/1DLM
pg. 161

Whalehead Club
1100 Club Road
Corolla, NC 27927
(252) 453-9040
www.bringfido.com/go/1DRM
pg. 162

Wright Brothers National Memorial
1000 N Croatan Highway
Kill Devil Hills, NC 27948
(252) 473-2111
www.bringfido.com/go/1DRE
pg. 163

HOTELS

Bald Head Island Limited
6 Marina Wynd
Bald Head Island, NC 28461
(910) 457-5002
www.bringfido.com/go/1DLC
pg. 158

Barkwells
290 Lance Road
Mills River, NC 28759
(828) 891-8288
www.bringfido.com/go/1DLR
pg. 157

Drury Inn & Suites Northlake
6920 Northlake Mall Drive
Charlotte, NC 28216
(704) 599-8882
www.bringfido.com/go/1DLN
pg. 161

Four Paws Kingdom
335 Lazy Creek Drive
Rutherfordton, NC 28139
(828) 287-7324
www.bringfido.com/go/1DLP
pg. 159

Grand Bohemian Hotel Asheville
11 Boston Way
Asheville, NC 28803
(828) 505-2949
www.bringfido.com/go/1DLG
pg. 159

Inn at Corolla Light
1066 Ocean Trail
Corolla, NC 27927
(252) 453-3340
www.bringfido.com/go/1DRK
pg. 162

Sandbar Bed & Breakfast
2510 S Virginia Dare Trail
Nags Head, NC 27959
(252) 489-1868
www.bringfido.com/go/1DRF
pg. 163

NORTH DAKOTA

ATTRACTIONS

Dakota Thunder
404 Louis Lamour Lane
Jamestown, ND 58401
(701) 251-9145
www.bringfido.com/go/1DYR
pg. 165

Dickinson Dog Park
455 8th Avenue SW
Dickinson, ND 58601
(701) 456-2074
www.bringfido.com/go/1DYW
pg. 165

Enchanted Highway
I-94, Exit 72
Regent, ND 58650
(701) 563-6400
www.bringfido.com/go/1DYV
pg. 165

Frontier Village
404 Louis Lamour Lane
Jamestown, ND 58401
(800) 222-4766
www.bringfido.com/go/1DYS
pg. 165

International Peace Garden
10939 Highway 281
Dunseith, ND 58329
(701) 263-4390
www.bringfido.com/go/1E2M
pg. 166

National Buffalo Museum
500 17th Street SE
Jamestown, ND 58401
(701) 252-8648
www.bringfido.com/go/1DYP
pg. 165

Salem Sue
N 8th St
New Salem, ND 58563
(701) 843-7828
www.bringfido.com/go/1DYU
pg. 165

Sandy, The World's Largest Sandhill Crane
299 5th Street NE
Steele, ND 58482
701-475-2805
www.bringfido.com/go/1DYT
pg. 165

Scandinavian Heritage Park
1020 S Broadway
Minot, ND 58701
(701) 852-9161
www.bringfido.com/go/1DYO
pg. 166

Seaman Overlook at Fort Mandan
Lewis & Clark Interpretive Center
2576 8th Street SW
Washburn, ND 58577
(701) 462-8535
www.bringfido.com/go/1DYN
pg. 166

HOTELS

Hawthorn Suites by Wyndham Minot
800 37th Avenue SW
Minot, ND 50701
(701) 858-7300
www.bringfido.com/go/1DYM
pg. 166

La Quinta Inn & Suites Dickinson
552 12th Street W
Dickinson, ND 58601
(701) 456-2500
www.bringfido.com/go/1DYQ
pg. 165

OHIO

ATTRACTIONS

Battelle Riverfront Park
25 Marconi Boulevard
Columbus, OH 43215
(614) 645-03800
www.bringfido.com/go/1E78
pg. 169

BrewDog Franklinton
463 W Town Street
Columbus, OH 43215
(614) 908-3077
www.bringfido.com/go/1E79
pg. 169

The Canine Country Club
29929 Lorain Road
North Olmsted, OH 44070
(440) 455-9337
www.bringfido.com/go/1DYZ
pg. 167

Hueston Woods State Park
6301 Park Office Road
College Corner, OH 45003
(513) 523-6347
www.bringfido.com/go/1DYX
pg. 168

Scioto Audubon Metro Park
400 W Whittier Street
Columbus, OH 43215
(614) 891-0700
www.bringfido.com/go/1E77
pg. 169

Scioto Mile
W Rich Street
Columbus, OH 43215
(614) 645-3800
www.bringfido.com/go/1E75
pg. 169

HOTELS

DogHouse Hotel & Brewery
100 Gender Road
Canal Winchester, OH 43110
(614) 908-3054
www.bringfido.com/go/1E76
pg. 169

**Hueston Woods Lodge
& Conference Center**
5201 Lodge Road
College Corner, OH 45003
(513) 664-3500
www.bringfido.com/go/1DYY
pg. 168

Metropolitan at the 9
2017 E 9th Street
Cleveland, OH 44115
(216) 239-1200
www.bringfido.com/go/1DZ0
pg. 167

OKLAHOMA

ATTRACTIONS

The Art Hall
519 NW 23rd Street
Oklahoma City, OK 73103
(405) 231-5700
www.bringfido.com/go/1E4Q
pg. 170

Bone Dog Boutique
100 NE 2nd Street
Oklahoma City, OK 73104
(405) 600-3460
www.bringfido.com/go/1DZ4
pg. 171

Literati Press Bookshop
3010 Paseo
Oklahoma City, OK 73103
(405) 882-7032
www.bringfido.com/go/1E4T
pg. 170

Little D Gallery
3003A Paseo
Oklahoma City, OK 73103
(720) 773-1064
www.bringfido.com/go/1E4R
pg. 170

Little Market Paseo
3004 Paseo
Oklahoma City, OK 73103
(405) 525-2688
www.bringfido.com/go/1E4U
pg. 170

Myriad Botanical Gardens
301 W Reno Avenue
Oklahoma City, OK 73102
(405) 445-7080
www.bringfido.com/go/1DZ1
pg. 171

**Myriad Botanical Gardens
Dog Park**
301 W Reno Avenue
Oklahoma City, OK 73102
(405) 445-7080
www.bringfido.com/go/1DZ3
pg. 171

Paseo Arts District
3024 Paseo
Oklahoma City, OK 73103
(405) 525-2688
www.bringfido.com/go/1E4O
pg. 170

Picasso Café
3009 Paseo
Oklahoma City, OK 73103
(405) 602-2002
www.bringfido.com/go/1E4V
pg.170

Prairie Arts Collective
3110 N Walker
Oklahoma City, OK 73118
(405) 436-5439
www.bringfido.com/go/1E4S
pg. 170

Riversport OKC
800 Riversport Drive
Oklahoma City, OK 73129
(405) 552-4040
www.bringfido.com/go/1E4W
pg. 170

HOTELS

**21c Museum Hotel
Oklahoma City**
900 W Main Street
Oklahoma City, OK 73106
(405) 982-6900
www.bringfido.com/go/1E4P
pg. 170

**Aloft Oklahoma City Downtown
Bricktown**
209 N Walnut Avenue
Oklahoma City, OK 73104
(405) 605-2100
www.bringfido.com/go/1DZ2
pg. 171

OREGON

ATTRACTIONS

Deschutes National Forest
63095 Deschutes Market Road
Bend, OR 97701
(541) 383-5300
www.bringfido.com/go/1DX6
pg. 174

Dog Mountain Trail
WA-14 at Milepost 53
Cook, WA 98605
(541) 308-1700
www.bringfido.com/go/1DU6
pg. 179

Ecola State Park
84318 Ecola Park Road
Cannon Beach, OR 97110
(503) 436-2844
www.bringfido.com/go/1DP7
pg. 177

Haystack Rock
Hemlock Street & Gower Avenue
Cannon Beach, OR 97110
(503) 436-2623
www.bringfido.com/go/1DP5
pg. 177

John Dellenback Dunes Trail
Eel Creek Campground
67760 Spinreel Road
Lakeside, OR 97449
(541) 750-7000
www.bringfido.com/go/1DPZ
pg. 175

Mt. Bachelor Ski Resort
13000 SW Century Drive
Bend, OR 97702
(541) 382-1709
www.bringfido.com/go/1DX7
pg. 174

Multnomah Falls
E Historic Columbia River Highway
Bridal Veil, OR 97010
(503) 695-2372
www.bringfido.com/go/1DU4
pg. 179

Proxy Falls
OR-242 W / McKenzie Highway
McKenzie Bridge, OR 97413
(541) 822-3381
www.bringfido.com/go/1E5I
pg. 181

Riverbend Beach Dog Park
799 SW Columbia Street
Bend, OR 97702
(541) 389-7275
www.bringfido.com/go/1DWX
pg. 176

Sahalie and Koosah Falls
McKenzie Bridge Drive
McKenzie Bridge, OR 97413
(541) 822-3881
www.bringfido.com/go/1DXB
pg. 181

Sand Dunes Frontier
83960 US 101
Florence, OR 97439
(541) 997-3544
www.bringfido.com/go/1DPY
pg. 175

Secrets of Portlandia
700 SW 6th Avenue
Portland, OR 97204
(503) 703-4282
www.bringfido.com/go/1DX0
pg. 173

Sellwood Riverfront Park
1221 SE Oaks Park Way
Portland, OR 97202
(503) 823-4000
www.bringfido.com/go/1DX3
pg. 173

Spinreel Dune Buggy
67045 Spinreel Road
North Bend, OR 97459
(541) 759-3313
www.bringfido.com/go/1DPW
pg. 175

Sunriver Resort
17600 Center Drive
Sunriver, OR 97707
(800) 801-8765
www.bringfido.com/go/1DX4
pg. 174

Tin Shed Garden Café
1438 NE Alberta Street
Portland, OR 97211
(503) 288-6966
www.bringfido.com/go/1DX2
pg. 173

Three Creeks Brewing
721 S Desperado Court
Sisters, OR 97759
(541) 549-1963
www.bringfido.com/go/1DXC
pg. 181

Three Sisters Wilderness
57600 McKenzie Highway
McKenzie Bridge, OR 97413
(541) 822-3381
www.bringfido.com/go/1DX9
pg. 181

Tour DeVine
3800 NE Three Mile Lane
McMinnville, OR 97128
(503) 687-3816
www.bringfido.com/go/1DWY
pg. 178

Tumalo Creek Kayak & Canoe
805 SW Industrial Way
Bend, OR 97702
(541) 317-9407
www.bringfido.com/go/1DWV
pg. 176

Village Bike & Ski
57100 Beaver Drive, Bldg #21
Sunriver, OR 97707
(541) 593-2453
www.bringfido.com/go/1E4X
pg. 174

Wanoga Sno-Park
Cascade Lakes National
Scenic Byway
Bend, OR 97703
(541) 383-4000
www.bringfido.com/go/1DX8
pg.174

HOTELS

Bennington Properties
56842 Venture Lane
Sunriver, OR 97707
(541) 705-2267
www.bringfido.com/go/1DX5
pg. 174

**Best Western Plus Hood
River Inn**
1108 E Marina Way
Hood River, OR 97031
(541) 386-2200
www.bringfido.com/go/1DU5
pg. 179

FivePine Lodge
1021 E Desperado Trail
Sisters, OR 97759
(541) 549-5900
www.bringfido.com/go/1DXA
pg. 181

Kimpton RiverPlace Hotel
1510 S Harbor Way
Portland, OR 97201
(503) 228-3233
www.bringfido.com/go/1DX1
pg. 173

McMenamins Hotel Oregon
310 NE Evans Street
McMinnville, OR 97128
(503) 472-8427
www.bringfido.com/go/1DWZ
pg. 178

Oxford Hotel Bend
10 NW Minnesota Avenue
Bend, OR 97703
(541) 382-8436
www.bringfido.com/go/1DWW
pg. 176

Surfsand Resort
148 W Gower Avenue
Cannon Beach, OR 97110
(503) 436-2274
www.bringfido.com/go/1DP6
pg. 177

William M. Tugman State Park
72549 Highway 101
Lakeside, OR 97449
(501) 759-3604
www.bringfido.com/go/1DPX
pg. 175

PENNSYLVANIA

ATTRACTIONS

Abe's Buggy Rides
2596 Old Philadelphia Pike
Bird in Hand, PA 17505
(717) 392-1794
www.bringfido.com/go/1DZ7
pg. 188

The Amish Farm and House
2395 Covered Bridge Drive
Lancaster, PA 17602
(717) 394-6185
www.bringfido.com/go/1DZ9
pg. 188

**Beau's Dream Dog Park
at Buchanan Park**
901 Buchanan Avenue
Lancaster, PA 17603
(717) 291-4841
www.bringfido.com/go/1DZA
pg. 188

Bushkill Falls
138 Bushkill Falls Trail
Bushkill, PA 18324
(570) 588-6682
www.bringfido.com/go/1DWT
pg. 184

The Constitutional Walking Tour
525 Arch Street
Philadelphia, PA 19106
(215) 525-1776
www.bringfido.com/go/1DZC
pg. 182

**D&L Trail at Lehigh Gorge
State Park**
Packer Hill Road (Parking Area)
Jim Thorpe, PA 18229
(570) 443-0400
www.bringfido.com/go/1DUJ
pg. 183

Geno's Steaks
1219 S 9th Street
Philadelphia, PA 19147
(215) 389-0659
www.bringfido.com/go/1DZF
pg. 182

Gettysburg National Military Park
1195 Baltimore Pike
Gettysburg, PA 17325
(717) 334-1124
www.bringfido.com/go/1DP8
pg. 185

Haunted Gettysburg Tours
27 Steinwehr Avenue
Gettysburg, PA 17325
(717) 253-5013
www.bringfido.com/go/1DPA
pg. 185

Knoebels Amusement Resort
391 Knoebels Boulevard
Elysburg, PA 17824
(570) 672-2572
www.bringfido.com/go/1DPB
pg. 187

Lehigh Gorge Scenic Railway
1 Susquehanna Street
Jim Thorpe, PA 18229
(570) 325-8485
www.bringfido.com/go/1DUH
pg. 183

Pat's King of Steaks
1237 E Passyunk Avenue
Philadelphia, PA 19147
(215) 468-1546
www.bringfido.com/go/1DZE
pg. 182

HOTELS

Battlefield Bed and Breakfast
2264 Emmitsburg Road
Gettysburg, PA 17325
(717) 334-8804
www.bringfido.com/go/1DP9
pg. 185

**Country Inn & Suites
by Radisson Lehighton**
1619 Interchange Road
Lehighton, PA 18235
(610) 379-5066
www.bringfido.com/go/1DUI
pg. 183

Genetti Hotel
200 W Fourth Street
Williamsport, PA 17701
(570) 326-6600
www.bringfido.com/go/1DPC
pg. 187

Hotel Fauchere
401 Broad Street
Milford, PA 18337
(570) 409-1212
www.bringfido.com/go/1DWU
pg. 184

Kimpton Hotel Monaco
433 Chestnut Street
Philadelphia, PA 19106
(215) 925-2111
www.bringfido.com/go/1DZD
pg. 182

Knoebels Campground
391 Knoebels Boulevard
Elysburg, PA 17824
(800) 487-4386
www.bringfido.com/go/1E81
pg. 187

**La Quinta Inn & Suites
by Wyndham Lancaster**
25 Eastbrook Road
Ronks, PA 17572
(717) 208-2453
www.bringfido.com/go/1DZ8
pg. 188

RHODE ISLAND

ATTRACTIONS

Antique Yacht Collection
31 Bowens Wharf
Newport, RI 02840
(401) 678-6740
www.bringfido.com/go/1DND
pg. 190

Beach Rose Bicycles
1622 Roslyn Road
New Shoreham, RI 02807
(401) 466-5925
www.bringfido.com/go/1DPN
pg. 189

Block Island Ferry
304 Great Island Road
Narragansett, RI 02882
(401) 783-7996
www.bringfido.com/go/1DPK
pg. 189

Block Island Taxi and Tours
Block Island, RI
(401) 466-2562
www.bringfido.com/go/1DPO
pg. 189

Cliff Walk
175 Memorial Boulevard
Newport, RI 02840
(401) 845-5300
www.bringfido.com/go/1DNB
pg. 190

McAloon's Taxi
Block Island, RI
(401) 741-1410
www.bringfido.com/go/1DPP
pg. 189

Mohegan Bluffs
Spring Street & Mohegan Trail
New Shoreham, RI 02807
(401) 466-2474
www.bringfido.com/go/1DPM
pg. 189

HOTELS

Blue Dory Inn
61 Dodge Street
New Shoreham, RI 02807
(401) 466-5891
www.bringfido.com/go/1DPL
pg. 189

Paws on Pelham
96 Pelham Street
Newport, RI 02840
(401) 845-9400
www.bringfido.com/go/1DNC
pg. 190

SOUTH CAROLINA

ATTRACTIONS

Captain Buddy's
Calhoun Street Fishing Pier
Bluffton, SC 29910
(843) 470-7700
www.bringfido.com/go/1DZG
pg. 192

Conestee Dog Park
840 Mauldin Road
Greenville, SC 29607
(864) 288-6470
www.bringfido.com/go/1E53
pg. 193

Drayton Hall
3380 Ashley River Road
Charleston, SC 29414
(843) 769-2600
www.bringfido.com/go/1DZK
pg. 191

Falls Park
601 S Main Street
Greenville, SC 29601
(864) 232-2273
www.bringfido.com/go/1E5F
pg. 193

Lake Conestee Nature Preserve
601 Fork Shoals Road
Greenville, SC 29605
(864) 277-2004
www.bringfido.com/go/1E52
pg. 193

Limoncello
401 River Street
Greenville, SC 29601
(864) 263-7000
www.bringfido.com/go/1E50
pg. 193

Magnolia Plantation & Gardens
3550 Ashley River Road
Charleston, SC 29414
(843) 571-1266
www.bringfido.com/go/1DZI
pg. 191

Mast General Store
111 N Main Street
Greenville, SC 29601
(864) 235-1883
www.bringfido.com/go/1E54
pg. 193

Pour Taproom
7 Falls Park Drive
Greenville, SC 29601
(864) 412-7400
www.bringfido.com/go/1E51
pg. 193

Swamp Rabbit Trail
601 S Main Street
Greenville, SC 29601
(864) 232-2273
www.bringfido.com/go/1E4Y
pg. 193

HOTELS

Aloft Greenville Downtown
5 N Laurens Street
Greenville, SC 29601
(864) 297-6100
www.bringfido.com/go/1E4Z
pg. 193

Montage Palmetto Bluff
477 Mount Pelia Road
Bluffton, SC 29910
(843) 706-6500
www.bringfido.com/go/1DZH
pg. 192

Wentworth Mansion
149 Wentworth Street
Charleston, SC 29401
(843) 853-1886
www.bringfido.com/go/1DZJ
pg. 191

SOUTH DAKOTA

ATTRACTIONS

Bear Country USA
13820 S Highway 16
Rapid City, SD 57702
(605) 343-2290
www.bringfido.com/go/1DPJ
pg. 195

Black Hills National Forest
1019 N 5th Street
Custer, SD 57730
(605) 673-9200
www.bringfido.com/go/1E57
pg. 196

Blue Bell Lodge
25453 SD 87
Custer, SD 57730
(605) 255-4531
www.bringfido.com/go/1DR7
pg. 197

Custer State Park
Wildlife Loop Road
Custer, SD 57730
(605) 255-4515
www.bringfido.com/go/1DR9
pg. 197

Reptile Gardens
8955 S Highway 16
Rapid City, SD 57702
(605) 342-5873
www.bringfido.com/go/1DPH
pg. 195

Saloon No. 10
657 Main Street
Deadwood, SD 57732
(800) 952-9398
www.bringfido.com/go/1E58
pg. 196

HOTELS
Hart Ranch Camping Resort
23756 Arena Drive
Rapid City, SD 57702
(605) 399-2582
www.bringfido.com/go/1DPI
pg. 195

Mystic Hills Hideaway
21766 Custer Peak Road
Deadwood, SD 57732
(605) 584-4794
www.bringfido.com/go/1E56
pg. 196

State Game Lodge
13389 US Highway 16A
Custer, SD 57730
(605) 255-4541
www.bringfido.com/go/1DR8
pg. 197

TENNESSEE
ATTRACTIONS
3rd Deck Burger Bar
151 Riverfront Parkway
Chattanooga, TN 37402
(423) 266-4488
www.bringfido.com/go/1DHX
pg. 72

Backbeat Tours
197 Beale Street
Memphis, TN 38103
(901) 527-9415
www.bringfido.com/go/1DZL
pg. 199

Cades Cove Loop Road
Great Smoky Mountains
National Park
Townsend, TN 37882
(865) 436-1200
www.bringfido.com/go/1DZO
pg. 201

**Great Smoky Mountains
National Park**
107 Park Headquarters Road
Gatlinburg, TN 37738
(865) 436-1200
www.bringfido.com/go/1E7X
pg. 201

National Civil Rights Museum
450 Mulberry Street
Memphis, TN, US, 38103
(901) 521-9699
www.bringfido.com/go/1DZN
pg. 199

River Rat Tubing
205 Wears Valley Road
Townsend, TN 37882
(865) 448-8888
www.bringfido.com/go/1DZQ
pg. 201

Walkin' Nashville
414 Union Street
Nashville, TN 37219
(615) 499-5159
www.bringfido.com/go/1DQ5
pg. 198

HOTELS
Dancing Bear Lodge
7140 E Lamar Alexander Parkway
Townsend, TN 37882
(865) 448-6000
www.bringfido.com/go/1DZP
pg. 201

The Hermitage Hotel
231 6th Avenue N
Nashville, TN 37219
(615) 244-3121
www.bringfido.com/go/1DQ6
pg. 198

The Peabody Memphis
149 Union Avenue
Memphis, TN 38103
(901) 529-4000
www.bringfido.com/go/1DZM
pg. 199

**Residence Inn by Marriott
Chattanooga Downtown**
215 Chestnut Street
Chattanooga, TN 37402
(423) 266-0600
www.bringfido.com/go/1DHW
pg. 72

TEXAS
ATTRACTIONS
Bad Wolf Ghost Tours
300 Alamo Plaza
San Antonio, TX 78205
(805) 757-0512
www.bringfido.com/go/1E6R
pg. 203

Cadillac Ranch
13651 I-40 Frontage Road
Amarillo, TX 79124
(800) 692-1338
www.bringfido.com/go/1DZY
pg. 209

Casa Rio
430 E Commerce Street
San Antonio, TX 78205
(210) 225-6718
www.bringfido.com/go/1E6T
pg. 203

East Beach
1923 Boddeker Road
Galveston, TX 77550
(409) 797-5111
www.bringfido.com/go/1E04
pg. 205

**Enchanted Rock State
Natural Area**
16710 Ranch Road 965
Fredericksburg, TX 78624
(830) 685-3636
www.bringfido.com/go/1DU2
pg. 204

Galveston Island State Park
14901 FM3005
Galveston, TX 77554
(409) 737-1222
www.bringfido.com/go/1E00
pg. 205

Get Hooked Charters
1445 Harborwalk Boulevard
Hitchcock, TX 77563
(409) 698-7112
www.bringfido.com/go/1E02
pg. 205

Hill Country State Natural Area
10600 Bandera Creek Road
Bandera, TX 78003
(830) 796-4413
www.bringfido.com/go/1DTY
pg. 204

Hobbit Café
2243 Richmond Avenue
Houston, TX 77098
(713) 526-5460
www.bringfido.com/go/1E5M
pg. 207

**Houston Arboretum
& Nature Center**
4501 Woodway Drive
Houston, TX 77024
(713) 681-8433
www.bringfido.com/go/1E5J
pg. 207

Inks Lake State Park
3630 Park Road 4 W
Burnet, TX 78611
(512) 793-2223
www.bringfido.com/go/1DU3
pg. 204

Lobo Del Mar Café
204 Palm Street
South Padre Island, TX 78597
(956) 772-7256
www.bringfido.com/go/1E08
pg. 206

Marina Bar & Grill
715 N Holiday Drive
Galveston, TX 77550
(409) 765-3033
www.bringfido.com/go/1E03
pg. 205

Memorial Park
6501 Memorial Drive
Houston, TX 77007
(713) 863-8403
www.bringfido.com/go/1E5L
pg. 207

Palo Duro Canyon State Park
11450 State Hwy Park Road 5
Canyon, TX 79015
(806) 488-2227
www.bringfido.com/go/1DZZ
pg. 209

Palo Duro Creek Ranch
11301 TX-217
Canyon, TX 79015
(806) 488-2100
www.bringfido.com/go/1DZW
pg. 209

Pedernales Falls State Park
2585 Park Road 6026
Johnson City, TX 78636
(830) 868-7304
www.bringfido.com/go/1DU1
pg. 204

Red Bud Isle
3401 Red Bud Trail
Austin, TX 78746
(512) 974-6700
www.bringfido.com/go/1DZU
pg. 202

San Antonio River Walk
849 E Commerce Street
San Antonio, TX 78205
(210) 227-4262
www.bringfido.com/go/1E6S
pg. 203

Sea Turtle, Inc.
6617 Padre Boulevard
South Padre Island, TX 78597
(956) 761-4511
www.bringfido.com/go/1E06
pg. 206

Sisters Grimm Ghost Tours
204 Alamo Plaza, Suite #T
San Antonio, TX 78205
(210) 638-1338
www.bringfido.com/go/1E6P
pg. 203

South Llano River State Park
1927 Park Road 73
Junction, TX 76849
(325) 446-3994
www.bringfido.com/go/1DU0
pg. 204

Stewart Beach Park
201 Seawall Boulevard
Galveston, TX, 77550
(409) 797-5189
www.bringfido.com/go/1E05
pg. 205

Yard Bar
6700 Burnet Road
Austin, TX 78757
(512) 900-3773
www.bringfido.com/go/1DZV
pg. 202

Zilker Botanical Garden
2220 Barton Springs Road
Austin, TX 78746
(512) 477-8672
www.bringfido.com/go/1DZT
pg. 202

Zilker Park Boat Rentals
2101 Andrew Zilker Road
Austin, TX 78746
(512) 478-3852
www.bringfido.com/go/1DZR
pg. 202

HOTELS

Best Western Plus Fredericksburg
314 E Highway Street
Fredericksburg, TX 78624
(830) 992-2929
www.bringfido.com/go/1DTZ
pg. 204

Emily Morgan Hotel
705 E Houston Street
San Antonio, TX 78205
(210) 225-5100
www.bringfido.com/go/1E6Q
pg. 203

Holiday Inn Express Canyon
2901 4th Avenue
Canyon, TX 79015
(806) 655-4445
www.bringfido.com/go/1DZX
pg. 209

Hotel Havana
1015 Navarro Street
San Antonio, TX 78205
(210) 222-2008
www.bringfido.com/go/1E6U
pg. 203

Hotel Saint Cecilia
112 Academy Drive
Austin, TX 78704
(512) 852-2400
www.bringfido.com/go/1DZS
pg. 202

La Quinta Inn & Suites Houston
Galleria
1625 W Loop South
Houston, TX 77027
(713) 355-3440
www.bringfido.com/go/1E5K
pg. 207

La Quinta Inn & Suites South
Padre Beach
7000 Padre Boulevard
South Padre Island, TX 78597
(956) 772-7000
www.bringfido.com/go/1E07
pg. 206

Red Roof PLUS Galveston
Beachfront
3924 Avenue U
Galveston, TX 77550
(409) 750-9400
www.bringfido.com/go/1E01
pg. 205

UTAH
ATTRACTIONS
Arches National Park
Arches Scenic Drive
Moab, UT 84532
(435) 719-2299
www.bringfido.com/go/1E0H
pg. 210

Bear River Migratory Bird Refuge
2155 W Forest Street
Brigham City, UT 84302
(435) 723-5887
www.bringfido.com/go/1DQ2
pg. 212

Best Friends Animal Sanctuary
5001 Angel Canyon Road
Kanab, UT 84741
(435) 644-2001
www.bringfido.com/go/1E09
pg. 211

Coral Pink Sand Dunes
State Park
12500 Sand Dune Road
Kanab, UT 84741
(435) 648-2800
www.bringfido.com/go/1E0E
pg. 213

Dreamland Safari Tours
1350 E Mountain View Drive
Kanab, UT 84741
(435) 644-5506
www.bringfido.com/go/1E0B
pg. 213

Moab Rafting & Canoe Company
2480 S Highway 191
Moab, UT 84532
(435) 259-7722
www.bringfido.com/go/1E0F
pg. 210

Paria Canyon Wilderness
Wire Pass Trailhead
US 89 & House Rock Valley Road
Kanab, UT 84741
(435) 644-1200
www.bringfido.com/go/1E0D
pg. 213

HOTELS
Best Friends Roadhouse
& Mercantile
30 N 300 W
Kanab, UT 84741
(435) 644-3400
www.bringfido.com/go/1E0A
pg. 211

Best Western Brigham City
Inn & Suites
480 Westland Drive
Brigham City, UT 84302
(435) 723-0440
www.bringfido.com/go/1DQ3
pg. 212

Quail Park Lodge
125 N 300 W (Highway 89)
Kanab, UT 84741
(435) 215-1447
www.bringfido.com/go/1E0C
pg. 213

Under Canvas Moab
13784 US-191
Moab, UT 84532
(888) 496-1148
www.bringfido.com/go/1E0G
pg. 210

VERMONT
ATTRACTIONS
Dog Mountain
143 Parks Road
St. Johnsbury, VT 05819
(800) 449-2580
www.bringfido.com/go/1E0J
pg. 217

Gondola SkyRide
7416 Mountain Road
Stowe, VT 05672
(802) 253-3500
www.bringfido.com/go/1DOO
pg. 216

Mad Tom Orchard
2615 Mad Tom Road
East Dorset, VT 05253
(802) 366-8107
www.bringfido.com/go/1E7F
pg. 215

Smugglers' Notch State Park
6443 Mountain Road
Stowe, VT 05672
(802) 253-4014
www.bringfido.com/go/1DOQ
pg. 216

Stowe Scenic Auto Road
78 Toll Road
Stowe, VT 05672
(802) 253-3500
www.bringfido.com/go/1DOR
pg. 216

Winslow Farms
161 Channing Lane
Pittsford, VT 05763
(802) 773-1003
www.bringfido.com/go/1E7H
pg. 215

HOTELS

The Lodge at Spruce Peak
7412 Mountain Road
Stowe, VT 05672
(802) 760-4700
www.bringfido.com/go/1DOP
pg. 216

The Paw House Inn
1376 Clarendon Avenue
West Rutland, VT 05777
(802) 558-2661
www.bringfido.com/go/1E7G
pg. 215

Wildflower Inn
2059 Darling Hill Road
Lyndonville, VT 05851
(802) 626-8310
www.bringfido.com/go/1E0I
pg. 217

VIRGINIA

ATTRACTIONS

Aspen Dale Winery at the Barn
11083 John Marshall Highway
Delaplane, VA 20144
(540) 364-1722
www.bringfido.com/go/1E7L
pg. 221

Assateague Explorer
Curtis Merritt Harbor
2246 Curtis Merritt Harbor Drive
Chincoteague, VA 23336
(757) 336-5956
www.bringfido.com/go/1DUD
pg. 220

Barrel Oak Winery
& Farm Taphouse
3623 Grove Lane
Delaplane, VA 20144
(540) 364-6402
www.bringfido.com/go/1E7I
pg. 221

The Cheese Shop
410 W Duke of Gloucester Street
Williamsburg, VA 23185
(757) 220-0298
www.bringfido.com/go/1DNQ
pg. 218

Colonial Williamsburg
101 Visitor Center Drive
Williamsburg, VA 23185
(888) 974-7926
www.bringfido.com/go/1DNO
pg. 218

The Dog Park
705 King Street
Alexandria, VA 22314
(703) 888-2818
www.bringfido.com/go/1DNH
pg. 219

Downriver Canoe Company
884 Indian Hollow Road
Bentonville, VA 22610
(540) 635-5526
www.bringfido.com/go/1DNN
pg. 223

Historic Jamestowne
1368 Colonial Parkway
Jamestown, VA 23081
(757) 856-1250
www.bringfido.com/go/1DNR
pg. 218

Mount Vernon
3200 Mount Vernon Memorial
Highway
Alexandria, VA 22121
(703) 780-2000
www.bringfido.com/go/1DUF
pg. 224

Potomac Riverboat Company
211 N Union Street
Alexandria, VA 22314
(703) 684-0580
www.bringfido.com/go/1DNG
pg. 219

Shenandoah National Park
3655 Highway 211 E
Luray, VA 22835
(540) 999-3500
www.bringfido.com/go/1DNM
pg. 223

Skyline Drive
US 340 & Skyline Drive
Front Royal, VA 22630
(540) 999-3500
www.bringfido.com/go/1DNI
pg. 223

Three Fox Vineyards
10100 Three Fox Lane
Delaplane, VA 20144
(540) 364-6073
www.bringfido.com/go/1E7K
pg. 221

Torpedo Factory Art Center
105 N Union Street
Alexandria, VA 22314
(703) 746-4570
www.bringfido.com/go/1DNE
pg. 219

HOTELS

The Alexandrian
480 King Street
Alexandria, VA 22314
(703) 549-6080
www.bringfido.com/go/1DNF
pg. 219

Big Meadows Lodge
Shenandoah National Park
Mile 51.2 Skyline Drive
Luray, VA 22851
(877) 847-1919
www.bringfido.com/go/1DNJ
pg. 223

Kimpton Lorien Hotel & Spa
1600 King Street
Alexandria, VA 22314
(703) 894-3434
www.bringfido.com/go/1DUG
pg. 224

Kingsmill Resort
1010 Kingsmill Road
Williamsburg, VA 23185
(866) 371-6732
www.bringfido.com/go/1DNP
pg. 218

Lewis Mountain Cabins
Shenandoah National Park
Mile 57.5 Skyline Drive
Elkton, VA 22827
(877) 847-1919
www.bringfido.com/go/1DNL
pg. 223

Salamander Resort & Spa
500 N Pendleton Street
Middleburg, VA 20117
(540) 751-3160
www.bringfido.com/go/1E7J
pg. 221

Skyland
Shenandoah National Park
Mile 41.7 Skyline Drive
Luray, VA 22835
(877) 847-1919
www.bringfido.com/go/1DNK
pg. 223

Snug Harbor Marina & Resort
7536 East Side Road
Chincoteague, VA 23336
(757) 336-6176
www.bringfido.com/go/1DUE
pg. 220

WASHINGTON

ATTRACTIONS

Cape Disappointment State Park
244 Robert Gray Drive
Ilwaco, WA 98624
(360) 642-3078
www.bringfido.com/go/1E0Y
pg. 225

Center for Wooden Boats
1010 Valley Street
Seattle, WA 98109
(206) 382-2628
www.bringfido.com/go/1E12
pg. 232

The Cove Restaurant
9604 Pacific Way
Long Beach, WA 98631
(360) 642-2828
www.bringfido.com/go/1E0Z
pg. 225

Discovery Bay Golf Club
7401 Cape George Road
Port Townsend, WA 98368
(360) 385-0704
www.bringfido.com/go/1DQD
pg. 233

Discovery Trail
210 26th Street NW
Long Beach, WA 98631
(360) 642-2400
www.bringfido.com/go/1E0W
pg. 225

Ewe-topia Herd Dog Training
6311 288th Street S
Roy, WA 98580
(253) 843-2929
www.bringfido.com/go/1DQB
pg. 230

Griffiths-Priday State Park
Benner Road
Ocean Shores, WA 98569
(360) 902-8844
www.bringfido.com/go/1E0U
pg. 229

J&A's Winery
19501 144th Avenue NE, #B500
Woodinville, WA 98072
(206) 409-4841
www.bringfido.com/go/1DNU
pg. 227

Jackson Beach
Jackson Beach Road
Friday Harbor, WA 98250
(360) 378-2688
www.bringfido.com/go/1E0N
pg. 226

JM Cellars
14404 137th Place NE
Woodinville, WA 98072
(425) 485-6508
www.bringfido.com/go/1DNV
pg. 227

Kenmore Air
950 Westlake Avenue N
Seattle, WA 98109
(866) 435-9524
www.bringfido.com/go/1E13
pg. 232

Lime Kiln Point State Park
1567 West Side Road
Friday Harbor, WA 98250
(360) 902-8844
www.bringfido.com/go/1E0Q
pg. 226

The Market Chef
225 A Street
Friday Harbor, WA 98250
(360) 378-4546
www.bringfido.com/go/1E0R
pg. 226

Methow Trails
309 Riverside Avenue
Winthrop, WA 98862
(509) 996-3287
www.bringfido.com/go/1E15
pg. 231

Olympic Sculpture Park
2901 Western Avenue
Seattle, WA 98121
(206) 654-3100
www.bringfido.com/go/1E14
pg. 232

Pelindaba Lavender Farms
45 Hawthorne Lane
Friday Harbor, WA 98250
(360) 378-4248
www.bringfido.com/go/1E0P
pg. 226

Quinault Rain Forest
353 S Shore Road
Quinault, WA 98575
(360) 288-2525
www.bringfido.com/go/1E0V
pg. 229

**San Juan Island National
Historical Park**
4668 Cattle Point Road
Friday Harbor, WA 98250
(360) 378-2240
www.bringfido.com/go/1E0O
pg. 226

Seattle Ferry Service
860 Terry Avenue N
Seattle, WA 98109
(206) 713-8446
www.bringfido.com/go/1E11
pg. 232

Susie's Mopeds
125 Nichols Street
Friday Harbor, WA 98250
(360) 378-5244
www.bringfido.com/go/1E0M
pg. 226

Warehouse Wine District
14700 148th Avenue NE
Woodinville, WA 98072
(425) 287-6820
www.bringfido.com/go/1DNS
pg. 227

Washington State Ferry
2100 Ferry Terminal Road
Anacortes, WA 98221
(206) 464-6400
www.bringfido.com/go/1EOK
pg. 226

HOTELS
Ace Hotel Seattle
2423 1st Avenue
Seattle, WA 98121
(206) 448-4721
www.bringfido.com/go/1E10
pg. 232

Earthbox Inn & Spa
410 Spring Street
Friday Harbor, WA 98250
(360) 378-4000
www.bringfido.com/go/1EOL
pg. 226

Iron Springs Resort
3707 Highway 109
Copalis Beach, WA 98536
(360) 276-4230
www.bringfido.com/go/1EOT
pg. 229

Lighthouse Oceanfront Resort
12417 Pacific Way
Long Beach, WA 98631
(360) 642-3622
www.bringfido.com/go/1EOX
pg. 225

Port Ludlow Inn
1 Heron Road
Port Ludlow, WA 98365
(360) 437-7000
www.bringfido.com/go/1DQE
pg. 233

Prairie Hotel
701 Prairie Park Lane SE
Yelm, WA 98597
(360) 458-8300
www.bringfido.com/go/1DQC
pg. 230

Rendezvous Huts
Cub Creek Road
Winthrop, WA 98862
(509) 996-8100
www.bringfido.com/go/1E17
pg. 231

Willows Lodge
14580 NE 145th Street
Woodinville, WA 98072
(425) 424-3900
www.bringfido.com/go/1DNT
pg. 227

WEST VIRGINIA
ATTRACTIONS
Blennerhassett Island State Park
137 Juliana Street
Parkersburg, WV 26101
(304) 420-4800
www.bringfido.com/go/1E18
pg. 236

Parkersburg Brewing Co.
707 Market Street
Parkersburg, WV 26101
(304) 916-150
www.bringfido.com/go/1E1A
pg. 236

Trans-Allegheny Lunatic Asylum
71 Asylum Drive
Weston, WV 26452
(304) 269-5070
www.bringfido.com/go/1DNW
pg. 235

HOTELS
The Blennerhassett Hotel
320 Market Street
Parkersburg, WV 26101
(304) 422-3131
www.bringfido.com/go/1E19
pg. 236

Stonewall Resort
940 Resort Drive
Roanoke, WV 26447
(304) 269-7400
www.bringfido.com/go/1DNX
pg. 235

WISCONSIN
ATTRACTIONS
Dells Boat Tours
107 Broadway
Wisconsin Dells, WI 53965
(608) 254-8555
www.bringfido.com/go/1E1B
pg. 239

Elroy-Sparta State Trail
111 Milwaukee Street
Sparta, WI 54656
(608) 269-4123
www.bringfido.com/go/1DUB
pg. 240

Estabrook Beer Garden
4600 Estabrook Parkway
Milwaukee, WI 53211
(414) 226-2728
www.bringfido.com/go/1DQI
pg. 238

Northern Sky Theater
Peninsula State Park
10169 Shore Road
Fish Creek, WI 54212
(920) 854-6117
www.bringfido.com/go/1DNY
pg. 237

Old Post Office Restaurant
10040 Water Street
Ephraim, WI 54211
(920) 854-4034
www.bringfido.com/go/1DO0
pg. 237

Tunnel Trail Campground
26983 State Highway 71
Wilton, WI 54670
(608) 435-6829
www.bringfido.com/go/1DUC
pg. 240

Milwaukee Boat Line
101 W Michigan Street
Milwaukee, WI 53203
(414) 294-9450
www.bringfido.com/go/1DQF
pg. 238

Milwaukee RiverWalk
101 W Pleasant Street
Milwaukee, WI 53212
(414) 273-3950
www.bringfido.com/go/1DQH
pg. 238

HOTELS

Baker's Sunset Bay Resort
921 Canyon Road
Wisconsin Dells, WI 53965
(608) 254-8406
www.bringfido.com/go/1E1C
pg. 239

Edgewater Resort
10040 Water Street
Ephraim, WI 54211
(920) 854-2734
www.bringfido.com/go/1DNZ
pg. 237

The Iron Horse Hotel
500 W Florida Street
Milwaukee, WI 53204
(414) 374-4766
www.bringfido.com/go/1DQG
pg. 238

Justin Trails Resort
7452 Kathryn Avenue
Sparta, WI 54656
(608) 269-4522
www.bringfido.com/go/1DUA
pg. 240

WYOMING
ATTRACTIONS
Black Dog Raft Company
529 No Name Alley
Jackson, WY 83001
(307) 699-4110
www.bringfido.com/go/1E1H
pg. 243

**Buffalo Bill's Restaurant
& Saloon**
1192 Sheridan Avenue
Cody, WY 82414
(307) 587-4221
www.bringfido.com/go/1E1G
pg. 241

Café Genevieve
135 E Broadway Avenue
Jackson, WY 83001
(307) 732-1910
www.bringfido.com/go/1E1K
pg. 243

Cody Trolley Tours
1192 Sheridan Avenue
Cody, WY 82414
(307) 527-7043
www.bringfido.com/go/1E1F
pg. 241

Cody Wyoming Adventures
1119 12th Street
Cody, WY 02414
(307) 587-6988
www.bringfido.com/go/1E1D
pg. 241

National Elk Refuge
675 E Broadway Avenue
Jackson, WY 83001
(307) 733-9212
www.bringfido.com/go/1E1J
pg. 243

HOTELS

The Cody Hotel
232 W Yellowstone Avenue
Cody, WY 82414
(307) 587-5915
www.bringfido.com/go/1E1E
pg. 241

Cowboy Village Resort
120 S Flatcreek Drive
Jackson, WY 83001
(307) 733-3121
www.bringfido.com/go/1E1I
pg. 243

INDEX

ACKNOWLEDGEMENTS

Writing a travel book in a normal year is a daunting task. Doing so in the midst of a global pandemic takes the challenge to another level entirely. Our book's second edition would not have been realized without the diligence of BringFido's talented editorial team. Thanks to Erin Ballinger, Lauren Barker, Jessica Chipriano, Zain Deane, Merritt Dempsey, Billy Francis, and Scott Tunstall for hours dedicated to researching, writing, editing, fact-checking, and re-checking details about the more than 750 dog-friendly locations featured in this book. We are equally grateful for Brenda Ernst's assistance with the book's layout, cover design, and photo curation. Special thanks to René Nedelkoff for her efforts in getting this edition to print. Finally, a big thanks goes out to all of the pet parents who responded to our photo requests and helped us fill these pages with pictures of smiling dogs enjoying their vacations.

PHOTOGRAPHERS

Ruff Guide to the United States - Second Edition

Editors Melissa and Jason Halliburton
Contributing Writers Erin Ballinger, Lauren Barker, Jessica Chipriano, Zain Deane, Billy Francis, Scott Tunstall
Art Director Brenda Ernst
Photo Editors Lauren Barker, Brenda Ernst
Copy Editors Zain Deane, Merritt Dempsey

Published by Kendall Media, Inc.
PO Box 1489, Travelers Rest, SC 29690
www.bringfido.com
www.ruffguides.com

Library of Congress Control Number 2020924804

ISBN 978-1-939726-02-5

Published 2021.
First edition published 2014. Second edition 2021.
Printed in the United States of America

10 9 8 7 6 5 4 3 2 1